HATTIE

For Susan Hill

Without whom this book wouldn't have been written. Your humour, guidance and friendship are sorely missed.

Hattie

THE AUTHORISED BIOGRAPHY OF
HATTIE JACQUES

ANDY MERRIMAN

First published 2007 by Aurum Press Limited
7 Greenland Street
London NW1 0ND
www.aurumpress.co.uk

A catalogue record for this book is available from the
British Library.

ISBN-10: 1 84513 257 2
ISBN-13: 978 1 84513 257 6

10 9 8 7 6 5 4 3 2 1
2011 2010 2009 2008 2007

Designed in Garamond by Roger Hammond
Typeset by SX Composing DTP, Rayleigh, Essex
Printed and bound in Great Britain by
MPG Books, Bodmin, Cornwall

CONTENTS

PROLOGUE

'Sweet as a Kiss on a Summer's Day'

S T PAUL'S, THE parish church of Covent Garden, designed by Inigo Jones, and affectionately known as The Actors' Church, has had an association with London's theatre community stretching back nearly three hundred and fifty years. It was thus entirely appropriate that on a bright, crisp day in November 1980, Monday the tenth to be exact, a large troupe of family, friends and fellow performers gathered to pay their respects to a much-loved actress and comedienne.

'A memorial service to celebrate the life and work of Miss Hattie Jacques' conducted by the church's chaplain, the Reverend John Arrowsmith, played to a full house on that day and was, according to Hattie's ex-husband, John Le Mesurier, 'a joyous occasion, full of laughter'. It was, by all accounts, a life-affirming event, which banished gloom and sadness to the wings, while humour and warmth took centre-stage. This is not merely show-business hype, but a sincere testament to the woman being honoured.

The service commenced with the congregation belting out a rousing rendition of *The Battle Hymn of the Republic*, a somewhat surprising choice for the 'Oh so English' Hattie. This was followed by a touching and amusing account of Hattie's life by John Le Mesurier, who stated, 'There are givers and takers. Hattie was a giver. She had an aura of kindness around her and also a very sharp and earthy wit.'

A choir of twenty regular artistes from The Players' Theatre performed 'A Musical Portrait' – a medley of music hall songs that brought Hattie to fame. They opened, apparently to the audience's amusement, with 'My Old Man Said Follow the Van', followed by several Players' favourites, and ended with 'Swing Low, Sweet Chariot'.

Kenneth Williams gave the address and told the following story. In the 1960s, he and other celebrities attended a fundraising event, arranged, as ever, by Hattie, for the Leukaemia Association at Chelsea Town Hall. The stars had to assemble around an icecream stall, cornets in hand, and were asked by the photographer to 'lick their own cornets and then turn and lick each others".

Williams remarked to Hattie, 'I don't fancy licking other people's cornets! They may have germs and I don't even know them . . .' Hattie responded by saying, 'Don't worry, if you catch anything, I'll introduce you.'

This anecdote received the laugh that Williams desired, and after several more reminiscences he ended on a serious note by quoting from the poem 'Welcoming Land' by Clemence Dane (Winifred Ashton).

> Then came exiles who fled from death.
> Hunted Huguenots, Jews from Spain
> To the wise island, drew sobbing breath,
> The easy air and smelled the may,
> Sweet as a kiss on a summer's day.

The last line of the poem held personal significance for Kenneth Williams and, in the diaries that he wrote in later years, Williams explained, 'Hattie's Christmas present to me showed special thoughtfulness. Months before I had told her how I had lost a greatly loved 78 rpm recording of Noel Coward reading 'Welcoming Land' by Clemence Dane. She'd scoured half the gramophone exchange and mart shops in London to find it for me. There it was on my plate on Christmas Day with a special message written on the sleeve. It was a joy to have it back again and when I played it and heard those precisely modulated tones talking about the hunted people who fled from persecution to this wise island – I knew the last line would forever symbolise Hattie for me.'

Following Kenneth Williams' tribute, the ensemble sang Sir Hubert Parry and William Blake's 'Jerusalem' – a hymn that typified Hattie's patriotic feelings for her beloved England. As the crowd slowly dispersed, composer and pianist Peter Greenwell, a Players' original and celebrated for arranging the music for Sandy Wilson's 'The Boyfriend', played a poignant version of 'Over the Rainbow' – Hattie's favourite show tune. (Judy Garland had been an acquaintance of Hattie's and one of her heroines.)

Hattie's friend and personal secretary, Martin Christopherson, was quoted in the press the following day as saying, 'She was not a very religious person – not irreligious, but she would not have approved of a formal memorial. She would have said, "Let's have something bright and jolly."' Bright and jolly it was. Today a splendidly efflorescent cherry tree planted in her memory grows nobly in the church grounds, and inside the church is a memorial plaque which states simply, 'Hattie Jacques 1922–1980'. An all-too-brief epitaph to an exceptionally talented, sometimes troubled woman, who was truly loved and whose adventurous spirit, extraordinary warmth and generous nature touched all who knew her.

CHAPTER ONE

A Kentish Girl

It is a most agreeable seaplace excepting those on the Devonshire coast, I ever saw . . . at present the place cannot contain above twenty or thirty strangers, I should think I have bathed four times, and I believe I shall persevere on. Sir Lucas Pepys says my disease is entirely nervous.

ACTRESS SARAH SIDDONS (1755–1831)
FOLLOWING A VISIT TO SANDGATE IN 1790

THE TOWN OF Sandgate is situated between Folkestone and Hythe and extends for nearly a mile and a half along the Kent coastline, boasting panoramic views of the English Channel. According to the town's official website, 'Beneath steep wooded slopes you will find an area teeming with naval, military and social history and a village with a fascinating mix of architectural styles.' It was in one of Sandgate's more imposing Victorian houses that, on 7 February 1922, Hattie Jacques made her first public appearance.

The Jaques family were living at 116 Sandgate High Street when Hattie was born, but she was actually born more or less opposite, in number 125 Sandgate High Street, which conveniently was a nursing home for a number of years. In the light of Hattie's later extensive charitable work, it is interesting to note that the property in which she was born is now owned by the multi-millionaire Roger De Haan, founder of Saga, who uses the premises as a base for the Roger De Haan Charitable Trust.

It is quite likely that Hattie's first adoring public was her mother and the delivering doctor. No applause, certainly no laughter, but just the necessary ministrations from the attendant staff, and perhaps later inquisitive attention from other mothers.

In fact, Hattie wasn't even known as 'Hattie' at this early stage in her life. She was given the affectionate nickname over two decades later and so when recorded on 18 February 1922 in Folkestone, the birth was registered in her real name of Josephine Edwina Jaques. It wasn't just her first name that was later changed. The family surname at that time was 'Jaques', and the more familiar form by which Hattie became known – 'Jacques' – was adopted by her and her brother Robin in later years in an attempt to recapture a little of the fashionable French derivation.

Hattie's mother, Mary Thorn, who was born in Chelsea in 1899, had met Robin Rochester Jaques while he was in the services and she was a Voluntary Aid Detachment nurse. The couple had their first child, a son, also called Robin, in 1920 (27 March). Mary's own father was Joseph Edwin Thorn, and Hattie was obviously named in her grandfather's honour. Joseph owned a jeweller's shop and pawnbrokers. His wife, Adelaide, Hattie's grandmother, was the daughter of William Brown, a deceased East End cheesemonger and his wife, Hannah, thought to be of Jewish descent.

On her father's side, Hattie's grandfather, Joseph Rochester Jaques was born in Northumberland and was described in the 1901 census as 'a billiard room manager'. His wife, Hattie's other grandmother, Florence Emily King (known as Flora), was born in Dartmouth, Devon, and was the daughter of a Newton Abbot bookseller. Hattie's father, Robin Rochester Jaques was born in Newcastle in 1897 and lived with his parents at 17, King John Street, Heaton, a well-to-do part of Newcastle to this day.

Hattie's background was not typically showbiz; only one family member had exhibited any interest in the theatre and had actually 'trodden the boards'. This relative, however, was Mary, her mother: the most important person in Hattie's formative years and also of great influence in her later life. She was a singer and performer, whose appearance in a concert party tour of the British Army of the Rhine at the Palace Theatre, Cologne, on 29 January 1920, in a pantomime of *Robinson Crusoe*, whilst seven months pregnant, was described in the Army's newsletter. Billed as Mary Jaques, Mary played Harry Hathaway,

> A smart young blade, with love he's crazy,
> For Crusoe's cousin, sweet winsome Daisy.

Mary's husband, Robin, had received a commission on leaving school and was based at the time in Germany, serving in the Army Education Corps. On their return to the UK, Jaques left the Army, only to enlist in the Royal Air Force. He was a dashing, good-looking man and a considerable athlete, who harboured hopes of becoming a professional footballer. He represented both the Army and the Royal Air Force at the highest levels of football.

In fact R.R. Jaques (the way all gentlemen amateurs' names were written) played for an Army side in a match against Chelsea Football Club in 1921, and a photograph of him appeared in the *Daily Mirror*, shaking hands with The Duke of York (later King George VI) at the auspicious opening of the Army Football Association's new Command sports ground at Woolwich.

In the early 1920s, RR Jaques played for RAF West Norwood in the Isthmian League and there are various accounts (as well as various versions of his surname) recording his prowess as a centre-forward. Under the headline 'Victory of West Norwood' on 14 November 1921, there is a report in *The Times* by 'Our special correspondent' which enthused, 'West Norwood beat Dulwich Hamlet in a match in the Isthmian League at Herne Hill on Saturday by two goals to one . . . West Norwood never quite settled down to any combined work . . . but R Jaques at centre forward played well. After the interval the attack improved and R Jaques with a clever single handed effort went through several opponents and scored his side's first goal with a low shot.'

After he represented the Army in a match against the French equivalent at the garrison ground on 7 April 1921, *The Times* correspondent reported, 'Before half-time Lieutenant Jacques, an aggressive, penetrating player, took advantage of a push pass sent straight ahead down the centre to make the score 3–1. The French goalkeeper came out and tried to fall on the ball, but Jacques' shot was not one of the sort to be turned aside by a mere nose or ear.' (The British Army went on to win the match 5–1.)

By the beginning of 1922, 'RR' had decided to switch services to the new Royal Air Force, founded four years earlier. He was now playing for RAF West Norwood, and another report in *The Times*, on 14 January 1922 (just three weeks before Hattie's birth) described how, 'Wimbledon and West Norwood will play their Surrey Senior Cup match at Herne Hill this afternoon. Wimbledon will have HH Allwright back in the side, and although West Norwood have been very successful in their home games, and even with their strong forward line, including RR Jaques and JH Lockton, the Corinthian (Corinthian Casuals) they will have to be at their very best to win.'

It seems that West Norwood did indeed scale the heights for they reached the semi-final of the Surrey Senior Cup, where they played Redhill at Sutton United's ground on 18 February. They beat Redhill but unfortunately lost the final 1–0 to a team, intriguingly named 'Metrogas'.

During 1922 Robin also played four times as centre-forward for Clapton Orient, then in the Second Division of the Football League, scoring twice. Presumably, as an amateur with an RAF career to maintain, he was only occasionally available to play, but he was clearly turning a few heads. In July 1923 he signed for Fulham who had finished nine places higher than Orient in the same division. Tragically he was never to fulfil his ambition of becoming a professional footballer.

The family had not been settled in Kent very long when they were uprooted. The Air Force List for June 1923 shows that Flying Officer Robin Jaques had been posted to Number 100

Squadron with effect from 3 April 1923. This Squadron (motto: 'Do not stir up a hornet's nest') had originally been formed by the Royal Flying Corps in September 1917, a year before the creation of the RAF, specifically for night bombing. The squadron was based at Spittlegate, Lincolnshire, and so Mary and the two children duly left their comfortable Sandgate home and moved into a tiny cottage in Newton, near Folkingham.

Flying Officer Jaques was still described as being 'Under Instruction' on his arrival at 100 Squadron and soon embarked on flying lessons under the tutelage of qualified RAF pilots. Jaques was taught to fly an Avro 504, which had been used in the early stages of the First World War for light bombing and reconnaissance missions.

On the morning of 8 August, less than two months after he had moved to Spittlegate, Flight Lieutenant Jaques took a solo flight in the Avro. After he had been up for about ten minutes, and at the altitude of about 1,000 feet, he attempted to execute a difficult manoeuvre. An RAF colleague, Flying Officer AN Macneal, later reported that the bank on the machine had increased until it was plummeting vertically. About three hundred feet from the ground, the machine appeared to come out of the dive, but fell back into it again and appeared to veer sideways, crashing to the ground at 11.45am.

Chief Flying Instructor AP Ritchie flew straight to the scene of the accident and found the machine smashed to pieces in a field between Cold Harbour and Old Somerby. Hattie's father lay dead just clear of the machine, 'His skull being smashed and neck broken and other injuries. He must have struck the ground with tremendous force. Death was instantaneous.' Ritchie later stated that Flight Lieutenant Jaques had completed approximately thirty hours of flying and was quite capable of taking the machine out for a solo flight. He did, however, feel that 'Jaques had lost his head' to try a spin at such a height. The death certificate states, 'Deceased while flying, crashed to the ground and was killed from injuries received and shock.' Theodore Norton, Coroner for the Grantham District, who returned a verdict of 'Accidental Death', said he was satisfied the machine was 'all right.' At the subsequent Court of Enquiry, the following statement was issued, 'The cause of the accident was, in our opinion, faulty application by the pilot of the controls and an error of judgement due to over confidence.'

It appears that Hattie's father, a somewhat adventurous character, flew his plane in the same way that he played football. On the field he played with verve and spirit, which meant that he was prone to taking risks – unfortunately this philosophy was much more dangerous when he was airborne and in control of a machine that he was only just learning to master.

The Grantham Journal reported the accident on 11 August 1923 and described Flying Officer Jaques' funeral: 'The remains of the deceased officer were laid to rest in Grantham cemetery yesterday with full military honours. The coffin was covered with the Union Jack on which rested the deceased's cap. Floral tributes included wreaths from the children Robin and Josephine . . . three volleys were fired and the last post was sounded. In attendance were the men of the 100 Squadron Spittlegate, the widow, Mary Jaques, Mr and Mrs J Thorn, [Mary's parents] the management of the Theatre Royal Grantham and a number of friends.' There was no mention of the children attending the funeral, nor of RR Jaques' parents being present. Although the family had only lived in the area for a very short time, Mary had already become involved with Grantham's Theatre Royal.

Following the death of her husband, Mary Jaques, who even before the accident had already expressed some feeling of isolation living in the country cottage, quickly decided to leave Lincolnshire. A young widow with two toddlers and no source of income other than a small RAF pension, Mary had very little option other than to seek help and support from her parents in London, who were more than happy to rescue their daughter and grandchildren.

It was under these truly unhappy circumstances that

Josephine, at the age of eighteen months, and her brother Robin aged three, were left fatherless, almost penniless and facing a very uncertain future.

CHAPTER TWO

Gold Bracelets, White Gardenias and Crystallised Velvets

GROUCHO *'When I woke up there was the nurse taking care of me.'*
CHICO *'What's the matter, couldn't the nurse take care of herself?'*
GROUCHO *'You bet she could, but I found it out too late.'*

THE MARX BROTHERS, *MONKEY BUSINESS*, 1931

JOSEPH THORN, HATTIE'S maternal grandfather, was born in 1875 in West Ham in east London, and by the age of sixteen he had followed his father into the pawnbroking business, being employed as one of three assistants to pawnbroker Edward Masters. At that time, he lived at 65 Brompton Road, Kensington, which is now the address of the jewellers Mappin and Webb.

Joseph and his wife Adelaide were married at Emmanuel Church in Forest Gate in east London on 6 September 1898 and started their married life at 159 Marlborough Road, Chelsea, where Hattie's mother Mary was born the following year. By the end of the First World War, the Thorn family occupied premises above their jewellery and pawnbrokers shop on the 'S' bend in the Kings Road, Chelsea. It was here, on the edge of World's End, that in the summer of 1923 the three Jaques refugees found themselves. Fortunately, the flat was large enough for Mary to occupy her own bedroom. Robin and Josephine shared a room, referred to as 'the nursery'.

Josephine, not yet two years old, was now facing a very different environment from her cosy Sandgate beginnings and the rural idyll of a Lincolnshire hamlet. Not only was World's End, in the heart of London's metropolis, there was very little green space. Chelsea had only thirteen acres of public open area, one of the smallest proportions of the capital. Robin and Josephine would have had no local parks or grassy expanses to explore, apart from the burial ground around St Luke's church in Sydney Street.

In fact, parts of Chelsea – now renowned as exclusive and sophisticated – were quite deprived in the mid-1920s. Much of the housing was poorly maintained and decaying, and there were areas of great poverty and deprivation, especially in World's End, which was described as an area of 'sordid courts and alleys, where century-old worn-out cottages were crowded higgledy-piggledy together.' If Chelsea's great outdoors wasn't terribly appealing, there were other compensations for the Jaques family and in particular Mary, whose theatrical interests were well served.

The Kings Road was peppered with theatres and cinemas, including the Chelsea Palace Theatre, which had opened in 1903 as a music hall called the Chelsea Palace of Varieties. With its easily recognisable terracotta dome and situated on the corner of Sydney Street, the Palace was an important local landmark. The theatre also staged plays, ballets and, in the year that the Jaques family moved to the area, it screened films. In addition, the celebrated Royal Court Theatre which occupied the east side of Sloane Square had been established for nearly forty years. By 1912, Chelsea had six cinemas or theatres which also showed films, four of which were within walking distance of the Jaques family home.

Chelsea was an exciting neighbourhood in which to live during the early 1920s. Its village atmosphere and liberal environment had attracted a bohemian crowd, and a cosmopolitan community of writers, artists and intellectuals had colonised the area since the beginning of the century. The first Chelsea School of Art had opened in 1895, and the infamous arrest of Oscar Wilde in Room 53 of the Cadogan Hotel in Sloane Street in 1895 remained an ongoing conversation piece. Noel Coward and latterly Quentin Crisp, also lived in Chelsea.

From 1926, men in drag were among those who flocked to the annual Chelsea Arts Ball, the height of decadence, which scandalised newspapers with outrageous behaviour each New Year's Eve. The balls were world-famous for their immoderately themed fancy dress, regular nudity and licentiousness and the way in which normal social conventions were shunned until 5am on New Year's Day.

According to her lifelong friend Bruce Copp, Hattie, from a very early age and certainly during her formative years, was quite used to seeing the parade of flamboyant characters that frequented her neighbourhood. In later life, Hattie was to surround herself with an ensemble of gay men, and she maintained that the Chelsea period in her life paved the way for her acceptance of the homosexual culture.

On 15 September 1926, three years after moving to Chelsea, Hattie was enrolled in the local Lady Margaret Primary School, just across the Kings Road in nearby Parsons Green. Headmistress Miss Moberley Bell described the establishment as pleasant and supportive, 'I think it is the kindness and friendliness we meet on all sides that makes Lady Margaret School a particularly happy place.'

The school had been in existence for nine years when Josephine Edwina Jaques, pupil 655, began her academic career. Pupil 654 was Kay Walsh (who played Nancy in the original film of *Oliver Twist*, and, later, married the film's director, David Lean). Hattie made one of her first film appearances in this acclaimed interpretation of Dickens' story. Hattie's brother, Robin, also attended the school. In 1992, he wrote to Brian

Owen, who was compiling a history of the school, explaining that he and his sister had changed the spelling of their surname to 'Jacques' as being nearer its French origin. Owen replied, acknowledging this fact and adding, 'One of our old girls, Biddy Parr, remembers Josie doing cartwheels in the school garden.' Even at this young age 'Jo' was quite chubby and outgoing, and the quiet and shy Robin – as slim as his sister was large – was somewhat embarrassed by the antics of his sister, who was already developing into a bit of a 'show off'.

According to writer and actress Anne Valery, who later lived with Robin Jaques for over twenty years, it was around this time that Hattie's mother started working as housekeeper for an auctioneer in Gunnersbury, near Chiswick. Anne is of the impression that he and Mary became lovers. Thus, in addition to maintaining this relationship and her work commitments, Mary could not always perhaps devote as much time to the children as she wanted, and it was eventually agreed that Hattie's maternal grandmother Flora come down from Newcastle to live in London and act as a nanny. She didn't live with the family but had a flat nearby. Robin described her as, 'An extremely large and loud woman who liked a drink and performed ribald songs in local pubs!' Such larger-than-life behaviour would, no doubt, have left quite an impression on the young Hattie.

The move south had worked. The family's finances were improving. Mary was now earning her keep but, more importantly, Joseph Thorn's jewellery and pawnbroker business was extremely prosperous. He and Adelaide provided not only financial stability for Mary and her two children but, more telling, the security of an extremely happy home life. The children were raised in what Hattie later depicted as a fairytale world. She recalled the shop at night as, 'An Aladdin's cave . . . the illuminated windows glittering with colourful gems and silver and gold bracelets.'

At the back of the shop there were dingy 'pledge booths' and a bare wooden counter covered in family heirlooms and bundles of personal items traded in, perhaps forever, by the harder-pressed inhabitants of Chelsea. According to Hattie, Joseph Thorn was, however, a kind man, who 'would accept a bundle of rags and pledges for a shilling each Monday and then would redeem the items for a shilling and an extra penny on the Friday night'.

Robin Jacques spoke of a 'blanket chute' which was provided for customers to pawn their 'expendable' bedclothes in the summer. The chute led to the cellar, and Hattie and Robin would spend happy hours using this as a slide, launching themselves down the chute and ending up in a heap of blankets and coverlets.

Hattie also remembered that, 'Some pledges were never redeemed and twice a year we had "a turning out" day. There'd be old wedding dresses, top hats and bits of uniforms. My grandfather allowed me to keep some of them and I had a lovely time dressing up. It made me even more determined to become an actress.' Every few weeks when the unredeemed pledges were sorted, her grandfather would let Hattie choose whatever she wanted, including such clothing treasures as bonnets, Spanish shawls, velvet cloaks, mandarin slippers and ballet shoes. Joseph also constructed a small swing for her in the nursery and on it she would pretend to be a swooping ballerina, or a fairy princess riding on a cloud.

Although her grandfather's philanthropic nature was important in forming Hattie's own generous nature and social awareness, it was her mother who was, at this time, even more influential. As soon as she was old enough to appreciate live performances, Mary would take her daughter to West End shows. Hattie's first memory of these days was watching a pantomime at the Lyceum on the Strand when June (later, Lady) Inverclyde played Cinderella. At the end of the last performance, the cast removed their wigs and head dresses. Hattie recalled that the realisation that the Fairy Godmothers and Ugly Sisters were real people, smiling across the footlights at the audience, had a profound effect on her.

The young Hattie was a very pretty child with enormous deep brown eyes and glossy dark hair. Aged nine, she hosted tea parties for her friends and on arrival each guest was swiftly bundled into fancy dress costume. The game they played after the cakes and jellies had been devoured was 'theatre'. Hattie later described those days with great fondness, 'I remember how I bossed and bullied at "the rehearsals" and I always claimed the major roles of fairy princesses and prima ballerinas.'

In July 1930 Hattie left Lady Margaret and transferred to Godolphin and Latymer School in Hammersmith. This girls school has produced its fair share of actors: Kate Beckinsale, Samantha Bond and Rebecca Lacey, as well as such television celebrities as Nigella Lawson and Davina McCall. The move to secondary education also coincided with the children moving from their grandparents' haven in the Kings Road to their mother's residence in Gunnersbury at Osborne House, 7 Oxford Road. According to Anne Valery, Mary's lover and employer was a rather austere character and a freemason. He apparently disapproved of books and music – other than Gilbert and Sullivan. It seems unlikely that Mary could have had a relationship with a man so disposed against the very things that she loved, but it's not entirely impossible.

It seems that neither of the young Jaqueses enjoyed the sudden change. Robin was decidedly unhappy in this uncultured environment and was duly dispatched to a masonic boarding school, which he hated. Possessing a unique talent for drawing, he desperately wanted to go to art school, but this was frowned upon and so he left school at sixteen and found temporary work as a potman in a Kilburn pub.

There is no account of how Hattie fared with her 'stepfather' and she never spoke about these times in later interviews. However, whatever her employer's views on music and the theatre, Mary certainly encouraged her daughter in pursuing her love of dance. Hattie was enrolled at 'The Dean Sisters Academy of Theatrical Dancing and Ballet', a local dance school, and by the age of twelve was the star pupil in ballet and acrobatic dancing and was also the principal dancer in all the Academy's shows.

Hattie and Mavis von Proschwitz, a schoolfriend from Latymer, attended performances at Sadler's Wells where they would have seen productions of *Swan Lake*, *Giselle* and *Les Sylphides*, featuring principal dancers such as Alicia Markova and Anton Dolin, under the leadership of the legendary Ninette de Valois. The two schoolfriends sat in the gallery, hair scraped back in the traditional style, wearing black velvet cloaks, pinned with huge red enamel buckles. Hattie recalled these days in a magazine interview in the 1960s, 'What a strange lot we were. We used to eat things like crystallised velvets because they were so frightfully decadent and buy ourselves white gardenias and daydream that they were from some admirer.'

Hattie collected photographs and reviews and, during her teenage years, created a beautifully bound scrapbook of ballet dancers and ballerinas – a labour of love to an art form that she so adored. She would have loved to have been a dancer, but despite her grace and dancing prowess, sadly Hattie's shape was already proving to be a problem in her quest to be a prima ballerina.

Hattie had been told that her 'puppy fat' would disappear with adolescence. She considered dieting but was told by the family doctor, 'The human body changes every seven years and the fat will just go away.' So Hattie waited until she was fourteen. 'On the morning of my birthday I woke up expecting to find that a miracle had taken place in the night. But I was still the same. And I remember telling myself how important it was not to cry.'

Hattie was teased mercilessly at school and often spoke of the cruelty of some of her fellow pupils. She was reduced to tears on many occasions. It was something that she never forgot and typified to her the 'barbarous quality' of children, 'Oh the agonies of being fat as a child!' she said later. 'Well, I'm very stubborn and I decided very early on that wasn't all that I was going to be. So I decided to be captain of the netball team . . . which I was. I was actually jolly good, you know.'

So what sort of schoolgirl was Hattie? Mavis von Proschwitz contributed an article to the Godolphin magazine in 1980:

Hattie was a pupil of the school in the thirties. There must be quite a few of us who remember her from that time. It would be difficult to forget her performance in Miss Lockwood's brilliant production of *Au Clair de La Lune*, where she stood at the window and mimed replies to Pierrot.

We knew her as Josie (rarely Josephine) and, for some of us, memories of her performing go back even earlier to the Preparatory. I first met her in Lower 3a. Our classroom was to the left of the headmistress's office and Miss Zachary often had occasion to peep in and quell the noise. There, Josie wrote and produced her first pantomime at the age of ten.

Rehearsals began in the outside porch of one of the cloakrooms, but this stage proved rather cramped (and cold) for the ever growing cast. Eventually we were allowed to stay in and rehearse in the dinner hour – a treat indeed — and finally the performance took place in the classroom, before an invited audience headed by Miss Luce.

In spite of her weight, Josie was a light dancer and excellent acrobat. She performed during the intervals of her production and I can still hear Miss Luce's anxious voice, 'Mind you don't hurt yourself, Josie', as Josie did the splits. It was an unforgettable performance for all present and there were also many dramatic moments behind the swing blackboard which served as our dressing room.

From then on, I knew of nothing more entrancing than to be Josie's audience and later to share in her dancing lessons and amateur music hall performances. Josie was a natural actress. She could re-tell the story of a film and make it sound more fun than the original. She was very sensitive about her size and had to learn early in life to make people laugh with her rather than at her. She was born to go on the stage and despaired of getting there.

Josie's ambitions lay in the world outside school. Within its walls, she was less sure of her aims and her audience. As regards work, I can only remember her love of French. She was a great enemy of school uniform, the navy pleated tunic and the black stockings. Seldom has a more battered school hat been stuffed into a school case on the way home.

Despite no longer living with Joseph and Adelaide, the family remained in close contact and visited regularly. There was an inseparable family bond and they even continued to take annual holidays together. There is a record of a summer break at a vegetarian holiday camp in Eastbourne in 1937 and although it's difficult to imagine that the decidedly carnivorous Hattie was taken with this idea, the family did return to the camp the following year!

As Mavis von Proschwitz predicted, Hattie's ambitions did indeed exist outside the confines of her school as she sought to make her mark on the world's stage. A professional career was still some way away, and so at the beginning of 1939, while still a schoolgirl, the seventeen-year-old Jaques joined 'The Curtain Club', a locally based amateur dramatic company. Within a few months, she had made her theatrical debut in a series of four one-act plays by the company. On 4 May 1939, at the Kitson Hall in Barnes, she was a member of the cast in *Fumed Oak*, written by Noel Coward. Described as the forerunner of his play *Blithe Spirit*, it is the story of a downtrodden husband and a domineering wife. Hattie played Mrs Doris Gow and, according to a review in the local newspaper, 'the young Josephine Josie Jaques cleverly managed to convey her character's world by voice and expression'. The same night she also appeared in the Curtain Club's production of *Borgia* and the critic reported, 'The audience at Kitson Hall on Saturday evening were treated to a varied and ably produced programme. In Claude Radcliffe's *Borgia*, set in a Roman palace of 1500 AD, the passion and cruel tragedy was ably expressed by Josie Jaques as Beatrice of Orsini.' Takings from the evening were donated to the Barnes and District Nursing Association. Not only was this Hattie's theatrical debut but it was also her first contribution to a charitable event – something that she was to repeat selflessly and generously for the rest of her life.

Hattie left Godolphin and Latymer School in the summer of 1939 without achieving great academic success but with an ambition to break into the theatrical world. Having given up the idea of serious dance, she studied hairdressing and cosmetic art – not because she had a particular interest or flair for the profession, but she considered that it might help in her theatrical aspirations.

Hattie worked as an apprentice hairdresser for a few months and even learned how to dress wigs for dowagers in Kensington! She also learned how to style her own hair in any historical fashion – something she admitted to finding invaluable in later years when directing shows at The Players' Theatre.

When war was declared in September 1939, any theatrical pretensions were out of the question. Hattie's mother had been a Voluntary Aid Detachment (VAD) nurse during the First World War and Hattie decided to follow in her mother's footsteps. The Voluntary Aid Detachment was formed in 1909 (Agatha Christie was once a VAD nurse) and in the ensuing years, thousands of members of the British Red Cross Society and St John Ambulance Brigade were enrolled in the Civil Defence Service. VAD nurses served in hospitals, first aid posts, shelters, rest centres and in the river emergency service throughout the war.

Hattie embarked on some basic first aid courses, obtained employment at Hammersmith Hospital and eventually joined the Red Cross (Detachment London 208, Brook Green Division, Hammersmith Division) on 9 August 1940. In that very month, according to the Red Cross archive, 'The Luftwaffe had failed to win control of the skies and invasion plans had to be postponed. They switched their tactics in the belief that the British Government would surrender if the civilians lost the will to fight. The plan was to destroy morale through heavy bombing, and between September 1940 and May 1941, over forty thousand civilians were killed and nearly one hundred and fifty thousand injured during air raids in Britain.'

During the Blitz, Hattie became a mobile VAD, attending bombing incidents, providing first aid nursing care and assistance to civilians. Her bubbly personality and no-nonsense approach must have given strength to many a victim of the Luftwaffe's shells. She was posted to an air raid post near King's Cross and then later transferred to Bethnal Green. One night, Hattie was at her post in Bethnal Green when the police called and asked if she could provide assistance to a young woman who was about to give birth in a public phone booth. Hattie was initially very wary, but came to the rescue, 'I was young and didn't know much about those things. I did the best I could. But it was an easy birth, and I was proud to have helped deliver a fine baby girl.'

In later years, Hattie sometimes used to wonder what had happened to the baby, 'Where she is now? I ask myself. What names did her mother decide on? Did she ever tell her daughter she was born in a telephone kiosk?' Unfortunately, Hattie never discovered the identity of the baby. The programme researchers on *This Is Your Life* when Hattie was the subject in February 1963 wanted to bring on the girl as a surprise guest, but were unable to trace her. Hattie's Divisional Commander, Miss Vivienne Catlow, did, however, appear on the television programme and remembered, 'Hattie was always a great asset and always cheerful.' (Hattie looked quite bemused and replied, somewhat blandly, 'It's been a long time.')

Hattie spoke fondly of her time during the Blitz, despite the suffering that she witnessed. Even back then she was the subject of humorous jibes about her size and while huddling in shelters and underground stations dressing wounds and such like would elicit comments such as, 'Blimey, good job Adolf hasn't got a bomb that size' and 'There'd be room for a whole family if you left the platform!'

At the beginning of 1941, Hattie left Oxford Road and moved into her own accommodation at 13 Thurloe Place, Kensington. In December she was presented with the War Service certificate. This award, which bore the facsimile signatures of the King and

Queen, was issued to personnel who had given satisfactory service for a period of over two years or for part-time service of not less than a thousand hours. Within a few months, however, Hattie received the following letter:

PUBLIC HEALTH DEPT
METROPOLITAN BOROUGH OF ST PANCRAS
22 MAY 1942

Dear Miss Jaques,

In accordance with instructions received from the Regional Commissioners of the Ministry of Health, the medical aid posts in shelters are to be closed and put on care and maintenance basis. It is much regretted that we are obliged to lose the services of those who have supervised so efficiently the health and welfare of shelterers and done such splendid work under air raid conditions, but it will be recognised by all concerned that the new arrangements are part and parcel of adjustments necessary to be made to meet the present phase of the national war effort. With the foregoing explanation, I have to advise you that your services as a shelter nurse will terminate on the 21st June 1942. On behalf of the ARP Committee I have to thank you for the very excellent service you have rendered during this difficult time

Yours faithfully

Maitland Radford
Medical officer of Health.

An accompanying letter stated how the Medical Officer very much regretted having to lose the services of personnel who had given such loyal co-operation and hoped that when they were instructed to re-open the medical aid posts, Miss Jaques would be willing to return to them, if possible. It ended, '*Mrs Green and I will be pleased to see you at the Town Hall and give you any help we can.'*

During the following year, Hattie decided to end her nursing career. In 1943 nursing staff were needed in convalescent homes and auxiliary hospitals, and Hattie had been requested to move to the Home Counties to work in a nursing home. She was adamant that this move wasn't for her, and she was duly discharged from the Red Cross. We shall never know whether if the young Miss Jaques had remained in the nursing profession she would have achieved the rank of matron in real life, a role indelibly associated with her from the *Carry On* films.

Her reason for leaving nursing wasn't that she didn't like the work, nor was it because she had decided to concentrate on a show business career. It was all much more straightforward. The sick and injured of England were deprived of the ministrations of young Nurse Jaques because of the love of an officer in the American Army, who did indeed prove to be a Major love of her life.

CHAPTER THREE

There's no Business Like Arc Welding

I can't get away to marry you today . . . my wife won't let me.

WAITING AT THE CHURCH; WORDS AND MUSIC BY
FRED W LEIGH AND HENRY E PETHER

MAJOR CHARLES RANDALL KEARNEY was a career soldier with the 112th Infantry Regiment of the United States 1st Army and he had met Hattie at The Players' Theatre. The Players' Theatre, which was to play a huge part in Hattie's professional and personal life, was a popular haunt during the war for servicemen on leave. When situated in Albemarle Street, it was a venue to which various Services Welfare Committees regularly brought wounded soldiers throughout the blackout to enjoy the Victorian songs and sketches. American servicemen, in particular, were drawn to the typical English entertainment, the unique atmosphere and Victorian music hall. And it was here that Hattie, just twenty-one years old, was swept off her feet by this dashing American officer.

When Hattie learned her nursing duties were to take her out of London, she was alarmed that their chances to meet would be limited. Because the Major's leave was infrequent and unpredictable, Hattie was concerned that if she left London it would be very difficult for them to pursue the relationship. So Hattie decided to seek gainful employment elsewhere.

In 1943, with so many men away fighting, there was a shortage of workers on farms and in factories – particularly for war-related production, and the British Government had decided to stop recruiting women into the Armed Forces. Instead, women could choose between factory work and joining the Land Army. Women were required to work in munitions factories or were conscripted to work in tank and aircraft factories, civil defence and transport. Jobs such as driving trains and ambulances, which had traditionally been seen as 'men's work', were now open to women. The Land Army was not a consideration as Hattie wanted to stay in London. She couldn't drive and so applied to do factory work. So, in the summer of 1943, she found herself employed as, of all things, an arc welder. Unlike her American counterpart, *Rosie the Riveter,* a fictional figure who was popularised in a song of the time, Hattie was an employee of a factory in the Holloway Road in north London.

Hattie spoke about her time as a welder in an interview with a South African magazine in 1979, 'I took on war factory work and I was taught how to handle a welding torch and make dainty items such as pontoon bridges. My pay packet seldom contained more than £3 or £4 and night after night I trudged home with my eyes stinging from the intense brilliance of the welding torch. It wasn't exactly dangerous war work but it was stressful. My mask was cracked and at the end of the day I'd go home absolutely blinded. The condition is known as 'arc eyes' and I suffered badly from it.'

Once Hattie had become a well-known celebrity, she was a popular subject for magazine interviews; she was always willing to talk to the press, with whom, despite their constant references to her weight, she had a very good relationship. Over the years she gave a huge number of such audiences, and, inevitably, there are discrepancies in the stories. Her time at the tank factory was reported in many periodicals, newspapers and magazines, and the stories vary. It may be that she had a tendency to romanticise her time behind the mask.

In one interview, Hattie remarks, 'There I was behind a workbench, wearing a mask and welding away, the only woman among hundreds of men.' In other articles, it is reported that 'all the other women looked at her flawless complexion, deportment and plummy voice.' Or that 'her posh voice made her stand out from the crowd, she always had a clean overall and refused to wear pins in her hair. The other workmates nicknamed her 'Lady Muck'. In all the interviews, however, Hattie maintained that, 'the girls sang as they worked . . . some of the old songs and I picked one up called '*Call Round Any Old Time*', which I sang at The Players' audition when I was 18'.

Although one would love to imagine the factory being transformed into a Hollywood set in some kind of Busby Berkeley musical extravaganza with our torch-wielding Hattie belting out a number while the begoggled chorus girls form a kaleidoscopic pattern around the star of the show, one wonders quite how much her factory experience really did lead Hattie to her career in show business as she always maintained. In fact Hattie didn't actually audition at The Players' until the summer of 1944 when she was twenty-two and long after she had left the factory.

Hattie has also been reported as saying, 'The factory was churning out parts for prefabricated bridges and I was horrified at the often shoddy workmanship. After a while I left, wanting no more part in the negligence.' This again does seem somewhat fanciful, although, in July 1944, a War Cabinet document acknowledged that the build quality of British tanks was not very good and there were rumours workers had seen much of their painstaking work end on the scrapheap. It is factually correct, however, to say that Hattie didn't work very long as a welder, because she had definitely left the factory by the end of 1943, and her 1944 diary refers to interviews and difficulties at the Labour Exchange. There was certainly a gap in time between leaving the factory and her audition at The Players'.

Hattie was introduced to The Players' Theatre by her brother, Robin, who was employed at there as a cloakroom attendant and lift operator. (In later years, Robin became a prolific illustrator for the *Radio Times* and over one hundred novels, perhaps best-known for his illustrations of the Hornblower books by C.S. Forrester.) It was one night in 1943 that Major Charles Kearney, who had been stood up by another English girl, introduced himself to the young and flirtatious Hattie. Although rather plump, she was tall and statuesque with sparkling eyes and a face that had been likened to Vivien Leigh. Charles was handsome and possessed a jaunty air, not unlike Hattie's father, whom she never really knew. He also bore a remarkable physical resemblance to RR Jaques. There was a strong mutual attraction between the US major and Hattie and they embarked on a passionate affair, which would be recorded in the 105 letters that Charles wrote to 'Jo' and in her own diary from 1944. Most of the correspondence is addressed to the Oxford Road address in Gunnersbury, although Hattie refers occasionally to a flat (address unknown) where she occasionally entertains Charles.

A letter to her in March 1944 is addressed to Miss Josephine Jacques and presumably it is about this time that she and Robin changed the spelling of their surname by adding the 'c'. Hattie was unemployed during this period and so had plenty of time to devote herself to her Major. . .

At the start of 1944, Charles was stationed in Herefordshire and reported that he had received her photo, which he put under his pillow. He requested that she come and visit him in Hereford. Hattie's diary from 6 January records that she and Charles enjoyed an assignation at the Mitre Hotel, Hereford, and she stayed the night with him. A note in her diary stating *'11 times . . . wonderful'* leaves little to the imagination but she seems just as excited about having sandwiches together before dinner! They spent the next two nights together and for the first time Hattie writes, *'Love Charles so very much'.*

It is not known exactly how far into the relationship that Charles revealed that he was married, but he doesn't seem to have led her on for too long. In a letter dated 15 January 1944, he wrote, *'You are very much a part of me'* but admits that she deserves a better fate and even encourages her to take a better offer if it comes along, '*You deserve to be happy, Jo*'.

Five days later he replied to her letter, hinting that for security reasons he cannot divulge where he is, '*Only you would think that I was living in a bed of roses and not missing you a bit. I am living in a pool of mud and missing you like hell. I am as close to hell now as I was as close to heaven when you were in Leominster with me. I can't tell you where I am. I wouldn't be playing the game.*' He also quoted Hattie's last letter, '*Darling, it won't be but a few short weeks until you will be in London. You mustn't be impatient. After all you are supposed to be a soldier. And whether you know it there is a war on. We must win this war, and if we are to do so, you must get me and London out of your mind until you have leave!*'

The diary is a fascinating insight into Hattie's life at the time. She was spending more and more time at The Players' and also regularly visiting her grandmother Adelaide. Her grandfather Joseph had died the previous year. The diary also contains the first mention of 67 Eardley Crescent, Earls Court, London, which was to be the family home for the next thirty-five years.

Hattie was a keen cinema-goer – 'the flicks' as she described it – and saw such films as *Wuthering Heights*, *Road To Morocco*, *Thousands Cheer* and *Phantom Of The Opera*. She was also being courted by other men – and, in particular, by a Lieutenant Appelby, who seemed to telephone regularly when Charles wasn't around. There was another suitor by the name of Earl (presumably another American soldier) and although Hattie met him for dinner at Quaglino's, it was Charles who Hattie really wanted. An entry on 10 February says it all, '*Please, God send me a man – God sent him! Met him at 5.10 am – drunk by 6.10 am.*'

Hattie also wrote a Valentine's Day card to Charles,

'My ownest own and dearest dear
My heart is in a whirl

I want to be your darling wife
Your loving little girl.'

Next to the word 'wife' is an asterisk with a note from Hattie, *'If you know what I mean.'* As Hattie never sent the card, it may be that she lacked the confidence to give it to him so early on in their relationship. She was also only too aware of Charles's marital status.

Soon after Valentine's Day, Charles wrote, having stayed with her in Gunnersbury, *'I felt quite alone when my train started away from you today. I just sat there a nice warm feeling thinking about you. Know what? This, my friend, is the first time in my life I have been faced with a problem I can't seem to solve. Honey, you are going to divert my attention from the war effort and we will be in the clutches of Hitler . . . I wonder what his clutch is like?'*

Charles was a heavy drinker, and there are several references to his seeking solace in alcohol, *'I am sitting here looking at my bed. I just know I won't sleep. I'll be afraid in bed alone now. I am not used to going to bed and going to sleep anyway, I am used to passing out.'* There are also jealous references to Hattie being with other men, *'Listen friend, I am under the impression that you are mine, if I am wrong, correct me. If I am right or wrong it is your fault, you make me feel as though you are mine, and since you are mine, you can do just as you please (only don't let me find out) . . . I don't know why I should love you though, you are mean to me. Always paying attention to other men when there are other men around.'*

Hattie has also informed him about an ex-boyfriend to which he replies, *'I am truly glad you wrote to me so frankly about your ex. I want you to always be frank with me. I shall always be that way with you. Not that I am glad that I came between you, if I did. Although I am not contributing much to your happiness, I will always want to do what will bring you happiness. So let's have this between us, I will always consider you faithful to me as long as you never do anything that would someday make you feel that you had been unfaithful to yourself.'*

An entry in her diary dated 20 February 1944 stated, '*To Nana's* (Adelaide) – *going to give me some furniture.* It seemed that the move to Eardley Crescent was getting closer. During the same month, Hattie made several trips to the Labour Exchange and was clearly in some kind of dispute. Towards the end of the month, she remarked upon a series of heavy air raids to which 'our hero' refers, '*And then too you were nearly bombed, and here I was safe many miles away. Jerry was certainly lucky, as, had I been in that vicinity, I would have gone up into the air in 'Superman' fashion, results 37 planes destroyed, women and children saved, another black mask on my fingers.*'

Despite his obvious attraction for her, Hattie was still very self-conscious about her size and had clearly described how she felt. She was consulting a doctor about diets and Charles replied, in confidence-boosting fashion, '*I don't know why you think I'll love you more if you are thin . . . I love you as much as I can now, you have nothing to worry about. What do you mean, you wish you deserved my love? Darling, you deserve more than I can ever give you, but I do give you all my love, my thoughts and myself. The rest of what you deserve may come some day. I only hope you can be satisfied with me until you do find what you deserve . . . Darling I think it is grand that you lost 4lbs, since you are so set on wanting to lose weight. I have only one thing to ask. No two things. First: Be careful, do as the doctor tells you don't try and double doses. Second: If you are intent on going thru with it, be faithful in the things he tells you to do. I want you to be successful if you want to be thinner. Don't get too thin, I want enough of you left to love. And don't change within yourself. Keep sweet like you are.*'

At the beginning of March 1944 Hattie received her first pay cheque from The Players'. This was not for payment as a performer, but for backstage duties. Hattie took up the story in a later interview: 'When I was twenty-two, I was helping in productions at The Players' in my spare time. I was asked to "sit on the book", which is theatrical slang for looking after the prompt book. I took it literally, thinking they wanted me to press it down because I was the heaviest – so down I plumped and forgot all about it and everyone went mad searching for the thing!'

Hattie continued to work at The Players' on an informal basis for the next few months but did not receive a regular salary. She returned briefly to the Red Cross station in Hammersmith where she worked for a couple of days. However, during this period of unemployment, Hattie was being helped financially by the Major, who gallantly wrote, *'No more talk out of you about spending all of my money. There wasn't much to start with and what I did have is our . . . our money . . . not my money.'*

Despite Hattie *'pitching woo with my darling'* at the Piccadilly Hotel, the pressures of the relationship were beginning to tell. *'You were a grand sort of person with me over the weekend,'* wrote Charles, *'Strange too. What made you different than you usually are? You weren't mean with me like you always were before. Your acting is improving or you are in love with me a little? How is mummy and granny? I send my love, tell them both to keep an eye on you for me.'*

Another letter, later in the month was somewhat gloomy, *'Darling, darling, your letter made me feel as though I am not being fair to you. I know I shouldn't love you like this, I have no right to. I know you have grown to love me and that someday we are going to be hurt. Both of us. It doesn't seem fair to any of us to look forward and hope that some way or another we shall be together forever. This is always a chance I know. But I don't think we should build on it . . . it is not easy for me either, but then, it shouldn't be easy for me as it is my fault entirely . . . I have been very happy loving you and being loved by you in return. We have had some wonderful moments together darling. Jo! I am sorry it has to be this way . . . I used to feel that I would never come out of this war alive, it would be easy that way, wouldn't it. At least you would know where I was. I don't think it would be hard that way, but there is a chance I may come out of this war alive. If I do darling, there is a chance that we can at least be in the same country together. It wouldn't be fair to you of course, to come over to the States so that you would be near me. I could feel as though I could look after you a little bit.'*

Hattie's response was to give her telephone number to an unnamed Colonel which she later regretted, but which she made sure Charles knew about! In April of 1944, there is first mention in Charles' letters of his wife and daughter, *'Lets see, you should have those photos by now, when you send them to me, I'll take all those other girls pictures off my mantle, all but Ruthie's* [wife] *and Judy Kay* [daughter]. *I must show you the pictures they sent me. I meant to mention it before. They are sweet as sugar, you will love them. Judy Kay looks like something from heaven. Little chubby mug she is . . . I have about ten minutes yet to finish this and write Ruthie and Judy Kay. Bet they are mad at me. I haven't written them since Saturday evening. See now what I am like. I allow my work to interfere with my pleasure.'*

It was surprising that Charles should mention his wife and daughter – certainly his wife – in such affectionate terms and one wonders how Hattie must have felt as the other woman in his life. Here and elsewhere one is left with the impression that they knew their love was hopeless, but maintained the pretence while it burned brightly. After the mention of Judy Kay, it seems that Hattie must have written to him about her desire to have a child with him. His response was unsentimental, *'Honey you don't want to be a mother ever. I know you wouldn't like it. Anyway it might look like me, then what would the poor thing do? You would have to drown it.'*

Charles got back to basics with his next letter, *'Darling I am hungry for you. I need you even if it is only for a couple of hours. Been so long since I have seen you. Yet it has only been three weeks. Remember when we had planned on seeing each other once a month, then it got to be twice a month. Think of all the grand times we have had since then. Of course they are only samples of the good times we are going to have, that is if I don't continue to grow older each day.'*

He and Hattie were able to spend some time together in a hotel in Bristol in the first week of May 1944. Hattie was now spending part of her time in Gunnersbury and the rest at Eardley Crescent. But later in the month, on 23 May, she made a mysterious visit to a private address in Streatham, south London where she underwent *'a slight op'*. The following day an entry states, *'No go'*, and then on 25 May, *'things happened . . . Robin came – terrible pain all the time'*.

Hattie received a visit from a doctor the following week, and on 20 June, a month after her operation, she complains of *'hurting like hell and Goddamm awful pains.'* There is no record of Hattie involving or even informing Charles of her experience and indeed there is no correspondence from him during June. Not surprising as the 112th Infantry were involved in a slightly larger affair: the D Day landings in Normandy. Hattie consoled herself in the company of her brother, made a visit to the Tropicana Club and spent more and more evenings at The Players' Theatre.

On 27 July 1944, Hattie officially moved from Gunnersbury, and her permanent address became 67 Eardley Crescent, Earls Court, London, SW5. This was a sprawling, early Victorian house in a very nice part of London and there are conflicting stories about how the Jacques family were able to purchase such a lovely house. Hattie's mother Mary Jacques was the official owner and may have been the beneficiary of some money from her father's estate following his death the previous year. Anne Valery is of the opinion that Mary's freemason auctioneer and lover purchased the property for her. There is no record of what happened to him, but he certainly never lived there.

Another – and even more significant – event took place in July 1944, which was to change Hattie's life forever. As we know, she had been frequenting The Players' Theatre regularly both as a member and also behind the scenes. Hattie had never given up on her ambition to make it as an actress, but apart from her days with the 'The Curtain Club' and the odd song at the tank factory, she hadn't made any public appearances and, more importantly, had still not performed professionally. Whether it was recalling the music hall songs she learned as a welder or whether encouraged by her brother Robin, or both, something now prompted her to try to make her break into show business.

Hattie plucked up courage to approach the then chairman of The Players' Theatre, Leonard Sachs, and asked for an audition. Sachs agreed, and Hattie described what happened next in an interview in *The Daily Mirror* in 1958, 'I went along to the audition in 1944 – not exactly the norm of the slim young ingénue. I sang 'Call Round Any Old Time' and then 'A Little of What You Fancy Does You Good', a song made famous by the saucy music hall star Marie Lloyd.' According to Hattie she gave Sachs 'an oysters and wine flash of her black eyes' and flounced into the songs. Sachs recalled the event on Hattie's *This Is Your Life,* describing Hattie resplendent in a large white jumper with a bright red dragon emblazoned on the front. Hattie was extremely nervous, but even so, Sachs couldn't believe his luck. He had seen so many 'would-be' thespians who were great in their own front rooms but just weren't talented enough to appear professionally. And he needed someone to sing Marie Lloyd songs, 'Hattie was marvellous,' he recalled, 'With a lovely presence and singing voice.' She auditioned on the Thursday and Leonard Sachs put her straight on the bill the following Monday night.

This was the start of Hattie's professional career as a singer and comedienne. From then on she became a regular and in years to come was The Players' most popular performer. She was barely ever out of work after the summer of 1944. However, this was just the beginning of her career, and her salary reflected the fact that she was a newcomer. Her wage was just £4 a week but she was also rewarded with a sandwich and a coffee at every performance . . .

After a gap of nearly two months and towards the end of July, Charles wrote again from France. Hattie had obviously informed Charles about her debut at The Players' and he responded encouragingly but dispassionately, '*Glad you are finding something that you like. Keep it up and maybe one day I can be in your audience. I'll cheer you on.*'

The tone of the rest of the letter isn't exactly optimistic for their future: '*my time is pretty well taken up. My thoughts very seldom dwell on 'leave'. Not like me huh? Of course I don't look for a leave now until it is all over and I am back in the States. But then one never knows in this game. I am afraid that sounds kind of sober but it isn't meant that way. I am becoming quite a field soldier, I would give up a lot to get dried out once again . . . have been away from the HQ twice since I have been here. Of course I haven't seen much of Paris or stuff like that there . . . I will try and write you once a week, see you when and if I can. Then when the time comes for us to stop writing I'll let you know. I have said time and time again that you would probably think me a rat when the time came. But I knew and wanted you to know that these are the two people I can't bring myself to hurt. You know who the other one is. Sorry it has to be this way sugar. But it does.'*

Hattie obviously didn't take too kindly to his missive for her response, in his words was to *'bawl him out'*. In a letter dated 8 August 1944, the Major writes, *'Received the picture and the French book yesterday. You read my letters too well I see. I was of the opinion that it would be easier on both of us if we broke away gradually. You know very well if I have the opportunity of leave, I'll hurry back. But it does seem so remote. Sugar mine, you know there isn't anything we can do about this, but if you are content to go on and hope I am not going to fight you . . . I have missed you sugar puss, I do love you . . . it is still a hope-less love.'*

Hattie wrote to him in November, asking him if he could visit her at Christmas, but Charles was dismissive, saying that she was teasing him, *'That, I think is the meanest thing you could do to a soldier whose absence might mean the war would continue a week longer.'* He did, however, suggest that he could take a trip to Paris and asked, *'can you make it?'*

Hattie couldn't make it. Since the summer, she had been appearing regularly in the 'Late Joys' revues at The Players' but in December 1944 she was due to make her first appearance in their annual Christmas pantomime. Hattie wasn't quite ready for a starring role as one of the fairies, a role that she would make her own in years to come, and instead had been offered a supporting role in *The Sleeping Beauty In The Wood*. The production featured the then doyenne of 'The Players,' Joan Sterndale Bennett, producer Don Gemmell, Daphne Anderson and Jean Anderson (no relation). *The Observer* reviewed the show's first night, describing the panto as 'amusingly mounted by this familiar and popular team, with a charming, smiling grace, and without buffoonery'.

Which is more than could be said for Major Charles Randall Kearney, who continued to exhibit an increasingly insecure nature, *'I am afraid to write this afternoon, 'cos I am frightened of what I might say!!! Can you imagine me believing that? I know all about this "out of sight, out of mind business." Here I am, only away from you for 6 months and you forget me. I know you no longer care for me and write only because you know it was me that threw the bomb at Hitler and nearly ended the war. You think, that on the strength of your knowing me I will be able to get you a job in Hollywood. You may have something there. I think I could get you a job there because someone is going to need to work to feed me as I am not going to turn a hand after this war. Besides you said that with my technique I should spend all my time in bed, and not at work.'*

There were no further letters until February 1945, most likely explained by the fact that the 112th Infantry were involved in the Ardennes Offensive, embroiled in the infamous Battle of the Bulge. When some respite from active duty allowed Charles to correspond, he wrote to Hattie, promising to spend a week with her in March. They had not seen each other for nearly a year. *'I have great plans for these seven days, think of all the loving you have coming, that which I have stored up for you, don't you wish you had saved yours instead of dissipating it away on those "Yanks" left behind.'* He apologised for the tone of his previous letter but reiterated that he didn't think he would ever see her again.

The two of them did spend a week in March 1945 together, but it appeared to end precipitously, *'Honey! I am sorry I was so foolish as to hurry thru our goodbye at the hotel, why! I acted like a little boy. I have dreaded saying goodbye, and why did I scamper away as I did, why did my tongue get thick and out of control when*

I meant to say 'I love you too, why? I dunno, only because I am me I guess and I hate 'good-bying' you.'

On 5 May Charles wrote to Hattie from a hotel in Germany, *'I should be able to contact you soon on my new address, however, should it be a time of some length don't disappear, you will hear from me. As you know, I cannot be explicit. I hate this type of letter, one that leaves you with all sorts of ideas, but you can be assured not one of them is correct . . . now that will confuse you as well as the enemy. Just hold tight sugar and remember your "mister" loves you and will write.'*

Two days later – the day before VE Day – Charles wrote the last piece of correspondence that Hattie was ever to receive from him, *'Well Sugar, tomorrow is the day, I wonder what the future holds forth to us, or rather for me. Have I told you they are going to give me the "bronze star"?'* (This was a big deal: the medal was a US Armed Services military decoration and the fourth-highest award for bravery, heroism and meritorious service.) *'I am surprised to hear the end of the war had finally arrived,'* he continued, *'Even though I have been looking for it since last Sept. Still can't believe it is over, but then the other boys are still at the other part of it. So I guess we shouldn't be too elated until that one is over. Of course that one isn't too close to home is it, seems kind of far away. Yet I guess it is pretty tough over there . . . every thing and everyone here is in a fog, wondering what will happen next. Be good darling, I will write you more, even though you can't write me for a while, love and kisses, your Mister.'*

The tone of this letter suggests that Major Kearney is returning to the United States, reinforced by the fact that he tells Hattie that she can't write him for a while – his wife Ruthie might intercept it. The feeling is that this is 'the kiss off', albeit expressed in benign terms. Charles was trying to let her down gently.

Hattie and Charles never saw each other again.

Daphne Anderson, who shared a dressing room with Hattie at The Players' (there were only two dressing rooms at the Theatre – one for men and one for the women), remembered that there was much gossip and chatter about boyfriends but Hattie never mentioned Charles. Hattie informed close friends that Charles had died before the end of the war. She told Bruce Copp that her Major had been killed in a bombing raid, and Joan Le Mesurier (later wife of Hattie's husband John), remembered a story about a car crash. In subsequent magazine interviews, Hattie spoke poignantly of 'a fiancé' with whom she was very much in love and who had been killed in action during the war.

The story was further dramatised in 1948 when a séance was held at Eardley Crescent. Among those present were Bruce Copp, Players' Theatre performer Bob Nicholls and a young couple who lived opposite. Lettered playing cards were laid out on the kitchen table and the participants all placed their fingers gently on a glass tumbler. Initially the glass remained stationary, then it slowly began to move and then it gathered speed, before whizzing around the table, picking out letters. At first, the words were indecipherable. Then, extraordinarily, a sentence formed. It was a message from Charles: his widow, Ruth had been aware of Hattie's existence and now that Charles was dead she wanted Hattie to have her wedding ring, a Kearney family heirloom.

Four weeks later, Hattie told Bruce Copp that she had received a package from the United States, containing a wedding ring with a letter from Charles' wife, Ruth Kearney. It allegedly revealed that Charles had told Ruth he was going to leave her and that he intended to marry Hattie after the war. Their marriage had been on the rocks for some time and she realised that there was nothing she could do to save it. She wanted Hattie to have the ring.

Bruce Copp, who tells the story, is insistent that the séance did take place but admits that he never saw either the letter or the ring. As he wasn't introduced to Hattie until after the war, he had never met Charles. Hattie, however, had told him that she and Charles were going to set up home together after the war and had even arranged an entry in the phone book at Eardley Crescent.

There is a further twist to the story. According to American records, a Charles Randall Kearney (born 30 August 1908 in Brockway, rural Pennsylvania, son of a railroad car inspector) died on 29 February 1984 in Stoneham, Massachusetts. He had married a Ruth Callista Klawuhn on 12 May 1932, and they had had a daughter, called Judy Kay, born around 1939, but they later divorced. It seems that Major Kearney had survived the war, returned to the USA, remarried and had another child with his second wife.

Hattie's story that Charles had been killed during the war may have been fantasy – a final and convenient way of dealing with her loss. She didn't need to explain why or how Charles had rejected her or why he was no longer in her life. Telling everyone he died may have been cathartic. Bruce Copp feels that it was unlike Hattie not to be totally honest, but understands that this was perhaps her easiest way of coping with the rejection of a man with whom she was desperately in love. According to Bruce, when he first met Hattie, she was indeed grieving in her own way for Charles and it took her a long time to get over her 'bereavement'.

Reading Charles's letters, one gets the feeling that their relationship was always doomed. There were moments when the lovers dreamed about being together forever, even to the extent of Charles finding work for Hattie in Hollywood. In hindsight, this seems like idle talk, but who can blame them for fantasising. This was a romance very much of its time: a wartime affair, when many promises are made and broken.

Hattie coped with the end of the affair in the only way that she could. As far as she was concerned Charles died, as heroes in wartime do.

CHAPTER FOUR

The Players' the Thing

I occupy the Chair, boys,
By jingo, I'm all there, boys,
With my rat-tat for order boys, I'm the idol of the Hall!
When eight o'clock is striking, the performance I begin
With a sentimental song or two to sing the people in;
And having done my turn I take possession of the Chair,
And all admire my shirt-front, snowy studs and curly hair!

THE CHAIRMAN

ACCORDING TO *Late and Early Joys*, the excellent history of The Players' Theatre, its precursor was the Evans' 'Song and Supper Rooms' of the 1820s which first introduced Londoners to the joys of cabaret. (Evans, a comedian at Covent Garden Theatre, had acquired the business from a Mr Joy, who was pastry cook to King William IV.) Charles Dickens, William Thackeray and W.S. Gilbert would later frequent the Rooms, 'singing the bacchanalian ballads of the time, over chops and ale'. Hot meals were apparently served up until three in the morning, accompanied by tankards of 'foaming ale or steaming glasses of grog'.

Evans' closed in 1880, but it wasn't until over forty-five years later that a club known as Playroom 6 opened at 6 New Compton Street, introducing a young aspiring actress called Peggy Ashcroft. In 1929 it was renamed The Players' Theatre and subsequently moved to 43 King Street in Covent Garden.

Peter Ridgeway and Leonard Sachs took it over later and

revived the 'Late Joys' cabaret, giving Peter Ustinov his first stage appearance. The first evening of *Late Joys* entertainment took place on 6 December 1937 and was true to its name. Evening performances began at 11.30pm, so that artists who had been otherwise engaged could attend. The waiters were actors or friends of the actors who either stage-managed, sold tickets or worked in the cloakroom. Following the outbreak of the war, a dais and a piano were moved into the basement, 'the show went on', and The Players' first pantomime *Whittington Junior and His Cat* was produced during Christmas 1939. However, as the war moved into its second year, air raids intensified, and the basement was purloined as a permanent shelter.

A lease was obtained for the basement of 13 Albemarle Street, Piccadilly – formerly the 'El Morocco' nightclub. Apart from 'The Windmill', The Players' was the only other theatre 'never to close' throughout the war.

A 'chairman', who introduced the acts, usually ran the proceedings, and it was his style and character that defined the atmosphere of the room. Leonard Sachs was the chairman when Hattie started to appear regularly. As *Late and Early Joys* recounts, 'Sachs' effervescent vitality and flow of repartee gave him a well-deserved reputation in handling the audiences and making them forget the Blitz. That gave as much to the entertainment as did the artistry of the company gathered there night after bomb-wrecked night.' Sachs was also responsible for the recruitment of a number of performers with whom he had acted, including Alec Clunes, Patricia Hayes and Bernard Miles. (Clive Dunn, who performed duets with Hattie at The Players', also acted as chairman and was described by various people as both the best and the worst chair The Players' had ever had. At least, as he himself says, 'I made some sort of impression!')

Don Gemmell, who was in charge of productions, gave Hattie her first contract in 'Joys'. Hattie was described as having exactly the right talent, outgoing personality and warmth to fit in immediately in a music-hall setting. However, her 'little girl' voice, although natural in tone, according to early reviews, 'barely reached to the back of the tiny auditorium.'

Leonard Sachs was something of a perfectionist when it came to the Victorian era and consequently the cast had to dress in exact period costume, no contemporary jewellery was permissible, and hair had to be styled in an authentic manner. Hattie was able to advise on hairstyles, having worked briefly with those Kensington dowagers.

In 1953, Leonard Sachs became the celebrated chairman of the BBC television show *The Good Old Days*, which was first broadcast from the City Varieties Theatre, Leeds. Sachs reached notoriety as the verbose chairman who, in his introduction of each act, would reel off a list of lengthy, plauditory commendations to the audience. Finally he would bang his gavel loudly and announce the name of the act who would then take centre stage. The audience not only wore period clothes and adorned themselves in false beards, stick-on moustaches and side-whiskers but were also encouraged to join in the songs.

The Good Old Days ran for thirty years, featuring over two thousand artists and was a faithful facsimile of an evening at the music hall. Funnily enough, there is nothing in the BBC written archive at Caversham to verify that Hattie ever appeared on the show. Even with all her subsequent radio and television commitments, it is surprising that she didn't perform her old Marie Lloyd songs.

In 1945 The Players' moved premises again, and following a press reception after the Theatre's opening night, the *News Chronicle* reported, 'The dear Players' are back in West Central again. They have taken the old Forum cinema, under the arches, in Villiers Street and converted it into their new home. It is bright and pink and noisy and suitable.' *The Morning Advertiser* described the same night as, 'Extraordinary scenes of riotous enthusiasm were witnessed last Monday evening at the re-opening of The Players' Theatre. To the strains of 'Slap, Bang! Here we are again!' the huge audience shouted itself hoarse and this wonderful entertainment . . . was rapturously launched in its new home.'

For the first two years under Leonard Sachs' management, the policy of giving new plays and revues a home was tried and tested. Gradually The Players' spread its wings, with two television broadcasts, one from Alexandra Palace, on 11 June 1946, which was judged to be 'quite good entertainment', although *The Evening News* stated that, 'We saw too little of the artists and too much of the audience'.

Up until now Hattie was still known on stage as Josephine Jacques, but it was a production at The Players' in 1946 in which she was given the nickname that she would adopt professionally for the rest her life and by which was always affectionately known by her fans. While appearing in a minstrel show, *Coal Black Mammies for Dixie* and singing 'The Robert E Lee' and 'There'll Be a Hot Time in the Old Town Tonight', 'Jo', as she was still known to friends had blacked up, and one of the backstage staff likened her to Hattie McDaniel, the rotund black actress in *Gone With The Wind*.

Hattie later recounted the story, 'Leonard Sachs announced the next artiste, "And now ladies and gentlemen, your own, your very own, Josephine Jacques," it never sounded right, even though it was my own name. "Josie Jacques" was too much like a "Gibson Girl" [a Gibson Girl was the idealised American girl of the 1890s as drawn by the artist Charles Dana Gibson], and when they called me "Jo Jacques" it sounded like a chap. I was "Belle" for a few weeks, then one night I wore black stage make-up and everyone said I looked like the big black American actress, Hattie McDaniel, so I became Hattie from then on.' She also confirmed this in 1980, in a television interview with presenter Tony Bilbow, shortly before her death.

Despite this, alternative versions of how Hattie got her name still exist; the dancer and singer Josephine Gordon thought that Betty Lawrence, the resident pianist at The Players', had been to see a show called *Panama Hattie* and told the then Josephine Jacques that she should be known as 'Hattie'. Hattie was also known to wear some of the more flamboyant costumes from The Players' wardrobe, in particular cloaks and wide-brimmed hats, and someone said that that was how she picked up the Hattie sobriquet.

Even after the Major's departure, Hattie continued to devote time to men in uniform. She did a show with some of her fellow artistes from The Players' for the Queensbury Air Services Club at the London Casino in Old Compton Street and also gave her time to other Army events, as a letter from the Headquarters of the Grenadier Guards attests.

EGGINGTON HOUSE
25–29 BUCKINGHAM GATE SW1
DEC 29TH 1945

Dear Miss Jacques,

This is to say thank you on behalf of myself and the Grenadiers for coming down to 'special area' to help give them their Christmas party. You must have realised at the time how much they were enjoying themselves and this letter is merely to reinforce the impression you took away with you. I thought it was kind of you to come and I hope this note will convey to you how much your visit was enjoyed
All the best for 1946
Yours sincerely
Peter Potter

In 1946, another young man, recently demobbed from the Army was to cross Hattie's path and would remain her closest friend for nearly thirty-five years. Bruce Copp had served throughout the war, achieving an extremely distinguished war service. He was mentioned in despatches for bravery in Tunisia and, following the North African campaign, was seconded to General Staff Counter Intelligence. He was in charge of two hundred staff, tracking down Nazis in Austria and was responsible for the arrest of conductor Herbert von Karajan, whose career had been given a significant boost when he had applied for membership in the Nazi Party.

Freddie Stevenson, an Army friend of Bruce's, had been offered a room in a house in Earls Court, but had found alternative accommodation and suggested that Bruce, who was also looking for somewhere to live, take up the offer. Bruce was, as he himself says, 'Slim and tanned and rather good looking'. One September morning he took a taxi from Paddington station and rang the bell at 67 Eardley Crescent. The door was opened by someone who Bruce described as 'a rather unattractive old queen'. This was Edgar Redding, who worked at Bermans (the theatrical costumiers) and rented a two-bedroom, first-floor flat in the house. Bruce asked about the vacancy, and in response Edgar looked Bruce up and down and said, 'All my stuff is in the spare room, we'll have to share one of the bedrooms.' Although Bruce himself was gay, Edgar was not his type; 'My heart sank. I thought this might cause problems. He did pounce on me later but I rejected him very nicely.'

Edgar invited Bruce in and showed him the room, after which he said, 'Oh, I'd better introduce you to the girl upstairs.' He called up to 'the girl' who, in turn, shouted in response, 'I'm just cooking breakfast. He can come up.'

Bruce went upstairs and saw a young woman in a blue crepe evening dress, worn as a dressing gown, in the middle of cooking a hearty English fry-up to which Bruce was immediately invited, 'When I first met her, she was standing by the cooker in full evening dress at nine o'clock in the morning. Admittedly it was an old tatty, stained dress that she wore as a housecoat . . . but that was typical Hattie.'

The two took an immediate liking to each other and soon formed a symbiotic friendship. Bruce moved into Eardley Crescent in September 1946 and initially shared the flat with Edgar Redding before moving to the top floor, which he shared with Hattie. Although Hattie's mother, Mary, had purchased the Eardley Crescent house, she remained in Gunnersbury and let out various rooms and flats as an investment.

Hattie, broken-hearted by the loss of Charles, consoled herself with a series of boyfriends. Both Hattie and Bruce indulged themselves in matters of the flesh and occasionally found themselves breakfasting with their conquests from the previous night. The lovers, mainly actors or models, were graduates from the Rank Charm School and included an actor with whom Hattie was to appear in future years in a number of *Carry On* films. Unfortunately, the actor was married to a mutual friend and so the affair had to be kept very secret.

The other reason for secrecy was that 'pupils' at the Charm School, J. Arthur Rank's institution for young film actors, were not only trained in the techniques of cinema acting but were also expected to behave themselves both on and off the set. Rank could actually suspend a contract if the gossip columns got wind of any damaging scandal. The actors were all disturbingly handsome, the actresses gorgeous, and graduates included sex symbols Diana Dors and Joan Collins and the more unlikely Christopher Lee. By 1946, in addition to the Charm School, the Rank Organisation also owned five studios, including Pinewood and Denham, a large number of production companies, its own distribution subsidiary and more than 650 cinemas.

Bruce described Hattie as very flirtatious and quite unabashed about her sexual needs. Even after she became better known, Hattie kept her name in the telephone book and received regular anonymous and obscene phone calls from men who liked 'large ladies'. Far from being angry or embarrassed by these calls, she used to play along with them, often jokingly encouraging the men and sometimes persuading Bruce Copp to participate on another telephone extension!

Bruce and Hattie, who were becoming close friends, decided to buy a dog and, following a visit to Battersea Dogs Home, came home with a cocker spaniel, which they called 'Guinea' (the amount they donated to Battersea). Bruce said that the dog was extremely intelligent, very well behaved and even attempted to answer the telephone when it rang! On occasions, they used to take him to The Players', where he was welcomed and spoiled. Once, Guinea got out of the house, crossed the road to the Earls Court tube station and, believe it or not, commuted to Charing Cross station, where, following his nose up Villiers Street, he entered The Players' Theatre. He ran on the stage while Hattie was performing and although the audience thought it was hilarious, the curtain had to be brought down. Leonard Sachs was apparently equally amused and began to think of ways the dog could be kept in the show! Guinea wasn't destined for a career in show business. Hattie felt it wasn't fair to leave him alone for long periods in the house and arranged for him to be rehoused in large country house with lots of company and grounds. She may have also been slightly concerned about him stealing her limelight . . .

Towards the end of 1946, Hattie was asked to join The Young Vic Theatre Company, described as 'a theatre for young people' in a play entitled, *The King Stag*, 'a comedy with magic and music' by Carlo Gozzi, starring Rupert Davies (later famous as Maigret) and first performed in Venice in 1762. Hattie was cast as Smeraldina, the Royal Butler's sister. The play opened at the Lyric Theatre Hammersmith on 26 December 1946 and after sixty-six performances, the company embarked upon a five-month tour of the provinces, Cardiff and Belfast. The tour, in association with The Arts Council of Great Britain, the National Theatre and The Old Vic, was produced by George Devine and coincided with one of the coldest winters ever recorded – snow covered much of the country for fifty-two days and, as a result, houses were not huge. Notices were good and included the following review in *The Times*, 'The Young Vic last night produced their first play and a very jolly one it proved to be, which the elderly will enjoy as much as the young.'

While Hattie was on tour, she offered Bruce the use her room if any of his friends wanted to stay. Freddie Stevenson took up the offer and stayed for a few days. One night, cruising the West End, he picked up a Guardsman and brought him back to Eardley Crescent, where they went to bed. Apparently things were not going all that well, physically, until the soldier, spotting Hattie's open wardrobe door, rummaged around and attired himself in some of her more rococo clothing, thereby ensuring a successful night of passion.

According to Bruce, the clothes actually fitted the Guardsman rather well, and when Hattie returned from the tour and was regaled with the night-time frolics, she wasn't at all put out – in fact she thought it was quite hilarious.

Hattie had learned to cook from her mother, who was more than at home on the range, and, what with Bruce's culinary flair, the Eardley Crescent house soon became renowned for its gastronomic treats. Even during rationing, the two of them managed to create mini-banquets from limited resources. Hattie introduced Bruce to The Players' in 1947 and he started working behind the bar, soon to become a very successful 'chargé d'affaires' of the supper rooms. He left in 1953 to establish his own restaurants: The Hungry Horse and The Matelot. Later Bruce ran the restaurant at Bernard Miles's Mermaid Theatre and was manager of the infamous Establishment Club.

Meanwhile back at The Players', a revue, *Players', Please*, was produced by Leonard Sachs in December 1947, in place of the usual Christmas pantomime. Starring Joan Sterndale Bennett, Vida Hope and Eleanor Summerfield, it featured Hattie in several numbers, including a duet with Bill Rowbotham in which they performed a sentimental song, 'After The War', written by Ronnie Hill. The reviews were glowing; *The Times* reported, 'Miss Hattie Jacques, besides powerfully and gaily driving home several songs which depend on their refrains, gives point to an effective satire on the surplus fighting energy which seeks an outlet in peace.' The *Daily Mail* said 'It is just the thing to go with the auditorium beer sipping, a heartily arty, uninhibited show.' Harold Hobson in *The Sunday Times* 'Scene after scene in its present revue is put on with a compelling evocativeness.' True to form, *The Stage* was full of praise, 'There are songs, sentiment, sense and satire that give delight.'

Hattie was now on top vocal form, and, comparing her voice to those early appearances at Albemarle Street, *Late and Early Joys* stated, 'Those members who in these times are in the habit of seeing the Joys from the bar on the shelf of the Villiers street Theatre may not be inclined to believe this, when every syllable of her robust ballads reverberates on the eardrums as she sets the house in a roar.'

Actor Clive Dunn made his debut at The Players' in 1947 and used to perform duets with Hattie – the most amusing being their rendition of 'I Don't Want to Play in Your Yard' in which Clive and Hattie were dressed as little girls, who had fallen out with each other and were no longer friends. Their performance was reprised some twenty-five years later on *This Is Your Life* for Clive. He had naturally forgotten all the lyrics, but Hattie was still word perfect!

As Hattie's performances became more assured, she quickly established a reputation as one of the most popular entertainers – if not the most popular – at The Players'. A regular chant of 'We want Hattie' rose loudly from the audience and she received habitual praise from the public and her peers. Patsy Rowlands recalled, 'Hattie had the audience in the palm of her hand. There was no stage door at The Players' and, at the end of the show, we had to exit through the audience. When Hattie left the Theatre, the crowds used to wait especially so that they could cheer her.' Patsy also spoke fondly of Hattie's laughter, which was so infectious that 'she set everyone off'.

However, with increasing confidence in her performances and receiving more and accolades, Hattie became further concerned with calibre of the entertainers who were employed at The Players'. Clive Dunn remembers that Hattie could occasionally be firm, even sarcastic, with her fellow artistes – she had become quite a perfectionist when it came to performances – and expected total commitment from other members of the cast.

Although instinctively sympathetic, Hattie, who didn't suffer fools gladly, was quite tenacious when she needed to be. Cast members reported that she soon developed a reputation of sometimes being over-fussy and wasn't backward in giving advice. And, like Leonard Sachs, she could become infuriated if a cast member wore a piece of jewellery that wasn't in keeping with the period productions. The ethos of The Players' was that if the song and performance originated from a particular year then the costume and accoutrements must be authentic. Patsy Rowlands reiterated the point, 'Hattie was a stickler for discipline and because it was supposed to be a Victorian Theatre, she did it strictly by the book. Everything had to be right. Make up, costumes, the lot.'

Ian Carmichael also started his career at The Players'; he remembers Hattie as a regular performer, but he himself used to 'pop in and out of the shows.' The Players' was a useful venue for actors, who, if out of work, could ring up Don Gemmell or Leonard Sachs and ask to be put on the bill for a week or two if times were hard. Carmichael sang light numbers such as 'I Must Go Home Tonight', 'There Are Nice Girls Everywhere' and 'I Do Like To Be Beside The Seaside'. He worked with Hattie in later years in *School for Scoundrels* and they both also appeared in *Celebrity Squares* in 1976. Ian remembers Hattie as very amusing and his memory is that he, 'never heard a cross word pass her lips'.

A description of The Players' during this particular era appeared in the *New Statesman*: 'Here in the atmosphere of mutton-chop whiskers, heavy moustaches, hot pies, hot dogs and glasses of beer, the hoarse ripe lusty voice of chairman Don Gemmell calls for our "customary warmth of welcome" for that darling of the Joys, Hattie Jacques, who is going to perform something about a cock linnet. There is a roar of applause as she comes on from the wings – there's a don't give a darn air about her that is sheer delight and a brawling boisterousness that sends the choruses ringing to the roof.'

Actress and dancer Josephine Gordon remembers the marvellous atmosphere of the theatre, but that the plumbing was a disgrace and the fire regulations non-existent. It would have been closed instantly if subject to today's more stringent health and safety checks. During songs and sketches, trains thundered overhead on the Hungerford Bridge and the chairman sometimes had to raise his voice above the din to make himself clearly audible. The show at The Players' would always end with a 'Scena' when most of the company would take to the stage, hold hands and, accompanied by the audience, would sing their theme song, 'Dear Old Pals'.

The singer Violetta joined The Players' in 1947 as a singer. It was here that she met her future husband, Gervase Farjeon, who came from a famous theatrical family. Violetta immediately warmed to Hattie. Hattie was by now adapting a number of shows and even wrote the lyrics for a special number for Violetta, entitled 'A French Bird'. (In fact, Hattie adapted so many Victorian plays and pantomimes during her career at The Players' that, at one stage, she considered giving up performing in the shows to concentrate on directing.)

Violetta was notorious for her poor memory when it came to names and thus called everyone 'mon petit chou'. Hattie teased her, 'I don't know . . . you and your Chou Chous.' This stuck, and Violetta is still known as 'Chou' to her friends. Violetta recalls Hattie as coquettish, very sexy for her size and a wonderful dancer, who went 'on point' when she played the Fairy Queen. Hattie had a particular interest in clothes and always looked elegant, 'Hattie was very proper and didn't care for bad language.'

Violetta also appeared in another celebrated production at the Villiers Street venue. A fellow Players' performer, Diana Maddox, suggested the Theatre find work for a struggling young writer who needed work. This young man turned out to be Sandy Wilson who had written a short play, *The Boyfriend*. The play was subsequently first performed at The Players', was a great success and critically acclaimed by Noel Coward. Sandy Wilson rewrote and extended the piece when the musical later transferred to the West End.

Violetta did her last show for The Players' at the age of seventy-five. Now a vivacious octogenarian, Violetta is a member of the University of the Fourth Age where she is studying painting, 'I've been highly recommended for my apples, you know!'

In the summer of 1947 an aspiring actor, relaxing over a few drinks in a West End pub in the company of fellow thespian, Geoffrey Hibbert, suggested a visit to The Players'. They arrived too late to see the show but drinks were still being served and they chatted to some of the regulars until it was 'throwing out' time. The actor John Le Mesurier enjoyed the unique atmosphere of the venue and decided to return to the theatre in due course, this time to take in the show. In his autobiography, *A Jobbing Actor*, he wrote, 'One of the leading lights was a remarkable girl called Hattie Jacques. She was bright and witty and vivacious and an entertainer to her fingertips. Hattie would have a go at any comedy routine, but at The Players' her star turn was a take-off of Marie Lloyd. Swaggering across the stage in a moth eaten fox fur, she could carry off an entirely convincing and hilarious rendering of "One of the Ruins that Cromwell Knocked About a Bit" or even better "Don't Dilly Dally". On that first evening I was quickly caught up with Hattie's ebullient good humour and sense of anarchic fun.'

After the show one night, John asked Hattie for a drink. This was surprisingly direct for a man who remained extremely passive throughout his life. As Anne Valery stated, 'It was usually the women who discovered him.' Hattie was initially taken aback by his approach and supposedly replied, 'No, I'm not thirsty.' However, she soon relented and the two of them spent the evening together. Within a few days, Hattie introduced Le Mesurier to Bruce Copp, telling him, 'I've met this man who's rather special.'

Le Mesurier was still married to June Melville. Miss Melville was a very beautiful actress who came from a famous theatre-owning family. She was erudite, elegant and entertaining – at least until about the fourth gin and tonic, after which she became less articulate, her make-up smudged, her elegant hat slipped to a jaunty angle and her mink stole slid off her shoulders.

One of the first evenings that John Le Mesurier and Hattie spent together was in the company of June Melville and Bruce Copp. The four of them went dancing at the Lyceum in the Strand and despite his wife's presence Le Mesurier was quite open in his admiration for Hattie, who was equally captivated. According to Bruce Copp, they spent the evening, 'nose to nose – they were completely oblivious to anyone else.' June Melville seemed resigned to what was happening and said to Bruce, 'Come on, let's leave them to get on with it.' Because her family had owned the Lyceum when it was a theatre, she and Bruce went off with the manager for a private tour of the venue and left Hattie and John to their own devices. Bruce says that June seemed to accept Le Mesurier's behaviour and felt that there was nothing she could do about it. Perhaps this wasn't the first time that this had happened and, by all accounts, Miss Melville was herself no angel.

John found Hattie irresistible and described her in admiring terms, 'Hattie made a virtue of size. She wore long, billowy dresses, often very revealing. It was as if knowing she was bound to be noticed, she wanted to make a real job of it. It was characteristic of her that on visits to Covent Garden, she outmatched the sartorial splendour of the wealthier clientele by enveloping herself in a black, swirling highwayman's cloak borrowed from The Players' wardrobe.'

Soon after their first meeting, Hattie went down to Chatham to see John appearing in *The Winslow Boy* (apparently, a regular gig for John in those days). She told him that she had to find out what he was like as an actor. Le Mesurier said that he knew why it was so important for her to see his work, 'I know what she meant – if two performers get together, they must share a professional respect, otherwise the relationship is doomed. Fortunately Hattie warmly approved of my efforts to put some life into a thinly attended matinee.'

According to John's third wife, Joan Le Mesurier, who was to become a close friend of Hattie's, 'John was swept into her life and overwhelmed. Later in her career, Hattie was to allow herself to be typecast, even caricatured, as obese battleaxes, so it may be hard to visualise the exotic, Junoesque and sensual figure at the time. She rather resembled Maria Callas, having the same colouring and flashing vivacity.'

After a series of exciting but ultimately unsatisfying sexual encounters, Hattie had finally replaced her cocksure American major with a man who couldn't have been more different in character: a charming, gentle, unassuming Englishman, albeit of French background, who was to remain a devoted friend for the rest of her life.

CHAPTER FIVE

The Green Light

I had a lovely dream last night – I dreamed the bed was made of marzipan and the mattress was marshmallow and the sheets were jelly and the pillows embroidered with lovely sugar violets . . . but I'm alright now.

SOPHIE TUCKSHOP, *ITMA*

THE YEAR 1947 was hugely significant for Hattie. Barely two months after meeting John Le Mesurier, another man came into her life – one who was to be of immeasurable influence. *That Man* Tommy Handley, one of Britain's most adored comedy celebrities, had been a radio star since the early days of *Radio Radiance*, a 1925 series of sketches and songs. The medium of radio was suited to his quickfire, scatter-gun approach, and in 1939 when the BBC Variety Department was looking for a comic to follow the successful *Bandwaggon* comedy show, Tommy Handley was the obvious choice.

In *The ITMA Years 1939–1949*, PJ Kavanagh sets the scene: 'The outbreak of the war was the catalyst of the half baked ideas that was to be *ITMA*. It was a time of officialdom and officiousness, that curious strain of self importance that a crisis brings out in the British was ripe for deflation and Tommy Handley with the voice of a disaster-prone con man, more bent that a six pound note and cheery with it, was the ideal man to do the deflating.' Writer Ted Kavanagh, who hailed from New Zealand and had originally wanted to train as a doctor, submitted a sketch to

Tommy Handley. The comic liked it, wanted more material and in partnership with an archetypal BBC producer – the pipe-smoking, corduroy-jacketed – Francis Worsley an illustrious triumvirate was born.

Apart from a love of puns, (traditional fare in British comedy), *ITMA* was innovative in that characters appeared and disappeared without explanation, and the pace was something new to radio. '*ITMA* bred a new style of comedy.'

It's That Man Again had originally enjoyed a pilot-run of four broadcasts in the summer of 1939, but these were not particularly successful, and following the declaration of war in September 1939, the three men felt that the series should reflect the difficult times and create a zany world away from the awful reality that confronted the nation on a daily basis. With the creation of numerous bureaucratic institutions that the war had inevitably precipitated, it was decided that Tommy Handley become 'The Minister of Aggravation and Mysteries, a part of the Office of Twerps'.

The ITMA Years states that 'the title for the radio show which was to produce more catchphrases than any other was itself taken from one of the moment.' It was a *Daily Express* headline used each time Hitler staked yet another territorial claim, and was increasingly on the lips of an apprehensive public.

Other original characters in the show were: Tommy Handley's secretary Dotty (played by Vera Lennox); Mrs Tickle, the office char, and Vodkin, the Russian inventor (both played by Maurice Denham, a graduate from The Players' Theatre); and Funf, a ubiquitous German agent (played by Jack Train). Later, Molly Weir and Deryck Guyler also joined the cast.

By 1947, *ITMA* was generating an audience in the millions and the team were in a position to be able to increase cast numbers and bring in emerging talent. Hattie, who by now had established herself as a regular at The Players', was invited to audition for a part in the show. She was paid a fee of five guineas to attend a thirty-minute reading between 4.30 and 5 pm on 18

September at Studio 3A, Broadcasting House. 'I was so anxious that Tommy Handley held my hand . . . it actually made me more nervous. I remember I was given a copy of *Picture Post*, opened at random, and Tommy and the producer Francis Worsley told me to read the article in as many different accents as I could, changing every two sentences or so. It turned out to be an article full of statistics about paddy fields in China! I can't tell you what a mess I got into – a sort of Stanley Unwin delivery, with a Japanese-Welsh or French-Irish accent. Tommy laughed so much I got the giggles.'

In fact, everyone in the studio fell about. The audition couldn't have gone better, and within the week, Hattie had received a telephone call at Eardley Crescent from Richard Stone at Felix de Wolfe's theatrical agency (with whom she stayed all her working life) to say that she had got the part. Bruce Copp was with Hattie at the time and says, 'She was absolutely delighted. I'd never seen her happier, professionally. I knew the exposure would make her into a star and she loved being involved in *ITMA*.'

It was initially planned that Hattie was to play a character named 'Ella Phant'. Ted Kavanagh thought that they would get laughs because of her size but as Hattie explained later, 'Being radio, and coupled with the fact that my voice was rather light – it didn't really work out. It wasn't until one show when Tommy was supposed to be passing through a department store and knocked over a speaking doll, which I was playing, that the audience reacted favourably. A large schoolgirl with a very little voice seemed to hit the spot . . .'

The series started in the autumn of 1947 and Hattie joined the cast as Sophie Tuckshop, the schoolgirl with a voracious appetite who over-ate to the point of sickness, only to report later, 'But I'm alright now'. Hattie couldn't believe that she was part of the *ITMA* team. She had never worked on radio before and was starry-eyed about working with Tommy Handley, 'He was a wonderful man and one of the finest radio performers. I was very raw and to have a teacher like that was a marvellous experience.

All the broadcasting was live and he would often ad lib in the middle of a show and have us all convulsed with laughter. This could be serious because we couldn't go over the time. But he would pick up the script halfway down the page so it didn't matter what we'd lost.'

A number of these ad libs were written beforehand, sometimes with Hattie's help during rehearsals. Tommy Handley and others would seek refuge in the Captain's Cabin in Norris Street – a pub which became the recognised hangout for performers and writers before and after recordings at the Paris Cinema, where many of the radio shows of the time were made.

A highlight of Hattie's first series was a visit by the Royal Family to Broadcasting House on 4 December 1947. The programme included a concert by the BBC Symphony Orchestra, followed by an episode of *ITMA*. The plot revolved around a tour of Broadcasting House, and naturally the script was full of Royal references. After the performance, the *ITMA* team was presented to the King, Queen and Princess Margaret.

Hattie soon established herself as a much-loved regular in the show and was now earning a steady salary of ten guineas per episode. She was also working at The Players'. She was spending most evenings in the theatre and during half the week was rehearsing and recording *ITMA*.

In addition to these commitments, in the spring of 1948, Hattie did a television version of *No No Nanette* at the BBC studios at Alexandra Palace and appeared in *Bates Wharf,* a Barbara Leneker play, at the Whitehall Theatre for the 'Under Thirty Theatre Group.' In autumn 1948, Hattie donated her time to a gala revue at Theatre Royal, Drury Lane to promote National Savings. The cast included John Mills and Moira Lister, and the show featured excerpts from opera and ballet, and revue pieces in which Hattie performed with Stanley Holloway.

Hattie made her film debut in *Green for Danger* in 1946 at Pinewood Studios (she was uncredited and made only a very fleeting appearance). This 'wartime hospital tale of murder most horrid' was directed by Sidney Gilliat and starred Trevor Howard and Alastair Sim.

The following year she was cast as Mrs Kenwick in *The Life and Adventures of Nicholas Nickleby,* but made more of an impact in the 1948 production of *Oliver Twist* alongside a couple of her colleagues from The Players' (Maurice Denham and Erik Chitty), where she appeared as a singer in the Three Cripples tavern. The film, starring Robert Newton, Alec Guinness and Anthony Newley is visually impressive and considered a classic of British cinema. The film was initially banned in the United States, however, on the grounds of Guinness' portrayal of Fagin which was considered anti-Semitic. Hattie appeared as a barmaid in the film *The Spider and the Fly,* but made a more telling contribution in the 1948 film, *Trottie True,* made at Denham Studios. In this she played Daisy Delaware in a story about a young music-hall performer from Camden Town who rises to be a duchess after success at the Gaiety Theatre. The film gave Hattie the opportunity to reproduce her music hall material with Bill Owen.

However, it was to The Players' that Hattie continued to devote most of her time. Leonard Sachs, who had since become involved in radio and television productions, resigned and handed over the running of the Theatre to Don Gemmell, Reginald Wooley and Gervase Farjeon. As the end of 1948 approached, it was decided that a pantomime should fill the bill at Christmas: a revival of an earlier success at Albemarle Street, *The Sleeping Beauty in the Wood.*

Hattie played one of her most favourite parts, The Fairy Queen Antedota, in this panto (she continued to play the pantomime fairy at The Players' until 1960) and received rave reviews. *The Times* reported that 'Miss Hattie Jacques must surely be among the funniest fairies – the long suffering with which she devotes the enchanted century to teaching her younger companions to dance so markedly in contrast to the umbrage taken at the merest hint of indecorum.' A critic from *The Stage* declared, 'Hattie Jacques must have a larger heart than any other pantomime fairy . . . certainly the best of the Christmas shows.'

A rather snide piece appeared in the *Sunday Pictorial*, 'Reinforce the stage supports. Abandon all your ideas of producing a flying ballet of elves strung on wires. Here comes the Fairy Queen to end all Fairy Queens. Underneath the Arches at Charing Cross, she sings roistering Marie Lloyd songs in The Players' Theatre.'

The relationship between Hattie and John Le Mesurier continued to blossom and although he maintained a bachelor pad in Gloucester Road, they were pretty much living together. They could not marry as Le Mesurier's divorce had still not come through, but both needed the security of a live-in partnership. Besides which, Le Mesurier didn't find living alone particularly easy – he was not the most domesticated of creatures and even making a cup of tea seemed to present a complexity of choices that bemused him.

The ever-diffident Le Mesurier was still, however, not without some doubts about making a commitment, 'When I moved in with Hattie it was not without some apprehension about the future. I loved her very much and had great confidence in her will to succeed. But would I be able to keep up with her barnstorming talent? In those early days, it was a question to which even the most generous observer was bound to respond hesitantly. Hattie was already making her mark outside The Players' in *ITMA* and films.'

The contrast in their respective careers caused some difficulties at the outset; Hattie was becoming a nationally recognised artiste and Le Mesurier was attempting to establish his career and struggling to break into films. In later years, he was to become an acclaimed actor, but during this time he wasn't nearly as well known as his lover. Hattie had no such qualms about their professional status. According to Joan Le Mesurier, 'Hattie made sure that he never felt overshadowed by her growing popularity. She always encouraged him and believed in his talent.' Le Mesurier himself, wrote, 'She was well aware of my fear of not being able to keep up. She was as sensitive as I was to people calling me Mr Jacques or assuming, correctly that it was she who was bringing in the best part of the family income.'

Following Le Mesurier's arrival at Eardley Crescent, Bruce Copp moved down to the basement, Edgar Redding occupied a bedsit in the attic and as described by Joan Le Mesurier, 'John was very contented. The household ran smoothly thanks to Hattie and Bruce's organising gifts.'

ITMA had meanwhile celebrated its three hundredth episode and the twelfth series began in the autumn of 1948. However, only ten shows were ever broadcast in what was to be the final series. On 9 January 1949 Tommy Handley died suddenly of a cerebral haemorrhage. The shocking news reached Broadcasting House just as a repeat of the latest episode of *ITMA* was going out.

Two weeks after Handley's funeral, Hattie, along with thousands of others, attended a memorial service at St Paul's Cathedral, where the Bishop of London paid a final tribute, 'He was one whose genius transmuted the copper of our common experience onto the gold of exquisite foolery.' Without Tommy Handley, *ITMA* could not continue, and although his death was quite clearly a tragedy in almost every respect, one man, although naturally saddened, felt a slight sense of relief: Ted Kavanagh, having delivered over three hundred scripts, later said he felt released from a life sentence!

Just a few days after Handley's death, Hattie received the following note from David Henderson, Drama Booking Manager, BBC:

Dear Miss Jacques
Re: ITMA

'I think you will realise that since the continuance of ITMA without Tommy Handley is unthinkable we have no alternative but to inform you that your engagement is determined under the provisions of clause 21 of your contract dated 29th November and December 1948. We have decided to give an ex gratia payment of 48 Guineas equivalent to your ITMA performance fees in respect of the cancelled programme. Although it is possibly unnecessary I would like to say how deeply all of us at the BBC share the feelings of artists and public alike over the circumstances which have brought ITMA to an end and particularly the feelings of these like yourself, who have been associated with it for so long.'

Hattie gave her own generous tribute following the comedian's death, 'I shall never stop being grateful for the opportunity of working with Tommy, who must have been one of the greatest radio performers we have ever known. I learned (I hope) so much from him. His timing was unerring, his generosity as a performer unlimited, and his warmth a quality the whole nation was aware of, as was evident at his funeral – the streets were lined with people unashamedly crying at the loss of a dear friend. All of us who worked with him loved him, and he loved and cared for us. He enriched our lives in every way, and I am proud to have been in his company.'

Hattie was affected by Handley's demise in another, more fundamental, way. It seemed that neither he nor other members of the cast ever declared their repeat fees to the 'Tax Man' and, following Handley's dramatic exit, his financial affairs were investigated by Inland Revenue. In fact, all the cast, including Hattie, were interviewed and after this she was always very careful in any financial dealings with the tax authorities.

Her stint on *ITMA* paved the way for radio producers to employ her on a number of other projects, and she appeared regularly on the radio during the year in shows such as *April Revue*, *Clay's College* with Deryck Guyler, and *The Bowery Bar*, produced by Charles Chilton.

John Le Mesurier had meanwhile achieved an amicable separation from June Melville, who had now agreed to a divorce. The hearing took place, rather appropriately, at the Law Courts in the

Strand, round the corner from The Players', and was brought on the grounds of John's adultery with Hattie. According to Bruce Copp, it was all terribly civilised. The only concern was June Melville's appearance as a witness: it was likely that if the case went on after lunch, she was more than capable of enjoying a few drinks during the recess. Bruce was given the task of keeping an eye on her to ensure this didn't happen. Unfortunately, June gave Bruce the slip, telling him she was going to see a friend at the nearby New Theatre. She did go there but also paid a visit to the theatre bar where she proceeded to get sloshed. Fortunately, she composed her self enough later in the afternoon to deliver her testimony in a loud and theatrical manner and was praised by the judge for her projection and coherent evidence!

In the autumn of 1949, John Le Mesurier received a telegram from June Melville, 'The cage is open darling, you can fly away now.' The divorce had at last been finalised. Le Mesurier informed Hattie and, within a week, she proposed to him. He recounted the moment in his autobiography, 'One day Hattie and I were shopping in Earls Court. Then she turned to me and said, "Don't you think it's about time we got married?" I responded weakly on the lines that I was more than content with our present situation. I was, of course, conscious of the failure of my marriage to June. But there was no arguing with a determined woman.'

It was more likely that Le Mesurier would just never have got around to it, especially after the failure of his marriage to June Melville (she married again, but died in the early 1960s following a battle with alcoholism) but Hattie wanted the security that she thought the marriage would bring. According to Clive Dunn, Hattie, who was always insecure about her looks and size, yearned for the reassuring presence of a stable partner. He also felt that Hattie mellowed and grew in self-confidence after she met Le Mesurier.

The couple were married at Kensington Register Office on 10 November 1949. Hattie wore a long brown dress, matching shoes, fox fur and a small violet hat. She was twenty-seven years old; John was ten years older. After the wedding, Hattie and John went on a week's holiday to Southsea. Le Mesurier described their bridal suite as, 'The front upstairs room of a typical boarding house run by a dear lady called Kitty Clisby who had worked with Hattie at The Players' as well as being a masseuse in the Turkish baths in Jermyn Street.'

The decade ended with Hattie following up previous successes at The Players' with another pantomime, *Beauty and the Beast*. An account from *Late and Early Joys*, describes Hattie's backstage persona, 'Hattie Jacques (The fairy Marrygolda) taking everything in her stride, carrying her enormous handbag that could contain half the sets and does contain heaven knows what, mislaying her script, leaving a valuable camera on the settee in the foyer, always losing something, seldom ruffled . . . learning her part sitting in the box office, over staff dinners, downstairs, upstairs, in taxis and dashing off to recordings of BBC programmes in between, eternally smoking . . .'

The Evening Standard reported, 'The audience took the pantomime to their hearts night after night for weeks. A particular event during the run was the visit of Princess Margaret. It was the evening of Queen Victoria's birthday and so unobtrusive was the Princess' visit that many people didn't know she was there.' The Princess 'joined gaily in the songs, laughed heartily at the Chairman and watched the cake being cut in honour of Queen Victoria.'

It was in a film released at the beginning of 1950 that Hattie really made her mark. In *Chance of a Lifetime*, Hattie was cast as Alice, a hard-bitten factory worker. Co-scripted by Walter Greenwood and Bernard Miles, it starred Kenneth More, Bernard Miles and Basil Radford. It told the story of a small engineering works manufacturing agricultural equipment, whose owner, having grown impatient by the demands of the workforce for better wages and conditions, walks out, giving them the opportunity to run the factory for themselves. After early optimism, the workers run into trouble and the owner returns to assist them.

Everyone mucks in, facing the uncertain future together. *Chance of a Lifetime* is a likeable film and avoids whimsy and senti-mentality, using locations in a real factory and credible characters. Although it is scarcely controversial by modern-day standards, the political message resulted in the film being denied a general release.

Ironically, Hattie's role was that of a welder and Bernard Miles assumed that she would have no idea of what that entailed. He hired a professional welder to show her and other cast members how to use the equipment. When he met Hattie pre-production, presumably with agent, Felix de Wolfe, to discuss her fee for the film, he offered an amount which he considered fair for seventeen days' shooting. Hattie's response to the director was, 'I've done this job, welding Bailey and Pontoon Bridges and I know how hard it is. That's not enough money!'

Bernard Miles had to improve his offer and, when interviewed on Hattie's *This Is Your Life*, nearly a decade and a half later, said, 'She was worth every penny and more. She is a born actress, witty, sensitive, and warm – she should be used constantly on screen and in plays.' He added, 'She has far more vivacity and sex appeal than any woman I know. She should be a straight actress and I predict she'll be snapped up by Hollywood soon – they'll know how to use her properly.' When this was repeated to Hattie on Terry Wogan's television interview in 1971, Hattie was suitably embarrassed and responded to audience laughter, 'Bernard is a bit strange. Still, I'm glad you said it again. I wish it was true.'

Hattie enjoyed working on the film very much, although in a postcard written to her mother, she reported, 'I have settled in – if that is the right description of being in a room between a mad deaf person and Peggy Ann Clifford (cast member). I am up at 6 o'clock every morning and then stand all day in a factory yard in the piercing wind on wet ground. The weather report says "cold", the script says, "summer", so we wear our little cotton frocks.'

Hattie had a small part in *Waterfront,* another film released that year. She played a singer in a kitchen sink drama, set in the slums of Liverpool's docklands. The film starred Richard Burton and Robert Newton, but failed to trouble the critics or audiences very much. Hattie then toured with Eddie Molloy in a musical comedy, *Please Teacher*. A review of a performance at The People's Palace, in Mile End Road 22 May 1950 noted, 'The humour in the show is smart, sophisticated and never vulgar. Hattie is a jolly, fat girl!'

The 'jolly, fat girl' adapted *Ali Baba and the Thirty-nine Thieves*, The Players' pantomime that Christmas. Reginald Wooley had discovered the book of the panto in the British Museum and copied it out in long hand! Apart from adapting the script, providing additional lyrics, Hattie also played Cogia Baba, Ali Baba's wife. Erik Chitty was Ali Baba and Johnny Heawood also featured as Miaza. Johnny Heawood was a dancer from Toronto, who had come to Britain during the war. He became a great friend of Hattie, who loved his flamboyant personality. Heawood went on to choreograph *The Boyfriend* and also worked on the film of *Guys and Dolls*.

'New members of The Players' will appreciate the rollicking knockabout fun, the brisk burlesque of grand opera, the cascades of excruciating rhymes and puns fetched from the ends of the earth and the dictionary . . . the pace of the production is, of course, the secret of infectious appeal . . . the carol singing by Hattie Jacques is as appealing as last year.' So *The Times* reviewed the Ali Baba panto. Further shows at The Players' in 1951 were *Apartments*, a play in which Hattie again played opposite Erik Chitty as a Mrs Tippity, and *The Crystal Palace* where Hattie was cast as the Duchess of Kent. Another production that year was crafted around Ruby Miller's 1918 performance in the musical *Going Up* and was described as 'an entrancing evening, a delightful reminder that Shaftesbury Avenue once held its own with Broadway'. Ruby Miller was then a youthful sixty-two!

There were further guest radio appearances in '*Fine Goings On*', Frankie Howerd's first-ever radio series. Written by Sid Colin and Eric Sykes and produced by the popular Jacques

Brown, the enterprise also starred Marjorie Holmes and a young Norman Wisdom. Unfortunately, Howerd had just made a disastrously nervy appearance on the Royal Variety Performance and he again failed to be funny. In fact, he became so depressed after these appearances that he considered giving up the business. Hattie also featured in another disappointing show soon after, – this time a BBC television pilot, a sketch show, featuring Bobby Howes and Zena Marshall and written by *ITMA's* Ted Kavanagh. The premise of the fortnightly show was that 'the hero will appear in the most extraordinary guises, burlesquing characters from fiction'. The show sank without trace.

Miss Jacques returned to the silver screen, making a fleeting appearance in *Scrooge* as Mrs Fezziwig, the wife of Scrooge's kindly old employer where she is seen, dancing gracefully during a party scene. The film was shot at the Nettlefold studios in Walton-on-Thames, Surrey and also starred Michael Hordern as Jacob Marley. George Cole is the young Ebenezer Scrooge. However, it is Alistair Sim's haunted portrayal of the infamous misanthrope that steals the film.

The year 1951 came to an end with another pantomime, *Riquet with the Tuft*. Described rather grandly as 'a grand comical, allegorical, magical, musical burlesque', the play was adapted by Joan Sterndale Bennett and Hattie, who also played the Fairy Queen. Reviews were good, 'It is delightfully sung, acted and staged and I suspect that Hattie Jacques and her co-author introduced most of the wit into this jolly diversion.' The *Daily Mail* reported that, 'the thing to chiefly admire here was the rhyming couplet. Whether used with resource or in desperation, it provided continual amusement.' The critic in *The Sunday Times* wrote, 'That is why the annual pantomime at The Players' Theatre is so welcome. It can always be relied upon to be one steady illumination in a crowded and disorderly sky.'

An article in *Harper's Bazaar* stated, 'Hattie Jacques, our very own and dearly beloved comedienne of The Players' Theatre, is the Fairy Queen in this year's pantomime . . . Hattie can be coy, sedate, or hideously blousy according to the style of ballad she sings.'

The idea of using a ventriloquist on the wireless does seem at first consideration a somewhat preposterous idea. However, the precedent had been set in America, when celebrated 'vent' Edgar Bergen and his comedy dummy starred in *The Edgar Bergen/Charlie McCarthy Show*. Bergen had been performing his ventriloquist act in US nightclubs since 1936.

Peter Brough and his protégé, the cheeky schoolboy, Archie Andrews, elegantly clad in a broad-striped blazer, had made guest appearances on shows such as *Navy Mixture* in the latter stages of the war with limited appeal, but it was not until 1950 that he was given his own radio show.

Hattie's involvement with Archie was the result of a visit to The Players' in 1948 by scriptwriter Eric Sykes, who was immediately captivated by her performance and described it in his autobiography, *If I don't write it nobody else will*. 'The place was in uproar as a buxom, extremely attractive young lady, gowned in the music-hall fashion of a high spirited housewife holding a bird cage, came on stage. She sang 'My Old Man Said Follow the Van and Don't Dilly Dally on the Way' with such radiance and vitality that she took my breath away. She was the darling everyone had waited for and well deserved the standing ovation she received at the end of her song. She had to sing it again, and this time the audience joined in. Incredibly, at the end of the number, she leapt into the air and landed in the splits as softly as an autumn leaf.'

Sykes was 'intoxicated' by her performance and knew that 'this evening was to be the beginning of a new flight'. Their chance to work together on a comedy series came two years later. Sykes had been commissioned to write a radio script for Peter Brough in June 1949, and a year later, on 6 June 1950, the first episode was broadcast. The show was scheduled to fill the slot previously occupied by the hugely successful *Take It from Here,* a tough act to follow. However, by the end of the first series, *Educating Archie* was entertaining an audience of twelve million listeners.

Incredibly, the programme was then broadcast for thirty weeks without a break. Hattie's fee for the first series of *Educating Archie* was twelve guineas, and for the second series fourteen guineas. In fact, the fee went up by two guineas with each series and she received half fee again for each repeat (now duly declared to Inland Revenue) as well as £3 7s 7d for five overseas broadcasts.

The theme of the show was Peter Brough being insulted by the haughty schoolboy in his unmistakable, high-pitched voice. Additional support and catchphrases were provided by Harry Secombe, Robert Moreton as Archie's tutor, and Max Bygraves as an odd-job man (*'I've arrived . . . and to prove it, I'm here'*). A thirteen-year-old soprano was the resident singer and went by the name of . . . Julie Andrews (no relation to Archie). Hattie was cast as Agatha Dinglebody and also played a selection of spinsters and maiden aunts. Later in the series Beryl Reid joined the cast in two roles: the dreadful schoolgirl Monica, and Brummie Marlene.

The two women enjoyed working together and became friends. A subsequent memo from producer Roy Speers suggested a show for Beryl and Hattie together: *'if, and when "Island Fling" is revived as a potential Home Service project some time next year, would it be a thought to cast Hattie Jacques and Beryl Reid in the respective roles taken by Angela and Hermione Baddeley, i.e. Aunt Beatrice and Aunt Babs? During "Educating Archie" they struck up a friendship and thoroughly enjoyed working together, and Beryl is too versatile a performer to be confined indefinitely to her "Monica" and "Marlene" characters. Needless to say both these artistes are appreciably cheaper than the Baddeley sisters.'*

Although a pilot recording was made with the two of them, a series never reached the airwaves. Beryl Reid remembers *Educating Archie* as a very happy project and confirmed that one of the great bonuses was working with Hattie, 'I felt much richer by working with her. A lovely, lovely lady. Dead sexy. She used to knit balaclavas for Harry Secombe.' The quirky Miss Reid never did explain why Harry Secombe needed a collection of hand-knitted balaclavas or why Hattie was so disposed to do so but

Hattie was the sort of person that if Secombe said he needed them, she would just do it – no questions asked!

Gilbert Harding, Bernard Miles and Dick Emery, as Grimble ('*I hate yew!*') all made appearances in later series. There was talk of Hattie and Dick Emery having a bit of a fling, which should not surprise anyone given Emery's reputation. After its first break, the show returned with a new tutor: a comedian who had been popular with listeners to *Bandwaggon*, Tony '*Flippin Kids*' Hancock. Max Bygraves left, and Alfred Marks took over. (By the end of the final series in 1958, Bruce Forsyth and Sid James had also been drafted in as Archie's tutor.)

Tony Hancock always found the notion of working with a wooden dummy somewhat disconcerting. Peter Brough suffered from varicose veins and standing for long intervals exacerbated the condition. Brough thought that being on the radio would give him some respite: he could work without the doll and just do Archie's voice. Hancock would have none of it. He was adamant that the dummy was present – even at rehearsals, 'I can't make the scripts live unless he's here.'

It was not a role that Hancock enjoyed. He played a character that didn't allow him any opportunity to stretch himself, he found the catchphrase somewhat stifling and he really was paranoid about the dummy. In the words of John Le Mesurier, Hancock felt 'that the doll was somehow exercising a personal spite'.

According to Bruce Copp, Hattie would return home from The Players' at about midnight, after which she cooked a very late supper. The doorbell at Eardley Crescent would then invariably ring about an hour later. It was Eric Sykes, who in order to make the deadline needed some help with finishing the script. Hattie usually managed to help Eric sort it out. Bruce used to attend rehearsals of *Educating Archie* and remembers Hattie showing Max Bygraves how to use the microphone, in this his first regular radio engagement.

For a number of years, Peter Brough had been involved in

organising the cabaret for the annual Windsor Castle Christmas party, and in 1951 Peter Sellers, Tony Hancock and Hattie Jacques performed. Tony Hancock went down very well, particularly with Princess Margaret, who apparently laughed so much, 'she was in danger of ruining her make-up'. Hattie was also involved in the following year's festivities at Windsor alongside Max Bygraves, Beryl Reid and Harry Secombe.

Hattie featured in *The Archie Andrews Christmas Show* which ran for forty-five performances at the Prince of Wales Theatre, between 21 December and 19 January 1952. There were two shows a day, very much geared to an audience of children, the first being at 11am and the second at 2.30pm. In addition to Brough and Hancock, Peter Madden and Ronald Chesney appeared. The cast were supported by a clown who doubled on drums, a magician, a pair of trick roller skaters and 'a man who made shadow pictures with his hands'. In the theatre programme, there is an advert for the Archie Andrews ventriloquist doll which is 'worked by an easily controlled device in his mouth which opens as in speech and his head turns. His arms and legs bend and Archie is smartly dressed in blazer and flannels.'

The popularity of *Educating Archie* cannot be overestimated; in 1951 Archie was inadvertently left on a train and subsequently disappeared. The 'kidnapping' created huge publicity: it made the headlines in the national newspapers. 'Missing' posters went up in shop windows up and down the country, and a £1,000 reward was offered by Peter Brough. Three days later, the culprit, fearing the nation's wrath, sent Brough an anonymous note: Archie could be found at the lost property office at Kings Cross station. Archie was discovered trapped inside a box, unable to speak or move, but otherwise unharmed and in rude health.

Educating Archie was one of a number of post-war radio shows which captured the mood and heart of the nation. At the height of its popularity a vast merchandising industry was launched: children licked Archie Andrews lollipops and washed with Archie Andrews soap. There were Archie Andrews comics and annuals, and the dummy's face appeared on mugs, ties and scarves. It's somewhat surprising that breweries didn't produce 'gottles of geer' in his name.

Educating Archie won the coveted Daily Mail National Radio Award as the 'outstanding variety series' of 1950, and the presentation, which Hattie and all the cast attended, took place at Grosvenor House on 5 December that year. The show went on to win this award for another three years running. At the peak of the show's success, *Educating Archie* pulled in fifteen million listeners and had a fan club of a quarter of a million children. The last radio performance was in 1958, when the show transferred, some-what unsuccessfully to television.

Peter Brough, as he readily admitted, wasn't the greatest of 'vents'. It was an accepted fact that Brough's lips could easily be seen to move during his act, which, although not so important in radio appearances, did discommode live audiences. Roy Hudd tells a story about the legendary comedian Sandy Powell. 'Powell was a lovely man, who I saw perform his hysterically funny ventriloquist act in Eastbourne towards the end of his career. Powell was once talking to Peter Brough and asked him where he was working next. Brough mentioned a venue in Sheffield, "Oh", said Sandy Powell, "You'll do very well there – the lighting is terrible."'

Hattie did a BBC radio play, *Arthur's Inn*, recorded at The Playhouse and broadcast in July 1952, but the most interesting project of the summer was a short film in which she and John Le Mesurier were cast together, which turned out to be a rather unusual departure for both of them. Filming began in July on *The Pleasure Garden*, a thirty-eight minute 'movie masque', a classic piece of fifties Bohemia, written and directed by an American poet, playwright and avant-garde film maker, James Broughton, who described the movie as 'A midsummer afternoon's day dream'.

The film was set in the statue-filled landscape of Crystal Palace Gardens, with its decaying bandstand, crumbling paving stones and stairways engulfed by thrusting shrubs, tangled weeds and brambles. The Gardens' statues, covered in ivy and moss, were also featured. The British Film Institute described the theme of the silent film as 'sexual desire endlessly frustrated by censorious officialdom . . . regularly offset by burlesque performances and cabaret-style lyrics, as well as by the appearance of the then relatively unknown John Le Mesurier and Hattie Jacques. Part psychodrama, part home movie, part parody, the film has an enduring charm.'

Hattie was cast as Mrs Albion (an archaic expression for England), a genial fairy whose magic touch releases uninhibited love to all she meets, and Le Mesurier as Colonel Paul K Gargoyle, the local bureaucrat who wishes to convert the Pleasure Garden into a cemetery. Two Players' veterans, Jean Anderson and Diana Maddox, also featured, as well as American actor/director Kermit Sheets. Bruce Copp played several bit parts.

Lindsay Anderson, the celebrated theatre and film director, also assisted in the production of the film and wrote an account of his experiences:

> The first practical step towards a Broughton production in London seems to have been a propitious encounter between two of his fans . . . who formed a committee and launched an appeal for five hundred pounds. Anyway it would scarcely have been true to the traditions of avant-garde cinema if we had started shooting with enough cash in the account to finish the picture.
>
> A visit to The Players' Theatre pantomime had implanted Hattie Jacques' Fairy Queen in Broughton's mind as an obsessive image of liberation and goodwill, and a happy expedition to the Crystal Palace Gardens some weeks later had somehow linked up with that, and set germinating further ideas illustrative of his favourite theme – the pursuit of love. By the summer there was a formidably large and diverse crew of pursuers waiting to be assembled in the garden. It was astonishing how many professionals proved ready to give their talents to the picture for nothing.
>
> Miss Jacques, of course, first and foremost, as Mrs Albion,

liberator and fairy godmother to the world; and at her heels a wonderfully game troupe from The Players' Theatre and elsewhere. As can be imagined scheduling was apt to present problems when one was dealing with a cast of professionals whose paid commitments had naturally to take priority over our requirements, and of amateurs with husbands to feed, or other jobs to attend to. I am prepared to bet that no British film made this year will sport a livelier or more delightful cast.

John Le Mesurier greatly enjoyed working on *The Pleasure Garden* and noted that the charm of the piece more than made up for the fact that no-one was paid for their time, 'This was just as well because all we got was the return fare from Victoria every morning for a month, the 8.40 from Victoria to the location at Crystal Palace and lunch in a nearby restaurant where we were served by an impoverished gentlewoman who wore rather bizarre hats. Hattie played the spirit of goodness and kindness, wanting everybody to have a nice time . . . she was dressed as a Fairy Queen throughout and I wore a top hat and long black overcoat and kept on smacking people thought to be behaving improperly.'

A memorable scene from the film is that of John and Hattie in their rather gothic costumes dancing gracefully in the dilapidated bandstand. The film was subsequently publicised as 'possessing an innocence which is irresistible to modern audiences'. This was not all hype, as the film won a prize for 'poetic fantasy' at the Cannes film festival in 1953.

Several more of Hattie's films were released in 1952. In *Mother Riley Meets the Vampire*, she was again cast with John Le Mesurier. The involvement of Bela Lugosi, a star of the silent films, is the most interesting element of this film. Lugosi had been doing a Dracula stage show in Brighton in 1951, which had closed due to lack of interest. The septuagenarian Lugosi, by now dependent on drugs and completely broke, was left stranded and had no option but to accept an offer to play a mad scientist in this Arthur Lucan vehicle. Old Mother Riley (Lucan's Irish washerwoman music hall character) must stop Lugosi, who is planning to take over the world with radar-controlled robots. Hattie plays a character called Mrs Jenks, and she, Mother Riley and Dandy Nichols perform an unlikely song and dance routine.

In *The Pickwick Papers*, Hattie is Mrs Nupkins, in a stellar cast that included James Hayter (as Samuel Pickwick), Donald Wolfit, Joyce Grenfell and William 'Dr Who' Hartnell. Hattie also appeared as Miss Quibble in *All Hallowe'en*, a thirty-minute short, directed by Michael Gordon, most famous for directing the Oscar-winning *Pillow Talk*, the Rock Hudson and Doris Day vehicle.

The comedy, *Our Girl Friday*, which was filmed in London and Mallorca in 1952 and released the following year, was based on *The Cautious Amorist* by Norman Lindsay and adapted and directed for the screen by Noel Langley. It charts the story of four shipwreck survivors, a young woman (the 'sizzling' Joan Collins), and three men marooned on an idyllic tropical island, and their inevitable amorous rivalries. Hattie appears very briefly as Mrs Patch, a Lancashire harridan and mother of Joan Collins (she was, in fact, only ten years older than Collins). Peter Sellers is the voice of the parrot and the film also features a young George Cole, Robertson Hare, Kenneth More (voicing a dreadful Irish accent) and a barely noticed Hermione Gingold. It's all rather dull with particularly flat dialogue.

Hattie's final film work that year was *The Love Lottery* (released in 1954), an Ealing Studios production about a film star (David Niven) who offers himself as a first prize in a lottery. Directed by Charles Laughton and starring Herbert Lom, *The Love Lottery* is a satire on the movie business, in which Hattie is cast as a chambermaid.

Meanwhile, Hattie was still recording *Educating Archie,* although a BBC memo, in November 1952, hinted at yet another production in which Hattie was to have a major, if not starring, role:

Memo from Miss M. Lipscomb Variety Booking Section
To Roy Speer

Subject Hattie Jacques 'Educating Archie'

'We should like to exercise the option we hold on the services of Hattie Jacques for further programmes in the above series. I know our option stands for thirteen, but . . . perhaps you could discover from her how many programmes she really will be able to accept, as I believe she's expecting what is known as a 'happy event' sometime in February . .

CHAPTER SIX

A Dotty Britannia
Gives Birth . . .

One day did two double takes
For standing there was Hattie Jacques,
Married her . . . good luck God bless
Creaking beds at Eardley Cres,
You did some plays with quite short runs
Hattie gave you two nice sons

CLIVE DUNN (EXTRACT FROM
'AN ODE TO JOHN LE MESURIER')

IN ADDITION TO her *Educating Archie* commitments and her
pregnancy, Hattie directed and also appeared in a Players'
revue, *The Bells of St Martins* which ran from 29 August to 29
November 1952. Hattie sang a duet with Douglas Byng – a
number by Michael Flanders, 'Spring in Whitehall' – and also
sang 'He Believes in Us' with Johnny Rutland. Alongside Joan
Sims, with whom she was to become great friends and work
regularly, Hattie appeared in a Derek Waring sketch, 'Charity
Begins at Home'. In this sketch Hattie had to slide vigorously
down a table, ending up by doing 'the splits'. Every night,
towards the end of the run, the cast all looked on nervously, being
aware of Hattie's fecund state.

Unfortunately the show had opened to distinctly average
notices, and although it did last for 107 performances, *'Bells'*

closed earlier than expected. This was something of a relief to John Le Mesurier, who was increasingly concerned at Hattie's onstage exertions.

The Players' pantomime that Christmas was *Babes in the Wood*, which Hattie directed but in which she did not appear.

Despite all her theatrical travails, Hattie's pregnancy was straightforward. She was in good health and sailed through her confinement in true 'Earth Mother' style. Hattie and John would cram themselves into their Morris Minor and take trips to the theatre and cinema right up until the time that she was admitted to the Queen Elizabeth Hospital. Le Mesurier stayed well away from the delivery room, which was probably a relief to Hattie and the nursing staff. He spent the evening of 22 March 1953 in the company of actor Denis Shaw, who, according to Le Mesurier, 'reserved his most memorable performances for the saloon bar'.

Le Mesurier later wrote, 'The hospital rang in the early morning to say that I had a son. Later I went around to greet the new arrival and was enchanted with Robin. Hattie was pale and worn out but it was not many days before she was back at work.' Hattie was actually back at Pinewood, filming *Up To His Neck* in which she played the unlikely role of the grass-skirted Rakiki, Tahitian girlfriend of Brian Rix. It was all very innocent – another desert island story. This time it was about a sailor, who was left in charge of a stores depot on a South Seas island, inhabited by hula girls, and is then forgotten about for ten years. The film featured Cyril Chamberlain, with whom Hattie later worked in a number of *Carry On* films and became close friends. Interestingly, the other *Carry On* connection was that of Peter Rogers, who worked on the film as a writer.

Apart from this project, Hattie did not work until the end of the year, when she hired several au pairs to look after Robin while she returned to The Players' stage for the Christmas pantomime, *Cinderella*. Hattie adapted the play and cast herself in the role of Fairy Fragrant. The reviews were universally good for her performance, although not quite so praiseworthy of her direction. *The*

Times stated, 'Miss Jacques as actress, playing a deliciously arch and absent-minded Fairy Queen, goes a long way to retrieve the failure of Miss Jacques dramatist'. The *Daily Mail* reported, 'Both birth and death have their pangs, but Miss Hattie Jacques' "traditional" version contains only pangs of merriment. As Fairy Fragrant, Cinderella's godmother, she sailed through it all like a Girl Guide captain who had lost her whistle. Whether it was traditional or not I leave to older and wiser judgement. Miss Hattie Jacques certainly peppered her script with some witticisms that I am sure my Grandfather never knew. But it was all rollicking good fun.' The *Daily Telegraph* described 'Miss Jacques was always a magnificent spectacle, and very funny to hear.' And *The Observer* stated, 'Hattie Jacques wanders in and out as an immense and absent-minded Fairy Queen, looking like a dotty Britannia.'

Hattie appeared in another radio play, *The Santa Claus Show*, broadcast live from the Playhouse Theatre on Christmas Day for which she received the fee of twenty guineas. The producer was a BBC legend: Denis Main Wilson.

In 1954 she had a contract for a voiceover for *Panorama*, appeared as herself at The Players' Theatre on *Tonight in Britain* – a tourist promotion film on the entertainment attractions of London, Stratford-upon-Avon and the Edinburgh Festival.

In the spring, Hattie and John took a short break to Paris, where they bumped into Max Bygraves and his wife Blossom, who were staying at the same hotel. Bygraves was having difficulty at the reception desk and Hattie, who spoke a little French, helped him out. The foursome later went to a club in the Latin Quarter. While Bygraves and Le Mesurier were in the toilets, Hattie and Blossom were approached by two male English tourists who asked them in pigeon French, 'Voulez-vous prendre un promenade?' To which Hattie replied in her dulcet tones, 'Why don't you take a running jump?' Not exactly Dorothy Parker, you might think, but Bygraves was impressed enough to repeat this anecdote on Hattie's *This Is Your Life*.

He was no doubt even more impressed with her later that year when they worked together in *Paradise Street,* a radio series produced by Roy Speer and recorded at the Paris Cinema. The show was a vehicle for Max Bygraves and featured Eric Sykes, with special guest stars such as Spike Milligan and David Jacobs in cameo appearances. The vehicle turned out to be more like an ambulance as only one episode has survived in the archives, which in this case probably <u>is</u> a reflection of its quality. Roy Speer also cast Hattie in *Archie in Goonland,* an equally unsuccessful one-off show, a sort of hybrid which combined *Educating Archie* and *The Goons* and was broadcast in June 1954.

In April 1954, Hattie directed The Players' Minstrels. Described as a 'Splendid Plantation Production in which Miss Hattie Jacques has gone to pains to recreate the authentic minstrel show with burnt cork , white gloves, banjos, a Mr Interlocutor, a Sambo, Bones, and the rest – the old soft shoe is much in evidence.' The *Daily Telegraph* reported it to be, 'perfect in period and style . . . an original and nostalgic show'. Although these shows were very much of their time and, for the most part, meant as meaningless fun, it's difficult not to be offended by white performers blacking up and portraying black stereotypes. It's equally difficult to believe that *The Black and White Minstrel Show* was still being broadcast on television as late as 1978.

Hattie and John made their first television appearance together in *Happy Holidays,* a comedy serial produced to run throughout the school summer holidays of 1954. Produced by the BBC for Children's Television, they played a married but childless couple, Mr and Mrs Mulberry who, for the summer, look after four children whose own parents are in Ceylon. At first, they all try to co-exist in the Mulberrys' cramped London flat but, finding it all too difficult, they take off for the seaside, and the action takes place at the end of a disused pier. In *Happy Holidays,* written by Peter Ling (the creator of two early TV soaps, *Compact* and *Crossroads*), Le Mesurier was the diffident dad, Hattie was cast as an affectionate but somewhat ditsy wife, and the pair were ably supported by Clive Dunn as the suitably named Mr Grimble.

The studio scenes were filmed at BBC Lime Grove studios, and the exterior beach shots at Walton-on-the-Naze, Essex. The six episodes were broadcast fortnightly on Saturday afternoons between 10 July and 18 September 1954. John Le Mesurier thought that the show had charm. Hattie's only recorded reminiscence of the show was that, 'The children are wonderful – particularly with all the business that is part of the plot. They never forget a thing.' Whereas most performers are uncomfortable, to say the least, whilst working with children, it was typically generous of Hattie to be so complimentary.

The following year, Hattie and John appeared in another television series, known collectively as *The Granville Melodramas*. Associated-Rediffusion had acquired an old music hall, the Granville Theatre, in Fulham, which was the first operational Independent Television studio. The conversion of the Granville Theatre for use as a television studio was rather primitive, and apparently the stalls floor retained its incline, creating much difficulty for the technicians, who, on occasions would lose control of their cameras! Hattie appeared in all seven episodes of *The Granville Melodramas,* a series of Victorian plays that proved surprisingly popular. The dramas also featured actor John Bailey, with whom Hattie and John struck up an immediate rapport.

Two films released in 1955 showed that Hattie loved to work no matter how small the role. In the frenetic farce *As Long As They're Happy*, starring Jack Buchanan, she popped up briefly as a 'party girl,' and in *Now and Forever*, featuring Janette Scott, Hattie was 'the woman in sports car with dog'. Brian Rix offered her a more substantial part in his production of *Plunder*, a play by Ben Travers in which Hattie played Mrs Howlett, a harridan housekeeper. The production, a Whitehall Theatre revival for BBC Television, was performed at the Riverside Studios as the Whitehall stage wasn't big enough to fit the four sets that were required for the television broadcast.

There were live television broadcasts from the Whitehall Theatre and, on occasions, the intervals extended longer than the normal theatrical performances. In order to keep the audience happy, Brian Rix used to employ Hattie and fellow Players' artiste John Hewer to perform duets and music hall songs from the Royal Box. In 1958, when Rix's number of Whitehall performances pipped the Aldwych's record, the farceur celebrated by giving every member of the audience a glass of champagne. He brought in a number of actors with whom he had worked over the years to serve the celebratory bubbly. Rix said that the audience loved being served by famous actors and were particularly delighted by Hattie's exuberant presence!

Rix has very fond memories of Hattie, whom he described as the consummate professional and great fun to work with. He employed her again in 1959 as another domineering character, Mary Brough in Ben Travers' *Cup Of Kindness*. He also remembers that Hattie was extremely sensitive about her weight and made quite sure that he and the rest of the cast were aware of her feelings. Two years later, Hattie appeared on Brian Rix's *This Is Your Life*, paying tribute to his charity work. She also accompanied him and Katie Boyle on a day's racing at Kempton when certain celebrities became owners for the day and won money for his charity, 'National Society of Mentally Handicapped' (now MENCAP).

Brian (Lord) Rix has spent a lifetime working for adults and children with learning disabilities and was subsequently awarded a knighthood for his services.

The first half of 1955 was taken up with radio engagements; between February and April 1955, Hattie appeared in nearly twenty episodes of *Mrs Dale's Diary,* for which she was paid six guineas for each rehearsal and broadcast. Her character, Mrs Leathers was 'a semi-regular', a somewhat blowsy and happy-go-lucky woman who hailed from 'a problem family'. As Hattie became busier with television and film parts, and as work in *Mrs Dale* was casual and booked by the episode, Hattie was unable to commit herself to the role. She was occasionally replaced by another actress, Betty Baskcomb who did a good impersonation of Hattie but eventually the character of Mrs Leathers was written out. Hattie also appeared in shows with the comedian Ted Ray and in a series recorded in Manchester, *You're Only Young Once*, for the North of England Home Service.

However, in the summer of 1955, Hattie embarked on a personally challenging project by agreeing to produce and direct the revue, *Twenty Minutes South* at the St Martin's Theatre in London's West End. The show, a musical satire on suburban life, was devised by Peter Greenwell, who also composed the music. The show also featured John Le Mesurier, dancer and choreographer Douglas Squires, Daphne Anderson and a young ballet dancer, Josephine Gordon.

Although Miss Gordon's background had been as a dancer at Sadler's Wells and she had never sung professionally, Hattie gave her the opportunity to extend her artistic repertoire. Hattie and Peter Greenwell conducted the audition and they were impressed enough to give Josephine her singing debut in *Twenty Minutes*. Hattie was extremely supportive and even made Josephine 'dance captain'.

Hattie was an encouraging and sympathetic director, but according to Josephine, certainly 'wouldn't stand any nonsense' and was professionally quite exacting, firm in her opinions and occasionally exhibiting a sarcastic side. This was Hattie's West End directorial debut and she was as nervous as Josephine Gordon. In addition, Hattie had the task of directing husband John, although organising him and telling him what to do must have been second nature – it was, after all, something that she had been doing constantly at home for the previous six years.

Josephine Gordon described Hattie as being 'terribly musical' and an extremely accomplished director. She gave everyone a first-night present and Josephine still has the pink china elephant that she received to mark her theatrical debut. She remembers Hattie's 'totally infectious' tinkling laugh. In later years, Josephine visited Hattie at Eardley Crescent when Maurice Browning, who wrote the book and lyrics for *Twenty Minutes South*, was employed as a personal secretary by Hattie. Maurice had a physical disability, caused by polio, and Hattie was instrumental in making sure that he was always looked after, to the extent of even procuring accommodation for him. Daphne Anderson, who had started at The Players' at roughly the same time as Hattie, remembers her as, 'a very encouraging and sympathetic director' and couldn't recall Hattie ever saying anything nasty about the cast.

John Le Mesurier enjoyed being directed by Hattie and playing a straight part opposite Daphne Anderson. He was quite taken with 'a dear young girl called Louie Ramsay who had great vitality and personality' and he described the experience as 'a happy, charming show . . . nicely put together by Hattie'.

Unfortunately the critics didn't all agree; although the show notched up over a hundred performances between July and October of that year, *Twenty Minutes South* received mixed reviews:

Daily Express: 'In spite of zestful dances and telling talent much of this is insufferably tame. It needs a touch of fantasy, a sharper edge of wit.'

Daily Telegraph: 'Unusually for a musical in London the excellent company had good voices and could use them. Hattie Jacques was responsible for a production in which sentiment and high spirits were very nicely balanced.'

The Times: 'This piece is well produced by Miss Hattie Jacques, but though generally pleasing it seems to aim at a higher mark than it ever succeeds in reaching.'

Daily Mail: 'Admittedly it has its good points. They include a few attractive songs, ably sung, some clever staging and a furiously energetic production by Hattie Jacques.'

The 'furiously energetic' Miss Jacques ended the year with a

Christmas panto back at The Players' where she was much more at home. Roger Hancock, brother of Tony, worked at The Players' in the early 1950s as a scene shifter and general dogsbody. He left the job temporarily just before actress and singer, Annie Leake was employed there. Annie soon became friendly with Hattie, who said to her, 'Roger Hancock's coming back to work here – he's just right for you!' When Hancock returned to The Players', Hattie played matchmaker – and extremely successfully too, as Roger and Annie have been happily married since 1955 . . .

Hattie appeared in two shows at The Players', *Chain of Guilt* and *The Two Mrs Carrolls* at the beginning of 1956. In May she was in *Albertine By Moonlight* at the Westminster Theatre with Bill Fraser, Emrys Jones and Geoffrey Palmer. In June she recorded a television tribute to Henry Hall in which she sang several numbers. A letter from the producer, John Warrington, expressed his thanks for her contribution: *'You gave a lovely performance in the Henry Hall programme. There has been such a wonderful reaction to your work. Hope we work together. I am returning 'The Spaniard who blighted my life' music. Yours, J. Warrington'*

Hattie received similar praise from BBC television producer, John Street, following her performance in *Pantomania* (aka *Dick Whittington*) on Christmas Day as the Good Fairy, 'How much I applauded your efforts to make *Pantomania* the undoubted success it seems to have been.' The panto, written and directed by Eric Sykes, also starred Frankie Howerd, Spike Milligan, Fred Emney, Sylvia Peters and Billy Cotton. The show was also crammed full of BBC personalities and presenters such as David Attenborough and chef Philip Harben.

However, it was a job in the autumn months of 1956 that significantly affected Hattie's professional career, for it was then that her association with Tony Hancock was initially established. Hattie had first worked with Hancock in the second radio series of *Educating Archie* between August 1951 and January 1952 and then made a guest appearance on *Calling All Forces* on 28 April

1952 when he was co-compère with Charlie Chester. The variety show had an audience of thirty million listeners worldwide and was a sort of early *Sunday Night at the London Palladium* for radio. It was for this Light Programme radio series that Ray Galton and Alan Simpson first started writing for Hancock, a partnership that, in my opinion, is the greatest in the history of British comedy.

A memo from the producer, Dennis Main Wilson of 1 May 1953 set the tone for the show, '*I believe we can entertain most of the people, most of the time without having to drop our sights – either intellectually or in terms of entertainment . . . this situation comedy would follow the misadventures of a central character and his associates based on reality and truth as opposed to 'jokes, merry quips and wheezes . . . a real life character in real life surroundings.*'

The British public were introduced to the first *Hancock's Half Hour* in November 1954. Hancock had played opposite Geraldine McEwen in a one-hour special, but it was Moira Lister who was cast as Hancock's girlfriend in the first series. Lister left after sixteen episodes and was replaced by Andrée Melly, who initially played a French character. Galton and Simpson felt that accent was distracting and so in the third series she became Hancock's English girlfriend. Ray Galton was amused that no-one ever said anything about the character's nationality switch, when devoted fans of the show were always the first to question him and Alan about any slight changes in the show's continuity!

Galton admitted that they found it difficult to write well for women and agreed that they had given Melly and Lister some uninspired lines (about which the actresses had gently complained). Hancock's character was such an unromantic one that they found it hard to make these relationships work. Hancock's inability to act as a lothario in any credible manner created difficulties for them in writing realistic dialogue. Galton and Simpson decided to cast a comedienne in the next female role. They wanted 'a funny woman' who wouldn't be yet another girlfriend. The writers discussed casting with Dennis Main

Wilson, and Hattie was the unanimous choice. They all liked and admired her; she had worked with Hancock in *Educating Archie* and already had a proven track record in radio.

Galton and Simpson created the character of Miss Grizelda Pugh, Hancock's rather hefty and overbearing secretary and a much better comedy foil for the star of the show. In November 1956, Hattie joined the illustrious cast of *Hancock's Half Hour*. Already well established were 'the lad himself' – Anthony Aloysius St. John Hancock of 23 Railway Cuttings, East Cheam; dim-and-distant Aussie relative, Bill Kerr; lovable rogue, Sid James (interesting to note that when Sid James first appeared on radio he was so nervous that for the first few recordings he pulled his hat down over his eyes to stave off embarrassment); and Kenneth Williams, who was there to provide the required 'superior' or 'snide' voices.

Hattie fitted in seamlessly, Bill Kerr was quoted as saying, 'Hattie delivered in sparkles' and everyone immediately realised how good she was. Her timing was fabulous, she had a great sense of humour and a beautiful speaking voice that aired indignity and protestation in the most dulcet of tones. As Miss Pugh, she had an edge and stood no nonsense in regard to Hancock's pomposity and idiosyncratic behaviour. Both Ray Galton and Alan Simpson were bowled over by her and surprised how extraordinarily graceful, attractive and sexy she was. Galton and Simpson – who remain modest and unassuming, despite their legendary status in comedy writing – are a little ashamed about how much they used Hattie's size in order to raise laughs. There were indeed a lot of references to Miss Pugh's butterball shape and vast appetite in the scripts: 'Look at her plate piled up there. You can't see her. Just her arms coming around the sides.'

Some of these scripts are now over fifty years old, and Galton and Simpson said that if they were writing the show today, they would have crafted Miss Pugh's character very differently. As ever, Hattie was always very professional, delivered the lines perfectly and never complained about the scripts.

On one occasion Hattie did take umbrage, as reported in Kenneth Williams' autobiography, *Just Williams,* 'Hattie's ample figure and jokes about her size were taken for granted. At one rehearsal, her lines called for her to talk about serving spotted dick, cabinet pudding and roly-poly for sweet. Hancock had to refer to her greediness, and she had to say, "No, I eat like a bird", and then Hancock replied, "A gannet, more like." We all laughed at rehearsal till an unsmiling Hattie asked, "Do we have to have these sorts of jokes in the script?" I suddenly realized how sensitive she was about allusions to her weight'. Williams also stated that 'Alan and Ray slanted her scenes differently after that.' It seems that Galton and Simpson were mindful of Hattie's feelings and rewrote the scripts accordingly. Williams added that the writers' willingness to accommodate all the actors contributed greatly to the success of their series.

Miss Pugh's first appearance in *Hancock's Half Hour* was the episode, 'The New Secretary'. In this script Hancock puts an advertisement in the local tobacconist's window: 'Secretary wanted, blonde, nineteen years old, 37-22-36 or nearest offer. Live-in. Five pounds a week (more if can type)'. In turn, Miss Pugh had described herself as, 'Twenty years old. 36-23-35. Have several times been mistaken for Anita Ekberg.'

Hancock is impressed, 'She sounds perfect!' and even when Bill points out her typing speed estimated at about eight words a minute, he remains committed to her, 'That's all right, you'll just have to dictate a bit faster to keep up with her.'

When Miss Pugh makes her entrance, Hancock is horrified and threatens her with the sack before she is even employed, 'Hop it before I set the dogs on you!' Miss Pugh is much scarier with her own threat of violence, and is immediately employed, 'Let's get down to business, shall we? Your hours are half-past nine to five-thirty.' Miss Pugh puts him right, 'They're eleven to half-past four. Hancock's timing is perfect – after a couple of beats, he replies nervously, 'Of course they are – I don't know what came over me.'

One of my favourite episodes, despite all the references to Hattie's weight, is 'Cyrano de Hancock', broadcast on 2 December 1956. Sid is behaving strangely and when questioned by Hancock, declares he's in love . . . with Miss Pugh. Hancock reckons Sid must be gravely ill, 'He's going . . . he's sinking fast' and suggests Bill Kerr loosen Sid's boots. Sid isn't ill at all but simply besotted with Hancock's secretary. He hasn't yet had the wherewithal to tell Miss Pugh how he feels, 'I'm very bashful – especially with skirts. My legs turn to jelly.' Hancock, in an aside, quietly responds, 'Crushed to jelly, more like.'

Hancock suggests that Sid woos Miss Pugh with something romantic, maybe a like a tandem ride, then reconsiders, 'You'll need legs like oak trees to shift her.' Sid is besotted with his 'little dove', Grizelda, but for once in his life, is paralysed with fear. Hancock shows Sid how to make a chivalrous marriage proposal which Sid is supposed to emulate later. Inevitably, Miss Pugh is convinced that Hancock is proposing to her. Hancock is horrified, 'I wasn't proposing, I was demonstrating. It's Sid who wants to marry you Grizelda.' Miss Pugh responds politely, 'I'm sure he does and I'm very flattered.' Hancock's reply isn't so diplomatic, 'I don't want to marry her – not my hammer – great big ugly thing.'

Miss Pugh is undeterred and sets a date for the wedding ceremony making all the arrangements, efficiently sending Hancock all the bills. Despite all Hancock's protestations, Miss Pugh refuses any contact and reports back to Sid, 'She's told me it's unlucky to meet before the wedding – I told her it will be unlucky to meet afterwards.'

Hancock embarks upon a series of letters using various excuses to get out of his matrimonial commitment, 'I am weak in the head', 'I have the plague', 'My wife and fifteen children are arriving today from Afghanistan'. Miss Pugh is unmoved, 'If you don't marry me I'll sue you for every penny you've got.'

Eventually, Hancock finds himself at the Register Office, where an angry Sid is waiting for him, 'You'll never carry her across the threshold.' 'No . . . but a gang of us might,' replies Hancock.

Hancock appeals to the Registrar for mercy, but the attending bureaucrat is played by the inept, snide Kenneth Williams, who in a matrimonial mix-up ends up married to Hancock by placing a ring on Anthony Aloysius's finger.

There is no question that Hattie's formidable presence added a new dimension to the scripts. Hancock, no longer hampered by the constraints of a relationship, was a free spirit. The writers could be more capricious, and the character of Miss Pugh could take on the more established male characters. 'Grizzly' gave as good as she got and could also dish out the insults . . . with added spleen.

Sadly, Hattie's association with Hancock was short-lived. As with the other cast members who were gradually dropped as his self-destructive impulses multiplied, she was written out the show. Kenneth Williams was disappointed, 'I was surprised to be asked back to the new *Hancock's Half-Hour* because I'd not expected to return. I was dismayed to find that Hattie Jacques had been dropped from the cast and that my own contributions had been reduced to a trickle.'

Hancock's first wife, Freddie, described her ex-husband as having 'a ruthless streak in him which allowed him to cut out of his life all those who had contributed to it but were considered to be of no further use. Eventually, he decided that he himself was of no further use and the ruthlessness turned inward and destroyed him.' This opinion was confirmed by Spike Milligan who succinctly summed Hancock up, 'One by one he shut the door on all the people he knew; then he shut the door on himself.'

When the show transferred from radio to television the cast was further reduced, although this wasn't all due to Hancock's insecurities and was, in part, because of the practicalities of the medium. Galton and Simpson recalled, 'In those days, television was quite crude and it was all done live. What would take thirty minutes to do with four people and various situations on a radio show, would take twice as long on television. You can't have a regular cast without using them all the time, so we narrowed it down to just two . . . and concentrated mainly on the relationship between Tony and Sid James.'

Bill Kerr was dropped, and Kenneth Williams was employed for the first television series. Hattie played a peripheral part in the transfer to television, appearing mostly in the second series (April to June 1957) in a variety of roles and in one episode in the fifth series in which she was cast as an 'amorous fat lady'. Her fee for this, her last 'Hancock' appearance, was seventy-five guineas.

From a professional point of view, Hattie had high regard for Hancock's work. She described him as a comic genius and a remarkably warm performer, 'I used to watch him in the wings and match myself against him to see if I could come in on cue. But I was always a second earlier or later than him. I'd give anything in the world to have his timing. He knew exactly how far he could ride an audience for a laugh.'

However, she found him distant and extremely difficult to get to know. 'He he was a loner and yet he loved people about him and he was a marvellous audience, sitting and laughing as we all talked.' Hattie was, like the rest of us, saddened by the talent that was ultimately sacrificed in his quest to make himself into an international star. 'He was always at his best when playing Tony Hancock. But that wasn't enough for him, he always wanted new challenges. His films didn't quite come off and he thought that getting new writers and new actors would help. One by one he got rid of them and it didn't work. Sid James was very good and a dear friend but Hancock even thought he'd go without Sid. Tony wouldn't take criticism – he was badly advised to go against the things he was so marvellous at.'

John Le Mesurier was a regular in Hancock's supporting cast and Galton and Simpson described Hattie's husband as the perfect straight man and lovely to work with. Although Le Mesurier and Hattie never worked together on the show, they had been in cahoots on another project. One afternoon, Galton and Simpson were sitting around talking about where everyone was going on their holidays. Hancock said he was off to France, inevitably Sid was working, Bill was going home to Australia. Hattie was unusually quiet and so Ray Galton pressed her for an answer, 'Where are you off to, Hattie?'

'Actually, I'm having a baby.'

'Blimey,' said Sid, 'When?'

'Next week,' Hattie replied.

Ray reported that this was a shock to them all and although Hattie's natural reaction was to laugh it off, it was purely because of her size that no-one had noticed that she was pregnant, 'She must have felt very hurt.'

Hattie's second son, named Kim after the Rudyard Kipling book, was born on 12 October 1956. A photograph of him with Hattie appeared the following week in the *Evening Standard*. The domestically challenged Le Mesurier, who was working only occasionally at the time and who must have been aghast at the idea of changing nappies, was now faced with the prospect of having two young sons around the house. Help was needed, and consequently the household numbers at Eardley Crescent, which was always a hive of activity, increased alarmingly. Apart from the incumbent lodgers, various au pairs came and went, a cleaner was employed, and Hattie also took on a secretary to manage her finances and ever-burgeoning social commitments.

CHAPTER SEVEN

But Never With a Daffodil . . .

Charity, dear Miss Prism, charity! None of us are perfect.
I myself am peculiarly susceptible to draughts.

OSCAR WILDE, *THE IMPORTANCE OF BEING EARNEST*

THERE WERE VERY few periods in Hattie's working life when she wasn't gainfully employed (I avoid the term 'resting', which actors despise) but in the first few months of 1958 things were relatively quiet work-wise for Hattie. Apart from appearing on Harry Secombe's *This is Your Life* in January and regular appearances at The Players', Hattie found herself under-utilised. In February, her agent Felix de Wolfe sent two tickets for a performance at The Players' Theatre to the BBC booking department and this was followed a month later by a letter from Joyce Edwards at the agency to Harry Carlisle, producer of BBC Light Entertainment, 'After being very busy, Hattie could be free again from the middle of April. I'm sure you will have seen some of her extremely successful Saturday Spectacular shows and she would be very interested to discuss any possible shows that she could do for you.'

One would have thought that with the responsibility of her two young sons and a husband who she later described as 'my third child', Hattie would have been busy enough. But as much as she adored the children and managing social events at Eardley

Crescent, it was her work that provided the stimulation that she needed. It was her very next job which precipitated Hattie to iconic comedy status.

A historic pre-production meeting at Pinewood Studios on 20 March 1958, attended by producer Peter Rogers and director Gerald Thomas, was to change British film history. The film in question, *The Bull Boys*, originally written by John Antrobus and then re-written by Norman Hudis, was based on a story by the popular novelist and playwright RF Delderfield and concerned the experiences of a group of ill-matched National Service recruits. Robert Ross, in his informative book *The Carry On Story*, describes how 'Peter Rogers proudly declared, 'This is a British story and ought to be set in Britain throughout . . . the background will be for the most part amusing but the thread quite serious.' Rogers also stressed that this film was to be a low-budget production.

Production started on 24 March and was shot over a period of six weeks at Pinewood and on location at the Queen's Barracks in Stoughton, Surrey. The plot concerns the frustrations of Training Sergeant Grimshawe (William Hartnell) who is about to retire and accepts a bet that his last platoon of National Servicemen will pass out as 'Star Squad'. In comparison to later *Carry On* films, it is all rather tame; there are surprisingly very few jokes or even puns, and apart from the mincing Charles Hawtrey and a supercilious Kenneth Williams, there was very little to suggest what was to come in later productions. Dora Bryan is excellent as the lovesick canteen manager who falls for Kenneth Connor's Horace Strong. Hattie, with hair up in an intimidating beehive, makes a few brief appearances as the fearsome medical officer, Captain Clark, whose main pre-occupation is to convince the manically hypochondriacal Kenneth Connor that he is one of the fittest men in the platoon.

An interesting correspondence, highlighting the innocence of the film, is described in Robert Ross's book.

. . . another letter from Peter Rogers was to the British Board of Film Censors. He wrote: 'Can you tell me what it is about the line "Man does not live by sausage-rolls alone" to which you object?' The BBFC explained that, "We raised objection to the line 'Man does not live by sausage-rolls alone' because we usually dislike parodies of well-known Bible phrases. If it can be slightly rephrased it would avoid giving offence to anyone.

The Bull Boys, later re-titled *Carry On Sergeant,* which came from a line in the script, was a big box office success, and thus the immortal *Carry On* series was born.

No sooner had Hattie finished the filming of *Carry On Sergeant* than she began rehearsals on a theatrical extravaganza at the London Palladium – called *Large as Life*, it starred Harry Secombe, Terry-Thomas and Eric Sykes, who also wrote the sketches. Hattie was fourth on the bill, and the principals were supported by artistes such as Harry Worth, Dickie Henderson and Adele Leigh. The show, which was produced by Robert Nesbitt, ran from 23 May to 13 December 1958. The schedule was punishing: thirteen shows a week, twice nightly and three times on Saturdays. With this pressure, it's no wonder Harry Worth got piles, which may explain the review in *The Stage* where he was criticised (very unusual for *The Stage* to be negative about any performance in those days) for 'performing the same act as last year'.

Hattie appeared in sketches with Sykes entitled 'Military Tournament' and 'Concerto for Three Buffoons' and fared much better at the hands of the critic from *The Stage*, 'In my opinion, Miss Jacques is the finest woman sketch artist we have. She's wonderful!'

In a magazine interview of the time, the heading of which inevitably linked the title of the show with Hattie's dimensions, 'Laughter is Keeping Them Larger Than Life', she was asked about her size. Obviously irritated, she stated, 'I never tell anyone what my waist measurement is – I don't know it myself. I'd like to think that when producers are creating shows they don't just say we want a fat girl, let's get Hattie Jacques but that they might choose me because I can say the lines fairly well!'

Hattie didn't miss a single performance, which meant that the family were unable to take a summer holiday together and she also had her purse stolen during the run when a burglar broke into the dressing room. The purse, which had been a present from Peter Brough, contained fifteen pounds and family photos. Hattie was more than understanding, 'Oh well, perhaps he needed the money . . . but I am upset about the photographs of the kids and the old man.'

Towards the end of the production Hattie inveigled Harry Secombe into stirring a huge Christmas pudding at Cadby Hall, Hammersmith, portions of which were duly boxed and sent to a thousand 'needy' recipients.

While still appearing at The Palladium, Hattie began filming *The Square Peg,* a wartime comedy starring Norman Wisdom and featuring Honor Blackman and Terence Alexander and directed by John Paddy Carstairs. Wisdom delivers a rather sympathetic and understated performance as road mender, Norman Pitkin, who is conscripted into the army and becomes involved with the Resistance movement as a German General.

The film's highlight is a comic scene involving Wisdom and Hattie in which she plays Fraulein Gretchen Von Schmettering, an opera singer. A contemporary review stated, 'Miss Jacques is a splendid comedienne and it's very sad that she isn't in the film longer and oftener. For when she departs the movie cools again to amiable tepidity.'

Hattie had to get up at 5.30 in the morning to get to Pinewood Studios and didn't return home from the Palladium until well after midnight, when she would sit with the sleeping boys just to be able to spend a little time with them. In fact, for the first nine months of his life Robin was woken at 11.30 pm when Hattie or John returned from the theatre, had a feed and was given a bath as it was the only time the family could be together. Hattie always maintained that as long as the children had a routine they weren't affected.

Hattie also appeared with Norman Wisdom soon after in *Follow a Star* as singing and elocution teacher, Dymphna Dobson. Neither of these films were the happiest experiences for Hattie – apart from the physical exhaustion during *The Square Peg*, Hattie found Wisdom difficult and self-centred. In fact, he is the only person in the profession whom Hattie ever admitted to not getting on with. One can just imagine her saying, 'It's nothing personal – I just don't like him.' She wouldn't be the first in the business to hold this opinion of Wisdom.

The year ended with Hattie appearing in The Royal Variety Performance at the London Coliseum. The cast of the stage version of *My Fair Lady*, including Julie Andrews, Rex Harrison and Stanley Holloway topped a bill which also included Eartha Kitt, Pat Boone, Tony Hancock and The Beverley Sisters.

Hattie had now made her mark on 'the silver screen' and was very much in demand. Not only were her performances assured and consistently impressive, but she was always consummately professional and a popular member of any cast in which she worked.

As the 1950s ended, Hattie popped up in quite a few films: she made a brief appearance as a fortune teller in *The Navy Lark* and in the following year featured as haughty Agatha Potter in another naval comedy, *Watch Your Stern*, produced by Peter Rogers, directed by Gerald Thomas and featuring a number of *Carry On* regulars. *The Night We Dropped a Clanger*, filmed at Shepperton Studios, is a take-off of *I was Monty's Double* and stars Brian Rix in a technically tricky double role. Hattie plays Ada, a farmer's wife, yet another termagant. *Left, Right and Centre* is a Gilliat and Launder romantic comedy starring Ian Carmichael and Patricia Bredin, in which a male Tory candidate and a female Labour opponent fall for each other during a by-election. Alistair Sim and Richard Wattis add support, and Hattie is briefly seen as 'woman in car'.

In the celebrated *School for Scoundrels* Hattie is billed as Miss Grimmet, first instructress, also starring Ian Carmichael and Alistair Sim with solid back up from Terry-Thomas and John Le Mesurier.

Another *Carry On* film, *Carry On Nurse*, was released in 1959 and revolves around the comic misadventures of the patients and staff in the men's surgical ward of Haven Hospital, which is run by Hattie's indomitable matron. The ward consists of obsessive radio listener Humphrey Hinton (Charles Hawtrey) and pompous bookworm, Oliver Reckitt (Kenneth Williams). Leslie Phillips is Jack Bell and The Colonel is played by Wilfred Hyde-White. The most memorable part of the film is during the final scene when the irascible Colonel, who has driven the hospital staff mad with his constant demands, is the target of a practical joke. He is laid on his front and a daffodil, described to him as an anal thermometer, is placed carefully where the sun doesn't shine. Inevitably, Matron (Hattie) enters the Colonel's private room to discover the surreal scene, and asks what is going on. The unenlightened Colonel snaps, 'Come, come Matron, surely you've seen a temperature taken like this before?', to which Hattie replies, 'Yes . . . but never with a daffodil!'

Filming the gag wasn't easy, as Peter Rogers recalled, 'Poor Hattie got a fit of the giggles – and when one wag on the set made a noise like a champagne cork popping out of a bottle, as she lifted up the daffodil, she was a complete goner. Gerald (Thomas) tried take after take, but she couldn't keep a straight face. We had to abandon the shoot for the day.'

Unfortunately, Wilfred Hyde-White wasn't quite so amused. The indelicately placed daffodil had not been fully outlined in the original script, and the actor was not prepared for it. He was outraged, feeling that his integrity as an actor was being questioned and threatened legal action. Rogers reassured him there would be no actual shot of his or anyone else's bottom. The legal action was subsequently nipped in the bud and the daffodil gag stayed in.

Carry On Nurse was even more successful at the box office

than its predecessor. The budget was also approximately a quarter of the cost. The film was the highest grossing film in Britain in 1959, and even more surprisingly, it was a huge success in the USA, where a clever marketing ploy provided American movie theatres with thousands of plastic daffodils.

Leslie Phillips is full of praise for Hattie in his autobiography, *Hello*, describing her as, 'an interesting character with whom I worked on a lot of films . . . she was a splendid comic actress, perhaps because she always played it straight.' Phillips was equally impressed by the individual and experienced actors that made up the team but not by the 'crummy' wages. Towards the end of filming Peter Rogers intriguingly said to Leslie Phillips, 'I'm going to work out a really good contract.' By that Leslie Phillips therefore assumed that he would be on a percentage but he was wrong and ended up doing Carry Ons *Constable* and *Teacher* on the same 'lousy' money!

Carry On Teacher was released that same year. In this Hattie was cast as Grace Short, the maths mistress. The school inspectors threaten to sack the popular head master (Ted Ray) and this galvanises the pupils into sabotaging school events. The cast also includes Kenneth Connor, Kenneth Williams, Charles Hawtrey, Joan Sims, Rosalind Knight and Leslie Phillips and is the first totally original *Carry On* script by Norman Hudis. Drayton Secondary School in West Ealing was used for location shooting. The part of the unpredictable maths mistress gave Hattie a little more scope and, at times, was curiously modern in outlook. In alliance with her great friend Joan Sims, the two characters were given the opportunity to berate the male domain of education with comments about 'beating the men at their own game'.

Carry On Constable, which followed soon after, capitalised on the formula of *Carry On Sergeant*. Long-suffering police sergeant Frank Wilkins is lumbered with a farrago of somewhat hapless recruits who, due to an influenza outbreak, are sent as relief staff. The stereotypical characters are now well established: Charles Hawtrey is the effeminate, Special Police Constable Gorse,

Kenneth Williams' Constable Benson is somewhat camp and 'superior', although Hattie's character, matchmaker Sergeant Laura Moon, is a little more sympathetic. The film is also noteworthy in that it was in the role of Frank Wilkins that Sid James makes his *Carry On* debut. Kenneth Williams later described the film as 'mediocre and tired . . . I think everyone knew it'. However, the *Monthly Film Bulletin*, in an inspired prophecy, asserted, 'The Carry On series looks like becoming an anthology of all the slap-and-tickle music hall jokes that have ever been cracked.'

Hattie's next film at Pinewood was one that she later professed to be one of her most favourite. In *Make Mine Mink*, she played Nanette Parry, a rather butch, tweed-suited, etiquette teacher with a propensity for alpine hats. It's a rather charming farce about an eccentric dowager Dame Beatrice Appleby (Athene Seyler) who, with a band of comically unhinged confederates, embarks on a series of crimes, stealing expensive furs to raise money for her pet charities.

In the London borough of Kensington, ex-jailbird Lily (Billie Whitelaw) works as maid and general factotum for Dame Beatrice. Other lodgers include retired Major Albert Rayne (Terry-Thomas) who is desperate for an opportunity to experience another military mission, and Elspeth Duxbury is Pinkie, a timid repairer of china teapots amongst other items. Hattie and Terry-Thomas are terrific, forming a symbiotic comedy partnership, playing off each other with great skill and perfect timing. Although *Make Mine Mink* doesn't contain any belly laughs, it is consistently enjoyable and one 'film noir' scene featuring Terry-Thomas lurking in a shadowy dockside location, accompanied by *The Third Man* theme, is memorable.

Hattie recalled her time filming *Make Mine Mink* as one of the happiest experiences of her working life. She spent the whole time giggling at the antics of Terry-Thomas, with whom she got on extremely well. Apart from being with old friends Kenneth Williams and Kenneth More, she also liked Sidney Tafler very much. It was between shots that he advised Hattie that she should, 'Work to live . . . not live to work'. Although this recommendation doesn't now seem very original, Hattie would quote this liberally to friends as sound counsel. However, judging by her body of work, it appears that she herself never actually followed this maxim. After filming was completed, Hattie and John Le Mesurier flew to Tangiers for a second honeymoon, which was actually their first holiday together since their marriage ten years previously.

The premise of a group of disparate characters thrown together in unfamiliar circumstances, usually in an unlikely house share, is the stuff of modern-day comedy. The premise of the ITV situation comedy *Our House,* in which nine characters are each looking for somewhere to live and then decide to pool resources by purchasing a rundown old house together, seemed, at the time, to be a promising idea.

The show, conceived by *Carry On* writer Norman Hudis (who later moved to Hollywood to write episodes of *McCloud, It Takes a Thief* and *The Man from Uncle* amongst others) featured Hattie in the main role, playing Georgina Ruddy, a librarian who needed to make a great deal of noise at home to compensate for having to be quiet at work. *Our House* also featured some of the *Carry On* cast members, including Bernard Bresslaw, Charles Hawtrey and Joan Sims.

The series was produced by Ernest Maxin, a renowned figure in Light Entertainment who, at the last count, has produced and directed over three hundred television shows and is perhaps most famous for the *Singing In The Rain* sketch in one of the *Morecambe and Wise* shows. The hour-long sitcom was filmed weekly before a studio audience and there were three series, each consisting of thirteen shows. Maxin and Hudis worked out the storylines for the second and third series and were assisted in later shows by comedy writer Brad Ashton. Maxin wanted strong characters and interesting storylines that could also provide a dramatic element to the show.

Ernest Maxin recalled his favourite episode, 'A Thin Time', in which Hattie is attracted to a rather dishy male character and decides to go on a diet. In a gesture of friendship and solidarity, the other housemates all agree to go on similar regimes. It transpires, however, that all the housemates have hidden food around the house and, in the middle of the night, each is to be discovered raiding their secret food store.

In retrospect, Maxin agrees that the storylines revolved to a large extent around Hattie's weight. He realised that she was always very sensitive about her size, but she was always totally professional, a perfectionist who never moaned about the plots or scripts. Hattie was becoming resigned to the fact that she was forever to be cast in the 'fat' roles. However insecure she was about her size, she was always assured about her acting performances. She was always generous with other actors and was quite happy for them to get more or bigger laughs. Ernest Maxin describes Hattie as, 'A wonderfully sexy comedienne . . . but more than that, she was a marvellous actress who had an innate intelligence and a fantastic presence.' He also found her kind and aware, without an ounce of prejudice. He remembers her saying to him, 'You know, we come into this world not having any control about who our parents are or the colour of our skin. It's all a matter of luck if we're born in a country with education and medication.'

Although *Our House* wasn't wholly successful, Ernest Maxin has reason to remember the series with great fondness. Not only was it an enjoyable project to be involved in but he also fell in love and married Leigh Madison whom he auditioned for the show.

Although Hattie had dabbled in charity appearances, it was now that she became seriously involved in philanthropic activities. Maxin had discovered that the East London Spastics Society (now part of the cerebral palsy charity Scope) wanted to open a centre and needed funds. He approached Hattie to do a show at the Palladium, which he was planning to direct. The show was sponsored by Fords of Dagenham and the enormous cast included

Laurence Olivier. Not only did Hattie appear but she agreed to 'go on the knock' and actually tramped the streets, collecting door to door.

A letter from Laurence Olivier acknowledged her contribution:

8, Hamilton Place
London W1
17th August 1959

Dear Miss Jacques,
      Thank you for helping with 'Night of 100 stars'. It was another great triumph and I hope you enjoyed being there as much as I enjoyed seeing you
      Ever sincerely
      L. Olivier

Chingford Round Table sponsored a special charity performance of *Late Joys,* and another show, *The Midnight Stars,* also produced by Ernest Maxin, in aid of the East London Spastics Society was held three years later, featuring Anna Neagle, Ian Carmichael, David Kossoff, Dickie Henderson, Leslie Phillips, Frankie Howerd and the Tiller Girls.

Hattie was also involved in a Christmas concert at The Royal Albert Hall in aid of the *Evening News* 'Toy for a sick child fund'. The Royal Philharmonic Orchestra performed Haydn's Toy Symphony and according to the programme, soloists included Hattie Jacques, Alma Cogan, Michael Bentine and the unlikeliest performer, England international footballer, Billy Wright.

Apart from being president of the East London Spastics Society, Hattie also became involved with the Leukaemia Research Fund (LRF). An extract from the history of the LRF states, 'The London Branch was blessed with a show business personality in Hattie Jacques who, with her fellow stars, participated enthusiastically and successfully in raising funds. Every year a star-studded fundraising event was held at Chelsea Town

Hall and Hattie Jacques was very much the inspiration and driving force behind it.'

Although Hattie was not a great supporter of trade unions, she attended a fundraising event for the National Union of Journalists' widows and orphans fund and also spent a lot of time in pubs, not drinking but pushing over piles of pennies for various worthy causes. She helped out at Great Ormond Street Hospital for Children and opened a number of British Red Cross annual bazaars. Even at these events Hattie was defensive about her size, 'I hope I'm safe on this platform. A few weeks ago, I opened a Boy Scouts bazaar and stood on a specifically constructed stage to do it. It looked very nice and safe then suddenly it creaked and I fell through a gaping hole, lost and very confused!' And at an occasion to raise money for the Theatre Royal Margate she was reported as saying, 'I am very glad to bring my weight to bear on this cause'.

Although in later years there might have been some degree of displacement activity in her charity work, Hattie's motives were quite selfless. Joan Le Mesurier described her various enterprises, 'She found a role in which she could excel, being a great organizer she was always setting up schemes to raise money: there were art exhibitions with contributions by celebrities, variety concerts, dances and if that wasn't enough she would take short leases on empty premises and run charity shops, such as the one in King Street, Hammersmith, where she sold second-hand clothes for the Leukaemia Foundation.'

Despite all her charity engagements, Hattie still found time to work: The Royal Variety Performance in May 1960 was held at the Victoria Palace Theatre. The show, compèred by Bruce Forsyth, was an all-star event with a liberal sprinkling of American performers such as Nat King Cole, Sammy Davis Jr and Liberace. Hattie performed 'Stolen from the Crazy Gang', a sketch with Jimmy Edwards, Diana Dors, Benny Hill, Bob Monkhouse, Norman Wisdom and Alfred Marks.

Her next engagement was a somewhat more esoteric experience. Hattie starred in a BBC television production, *Pictures from the Insects' Life*, also known as *Insect Play*, by Czechoslovakian brothers Karel and Josef Čapek. The play, about a tramp who finds himself shrunk to the size of an aphid, is a philosophical satire in which insects represent various human characteristics. Josef Čapek, apart from being an accomplished artist, was one of the most influential Czech writers of the twentieth century. He also introduced and made popular the frequently used international word 'robot', which first appeared in one of his plays in 1921. Both brothers were avowed anti-Nazis, and Josef died in Bergen-Belsen concentration camp in 1945.

In mid-1960, Hattie began suffering stomach pains but she carried on working. In the autumn she was admitted to Hammersmith hospital, where she underwent surgery. Fortunately, the surgeons didn't discover anything sinister, but Hattie needed some weeks to recover. She had meanwhile been cast to play Delia King, the lead part in *Carry On Regardless,* and Peter Rogers had agreed a fee of £1,400 for her services. When it was clear that she couldn't fulfil her contractual obligations the script had to be re-written. Some of Hattie's lines were transferred to Joan Sims, and Hattie's part of Delia King was re-cast for Liz Fraser to play a younger, sexier character.

Despite the fact that she was still recuperating, Hattie wanted to make an appearance in the film, so a small cameo part was written, with her playing, quite fittingly, a hatchet-faced ward sister to Joan Hickson's matron. (This was a role reversal for the two actresses who, in *Carry On Nurse*, had respectively played matron and sister.) Hattie was paid one hundred pounds for her 'loyalty to the brand name' but agreed to waive her right to any screen or publicity credit.

Hattie's hospital stay was a blessing in disguise. The project turned out to be a somewhat disjointed effort and more a series of sketches than a well-plotted film. *Carry On Regardless* is set at the Helping Hands agency, where its owner, Sid James hires six unemployed people and a clerk from the local labour exchange as staff. Kenneth Williams was interviewed on the set by a journalist from the ABC magazine, *Film Review*. Williams is reported as saying, 'I will stick my neck right out and say that . . . *Carry On Regardless* is the funniest yet.' It is interesting to compare that quote with his diary comments after a cinema trip to see the film, 'Saw *Regardless* which was quite terrible . . . a disaster'.

John Le Mesurier visited Hattie in hospital, and Eric Sykes recalled a conversation between the couple that Hattie had repeated to him. Hattie was concerned that her husband had been looking after himself adequately whilst she was hospitalised, 'Have you?' she enquired, 'been eating properly?'

'Yes, not too bad,' he replied. Hattie suggested some scrambled eggs; John looked confused and asked, 'How do I do that?' Hattie explained, 'You put three or four eggs in a bowl, mix them up and then cook them.'

The following day John visited again and Hattie asked how he had got on. 'An absolute disaster. I put the eggs in a basin, mixed them up, put the basin on the stove and it cracked.'

Despite the dubious veracity of Le Mesurier's story, there is no question that 'Mr Jacques' wasn't quite as helpless as he pretended and that he used this affectation as a way of avoiding any kind of domestic duty or task that he found too boring. Their son Robin Le Mesurier, who refers to his parents by their familiar names, confirmed this, 'Hattie was the homemaker – John's vague act was sometimes overused in order to get out of doing household tasks. John was a professional in this respect. In fact he should have got a BAFTA for portraying vague.'

Although he was not the sort of father to involve himself obsessively in the lives of his two sons, the two of them loved him very much. John described the two boys in *A Jobbing Actor*, 'Our second son, Kim came rollicking and laughing into the world in October 1956, a trifle before his allotted time. He was always a funny boy and different in many ways from Robin, who like me is somewhat introverted. Kim seemed intent on becoming some sort of clown. He succeeded very well in that direction for a time and retains a wry sense of humour. Thank goodness there was no jealousy between the boys.'

Robin has extremely fond memories of his childhood at Eardley Crescent and of a devoted mother and a 'very nice' father who would play cricket with him and his brother on Barnes Common. On Saturday mornings Robin also accompanied his father to a record 'emporium' near South Kensington underground station where they would search for rare jazz 78s.

Robin also adored his grandmother Mary, who was now living in Margate (25 Trinity Square) in a house that Hattie had bought for her. It was a beautiful, old stone cottage, in an idyllic setting, with spectacular views of the sea. Both Robin and Kim would be packed off there for holidays while their parents were working. The seaside house was an equally social setting for family and friends, as Hattie described, 'She is one of those people who keep an ever open door – as we all do in this family, and so there are as many people in and out of the Margate house as at Eardley Crescent.'

Robin Le Mesurier feels that Mary was a huge influence on his own mother. She was a sweet and extremely kind woman who imparted 'her own values and sense of caring to Hattie'. She was certainly a homemaker but this extended beyond the housewifely duties to a nuclear family. Hattie loved to entertain and her generosity of spirit and kindness attracted a huge number of guests and visitors.

Not only did Hattie feed them to within an ounce of their lives, but also offered maternal nourishment. Friends needing advice, support and succour would flock to Eardley Crescent. Hattie's role as hostess was already reaching legendary status. Robin recalls his mother being like 'a magician', conjuring up a meal for large numbers, even though the fridge might have appeared almost empty to anyone else.

Sunday lunch at Eardley Crescent was an institution to which Grandmother Adelaide, mother Mary and an increasing number of friends would be invited. Clive Dunn has fond memories of those days, 'We used to have great fun and bloody great, table-creaking meals at Hattie's. Her grandmother, who was Jewish, was very funny. I remember her telling us a story about how she and Mary were shopping in town one very hot August day and the heat was so sweltering they decided to take cover under the awning to the entrance of Claridge's Hotel. The Commissionaire wished them a good afternoon and they got talking. Adelaide asked him, "How's business?"

The doorman replied, "Well apart from the King of Siam and a couple of other regular guests, it's all bit quiet."

Adelaide considered this for a moment, shrugged her shoulders and said, 'So what do you expect in a side street?'

Clive and several friends also remember another story involving Adelaide. After a huge delicious Christmas lunch that had included oysters, turkeys galore, all the trimmings, an array of fabulous puddings and desserts, Hattie would produce a yard-long chocolate log. When offered a piece, Adelaide said she couldn't possibly eat another thing. Hattie wouldn't take no for an answer, and Adelaide, finally yielding, agreed to a mouthful. 'Alright . . . but it's only to take the taste of the food away.'

The house at 67 Eardley Crescent was a perfect place to entertain. The four floors provided a great deal of space and its topography reflected its bohemian occupants. The house was (and still is) situated on the bend of the road so that all the rooms were intriguingly asymmetrical. John Le Mesurier described the family home as a 'comfortable, if rambling, pile with more stairs than were strictly necessary'. A walled back garden led straight on to the rear of Earls Court Exhibition Hall which some of the rooms also overlooked. The house was full of Victoriana, and Hattie's living room walls were painted a warm red, reflecting Hattie's glowing character perfectly. At the top of one of the flights of stairs was a huge wooden fairy with an hourglass figure in Hattie's image, a gift from The Players' Theatre.

The house dated back to 1820 and, according to Hattie, was once occupied by an eccentric old fisherman, 'the story goes that a hoard of sovereigns was once found in an old battered tin under the floorboards'. There was also a ghost. A couple of years after she moved into the house, Hattie would hear her name being called on the stairs. Not, 'Hattie', the professional name she had now adopted, not even 'Jo' which family and friends continued to call her, but 'Josephine' was the name the spirit called. No one ever called her that. Bruce Copp confirmed this, and Mary also said that she had heard her own name being called and was convinced that it was her late husband, Robin Jacques. Robin Le Mesurier sometimes occupied a bedroom on the top floor of the house and remembers hearing unexplained footsteps which was explained as 'a friendly ghost!'

Both Hattie and John were fully occupied professionally during the boys' formative years and relied on hired help to look after Robin and Kim. Apart from a constant stream of Spanish and German au pairs, there was also assistance in the unlikely form of actor John Bailey, a friend to both Hattie and John. John Bailey had been another graduate of the Rank Organisation but had lost his contract in unfortunate circumstances. John Bailey was gay and whilst travelling in Italy, had met the love of his life, a young Italian man, whom we shall call 'Leonardo'. This was the 1950s, when homosexuality was still illegal. Even more extraordinary was that Leonardo's parents had accepted their son's homosexuality and actually approved of the relationship.

John and Leonardo exchanged letters and it was arranged that Leonardo would come to London to study English. An Immigration officer at Heathrow asked Leonardo to show proof of the address where he would be staying in London. Somewhat naively, the young Italian showed the bureaucrat a letter from Bailey, which revealed not only John Bailey's address but also the intimate nature of the relationship of the two men. Leonardo was deported, John Bailey subsequently arrested and sentenced to three years in jail for 'importuning an alien for immoral purposes'. He was released after two years but found it very difficult to get acting work and survived by making curtains. He did later return to the stage and appeared in a couple of Dennis Potter television plays.

Hattie immediately came to the rescue, not only offering Bailey a room in the house but employing him as a male 'Mother's Help'. Neither she nor John Le Mesurier had any compunction in having him look after the boys. Robin Le Mesurier says that Hattie was completely without any prejudicial feelings when it came to gay men and that 'a friend of Hattie's' took on exactly the same connotation as 'a friend of Dorothy's'.

When Bailey later moved out of the basement flat, a Players' contemporary, Stella Moray, moved in and stayed for some years. This arrangement wasn't quite so successful, as Stella, who was a well-known stage actress, appearing in *Funny Girl* opposite Barbara Streisand and also in *Robert and Elizabeth,* used to irritate Hattie by her untidiness in the bathroom. However, her main fault was to occasionally criticise Robin and Kim's behaviour – something which Hattie considered unforgivable. Hattie actually wanted Stella, who died in August 2006, to move out sooner but never had the heart to ask her.

The boys' school days could not exactly be described as the happiest of their lives, as John Le Mesurier noted, 'Robin and Kim disliked almost every moment of their formal education. They started at the Froebel school in Redcliffe Gardens, very near where they were born in the now defunct Queen Elizabeth Hospital. After Froebel, Kim went to pre-prep school just off Sloane Square. He did not acquire much academic knowledge, then or later on, when we moved him to a far too big comprehensive in Holland Park. A number of actor friends had sent their offspring there and I thought it would be great idea for Kim to mix with children of varied colours, creeds and social backgrounds. But the whole exercise was a fair disaster. We discovered . . . far too late . . . that when he should have been in class he was, as often as not, smoking pot with his friends in Holland Park.' This was just the beginning of Kim's experimentations with drugs that sadly was to feature throughout his life.

Kim was also unhappy with his given name. He never liked it and was nicknamed 'Jake' (Jacques) at Holland Park Comprehensive, which he used ever afterwards.

Robin fared little better at Westminster City School, where he was subjected to routine teasing and bullying, including having a compass stuck in the back of his neck by an unknown assailant. The other pupils, who would see both John and Hattie regularly on television, assumed that the family were very rich and gave Robin a hard time. Robin maintains that the family were certainly comfortably off but not nearly as wealthy as his contemporaries assumed.

In later years he and his friends loved to spend time at Eardley Crescent; Hattie would be on hand to provide meals at all times of the day and night, the regime was liberal and typical teenage behaviour, frowned upon in most houses, was more than tolerated.

Neither Hattie nor John were very helpful when it came to the boys' academic aspirations, 'Some parents are very good at helping their children with their homework but Hattie and I failed miserably, as neither of us could add up or do simple subtraction, let alone cope with the mysteries of Latin, algebra or chemistry . . . so what the boys learned from us were things like what was right and wrong and hopefully how to say "please" and "thank you". I have always believed that good manners and a certain amount of charm can take anyone anywhere they fancy.'

Joan Le Mesurier wrote that although life in Earls Court was rather exciting, both he and Hattie later regretted how little they saw of their sons when they were very small and found that, 'Along with success the carefree days had flown . . . while the boys struggled with the mysteries of the classroom, I was away on exotic locations such as Athens, Budapest or Nice.'

Life at Eardley Crescent was, no doubt, fun, but it was also chaotic at times. Robin remembers, when later sharing a room with Kim, being woken up regularly in the middle of the night by the likes of Peter Sellers, Spike Milligan, Michael Bentine and various jazz musicians jamming loudly somewhere in the house.

There was a lot of dope-smoking and pill-popping, but for Robin it was 'just the norm'. Robin describes his childhood as 'charmed' and would never have swapped this bohemian lifestyle for a more traditional upbringing. He and Kim were extremely close when young, drifted apart in teenage years when he described his brother as 'a lost soul' before regaining an affectionate fraternal relationship.

As lovely as John Le Mesurier was, he must have been infuriating to live with. His passivity and enigmatic behaviour caused Hattie some headaches – there were times when he supposedly went missing for hours or days on end and when questioned by Hattie about his whereabouts, was supposed to have replied, 'Time goes so quickly when you can't see daylight.' The mysteries of the night and its inherent darkness seemed to bring out the romantic in him. Joan Le Mesurier reported that he once 'took a fancy to a Greek actress who in the full light of day turned out to be not the Greek Goddess, but a moustachioed creature with a dodgy eye. John admitted this very brief infatuation to Hattie who laughed so much that she broke a plate whilst washing up and said, "You really shouldn't be allowed out on your own"'

Fortunately John had a wide circle of friends and didn't venture out much on his own. One of his closest pals was Hattie's brother, Robin. The two of them used to do the rounds of Soho clubs, ending up at their favourite haunt, Ronnie Scott's jazz club, which was then in Gerard Street. Both were huge fans of the incomparable pianist Bill Evans and never missed an opportunity to see him play live. John had another companion he used to take to Ronnie's: a golden Labrador puppy called 'Blades', given to him and Hattie by dancer Brian Blades. John would take the dog with him everywhere, but Blades was particularly welcomed at the jazz club where the waitresses would provide him with a bowl of water. Ronnie Scott even made him an honorary member. However, Blades like his predecessor Guinea, was 'retired' to the country. Owing to Hattie and John's work commitments, they were away for long periods and didn't want to leave him in kennels, so Blades moved to a village pub in Northamptonshire where he apparently developed the unusual trick of picking up ladies' handbags and depositing them behind the bar for safekeeping. At least that was the landlord's story.

Apart from Blades, sons Robin and Kim and husband John, Hattie was in still more demand as a mother figure and was 'mum' to some rather unlikely offspring. When she was appearing in a show in Dudley, Hattie discovered that two tiger cubs in the local zoo were motherless, 'It was absolutely nothing to do with me but I traipsed around the town trying to find "a bitch in milk" to foster the tiger cubs. Can you imagine peoples' faces when I asked for that?'

In November 1960, Able Seaman Conroy of *HMS Victorious* wrote to Hattie. His letter in the most exquisite italic handwriting, requested the following:

> Dear Hattie,
>
> On behalf of the seaman aircrew 825 squadron, I am writing this letter to you. We are a helicopter anti-submarine unit and are all fans of yours and, when possible, see your films, television programmes and listen to your radio shows all of which we enjoy. Our request is, would you condescend to adopt us? We will have a photograph taken of the aircrew and send you a copy.
>
> We would very much appreciate if you could send us a signed photograph of yourself.
>
> Hoping that you can grant our request
> Yours faithfully
> Rodney F. Conroy

Inevitably Hattie agreed to the request; Able Seaman Conroy wrote again in January 1961 thanking the actress for her letter and the signed photograph. In an accompanying note, Hattie had obviously asked if the squadron had another 'mum' and the serviceman replied, *'We haven't got another "Mum", as we had decided to have you, or no-one'*. He continued, *'We were all tuned in to "Juke Box Jury" just recently to watch you and, as usual, our "Mum" was a hit.'* Able Seaman Conroy sends his regards to *'Dad and the kids'* and signs off with a PS, *'We aren't trying to find out your age (we know you're twenty-one) but could you please tell us when your birthday is?'*

There is no record of any further correspondence from Hattie . . .

CHAPTER EIGHT

Driven to distraction

'There's a speed limit in this State, Mr Neff. 45 miles an hour.'
'How fast was I going, officer?'
'I'd say around 90.'

BARBARA STANWYCK, IN RESPONSE TO FRED MACMURRAY'S
ADVANCES IN *DOUBLE INDEMNITY*, 1944.

IN MARCH 1959 Hattie and Eric Sykes made their first tele-vision appearance together in *Gala Opening*, a one-off, sixty-minute spoof of a variety extravaganza at 'The Floral Hall, Grapplewick'. They had worked together before in radio and on stage. It was the same year that Sykes, along with fellow comedy writer Johnny Speight, created the pilot of a situation comedy, which was duly commissioned by the BBC following support from Frank Muir and Denis Norden, who were then acting as comedy consultants to the Corporation. The first episode of *Sykes and A . . .* was screened on 29 January 1960 and would run for nine series (sixty episodes) over the next five years. It was the start of a twenty-year partnership between Sykes and Hattie as the Sykes show was to return in 1972 (in colour) for another seven years with a different title, *Sykes*, but using some of the original plotlines.

Sykes avoided the usual husband-and-wife format, realising that by casting Hattie as his sister, and even more amusingly as a twin sister, more humorous situations could be exploited. *Sykes and A . . .* is a gentle comedy, set in 24 Sebastopol Terrace, in the

London suburb of East Acton, in which the devoted siblings become entangled in a series of engaging storylines. The show got very good ratings and was one of the most successful situation comedies of its time.

The show is well described by Graham McCann in *Spike and Co.*

> Eric is a playful, naïve, devious eternal adolescent and Hattie (often shortened to Hat) a decent sort of soul who found most of the world around her far too brash and bewildering and put up with Eric's antics because he was . . . after all, her twin brother. Both characters were unmarried and seldom seemed to work but each one laboured under the private delusion that the other was in greater need of grown up guidance and help.

Eric and Hattie were also well served by supporting actor, local policeman Deryck Guyler and waspish neighbour Richard Wattis – a part that was initially offered to John Le Mesurier but turned down because of his wish 'to make it without Hattie's help'.

Johnny Speight, John Antrobus and Spike Milligan, all members of the illustrious Associated London Scripts agency, where incidentally my late father, Eric Merriman, also worked, had contributed to the scripts in the first two series, but Sykes took complete control of the writing in the third series. However, as the show continued to build on its success, some problems arose. Although Hattie enjoyed working with Eric and was grateful for the nationwide exposure, she was left to ponder the dilemma that only popular actors experience: the show was bringing in high ratings and seemed destined to 'run and run' but as a result Hattie was concerned about being typecast. She also felt that that Sykes was being 'pandered to' and even more importantly, she was also in demand elsewhere.

A memo from BBC producer, Dennis Main Wilson to Bush Bailey (Artists Booking) in February 1961 attempts to address these issues:

Further to our conversation with Eric Sykes suggesting that Eric should have a friendly chat with Hattie Jacques about the long term planning of the show for the winter and beyond, I have also had a word with her agents – with the following disclosures.

Hattie is scheduled to start filming almost immediately, but has told her agents categorically that she wishes to do the next Spring series of six, and that the film company must make its arrangements to fit the filming around her commitments for us. We should hear within the next 24 hours the final outcome of this.

Her agents also made the following points:

1. Hattie has to decide how much of her life she should devote to supporting Eric when in films she is in a strong position to go all out for herself for big money and prestige.

2. She has two major films on offer at present, and more to come.

3. In 'Our House' she gets much more than the Sykes show (Hattie tells me she gets 500 pounds per show, plus transcription repeats)

4. Apparently she feels rather hurt that everybody is making a tremendous fuss of Eric and <u>his</u> availability, and nobody is giving any official regard to her.

5. Nonetheless she is still immensely pro Corporation and pro the Eric Sykes show.

Having pointed out the enormous growing prestige of the Sykes show, and its almost unlimited potential, Hattie's agents suggested – and I feel that this would be a good idea – that it would be a good move on our part if you and H.L.E [Head of Light Entertainment] were to invite Hattie and her agent up to see you and discuss long term plans. I am sure that more would be achieved in half-an-hour with all cards on the table than distant telephone calls and under-the-counter chats from Eric Sykes.

Although Hattie was being offered more lucrative television and film work, her friends maintain that her agent, Felix de Wolfe, was reluctant for Hattie to make a break from Sykes and give up a secure working relationship. Hattie was in two minds but was, above all, extremely loyal to Sykes with whom she had built up an excellent working relationship. After further correspondence and a reassuring meeting with BBC executives, Hattie decided to let matters rest.

Although she was persuaded to stay with the show, Richard Wattis became a casualty of the fourth series. There had been some criticism of his current fee which had increased to two hundred guineas a show (fifty guineas more than Hattie's fee). Wattis' agent now asked for an even bigger amount per show – something which the BBC felt to be 'intolerable'. It was agreed by everyone that Hattie Jacques was indispensable, and pressure was put on Eric Sykes to write Richard Wattis out the show which he duly did, although Sykes, rather honourably, refused to replace him with another actor. Wattis didn't return to the show until 1972.

Further negotiations in regard to Hattie's salary were carried out in May 1963. Joyce Edwards at the Felix de Wolfe agency asked for six hundred guineas per episode. In response, Bush Bailey stated, *'I still consider she is worth 500 guineas for this next series. I don't think we can consider her as a supporting artist to a star. Although Joyce Edwards (Felix de Wolfe agency) says she would be reluctant to accept anything less than the terms stated I think she would probably compromise with 500 guineas for the thirteen. As far as 1964 is concerned, and the balance of the thirteen programmes still to be recorded, I am quite sure she would be prepared to give us advance notice of any ITV offer that may come . . . there has been no doubt that she (Joyce Edwards) would prefer Hattie to work for us rather than ITV and this is also Hattie's wish. I believe she thinks she has been wrong in not approaching the BBC about a series for Hattie but she hoped that we would make an approach about it and, of course, ITV have done so instead. She is obviously of the opinion that Hattie is one of the leading comediennes in this country and perhaps after this next ITV series we shall all agree.*

There is no doubt that the offer contained in my letter of 20th May has been firmly turned down. Do you agree that I should offer her 500 guineas for the next thirteen?

Tom Sloan, Head of Light Entertainment, was drawn into the argument and wrote, *'Jacques agent is being greedy and uncompromising. Her fee has risen from 100 guineas in 1960 to 325 guineas in Jan 63. I think this should be our firm and final offer. We must be prepared to lose her if necessary, although I hope it doesn't come to that.'*

Fortunately, it didn't come to losing Hattie. A compromise was duly reached at 500 guineas for shows recorded in 1963 and 600 guineas for shows to be recorded in 1964. The BBC also wanted Hattie to sign an option for 1965 but Hattie was reluctant to commit to being available for a whole year. She did, however, appear in the ninth series which ran from 5 October to 16 November of that year. Sykes was offered a further, lucrative, long-term contract, but following a disagreement with the BBC about scheduling and ratings decided that he had had enough and sensibly realised that it would be best to stop while the show was still successful.

Eric Sykes described the show as, 'pure Walter Mitty, I can live out the fantasies of most ordinary chaps. Our programme is a place where nobody is going to do anyone any harm and where no-one is in pain. It is simple, enjoyable and pleasurable escapism and everyone needs at least half an hour of that a week, don't you think?'

The show received many plaudits during and after its initial sixty episodes; writer and broadcaster Russell Davies pointed out that *Sykes* was actually quite surreal at times and not quite as suburban as it at first appeared. Bob Monkhouse was particularly impressed by Hattie's acting skill and felt that she really didn't have much to work with, cast as 'a straight woman for Eric who needed a feminine presence without being threatened sexually. She invested all her personal charm and bearing and it was a miracle that she made the part what she did.'

Sydney Lotterby, who directed two of the series, was a huge fan of Hattie's understated work and felt that she suffered from typecasting throughout her career. He described her as, 'a lovely, softly spoken, woman who was a joy to work with. There was never a cross word with Hattie.' Sykes was also the first to credit his acting partner's attributes, 'Hat, to me had so much talent, it oozed out of her. She had a "puckish" sense of humour and was such a giggler. Hattie was brilliant . . . whatever I wrote she delivered as if it had been scripted by George Bernard Shaw and if a line was really appalling she would suggest another one – strangely, exactly the one I would have written had I thought about it first.'

According to Bruce Copp, Hattie contributed more to the scripts than just the odd line – something that was never recognised, although this is denied by Eric's then secretary, now theatrical agent Hilary Gagan, who used to type the scripts. There is no doubt, however, that the two of them possessed a kind of telepathic understanding, 'We'd sit around the table on the Tuesday, read through the script and sometimes, just as I was about to turn over the final page for the last bit of dialogue, Hattie would put up her hand and stop me. Then she'd come out with the next line – and we'd turn it over and there was that same line, She'd anticipated it just as I'd written it.'

The relationship between them was generally good, certainly in a professional sense, although they did not mix socially, 'We rarely see each other outside working hours. We have lunch together occasionally but he has his family and I have mine and they keep us occupied.' Sykes was quoted as saying, 'In all the time we worked together, I only went to her house three times and she came to mine maybe twice. We are very different people. Hattie loved being among people. There was always a crowd around her. She was as extrovert as you could get. I'm not like that. I'm basically shy. I like being alone. You couldn't say we had a lot in common, but she was a great lady.'

They did, however, appear together at various charity events; Eric and Hattie were asked to appear as guests of honour in a local parade in Royton, Lancashire, near to Sykes's home town of Oldham, 'Hattie and I arrived at the Royton Town Hall to a warm welcome. When one of the civic dignitaries asked Hattie what she would have to drink, she thanked them and asked for a whiskette, and ice was broken in both senses.' Unfortunately their vehicle broke down in the middle of the parade and, 'as if nothing had happened, Hattie was deep in conversation with the crowd . . . and I wished I had something to read.'

Another fundraising outing also nearly ended in tears for Hattie, 'When Robin was a small boy I took him along with me to a police charity function. At the end of the evening they presented me with a special pair of handcuffs as a gift. The next morning Robin got hold of them and locked himself up. It was a bit of a joke at first until we realised we couldn't get them off. When I carted him down the street to the nearest police station he yelled at passers by, "I haven't done anything, missus, please don't lock me up!" It was really embarrassing, even if it was funny. And when we did finally get to the police station they didn't have a key to undo the cuffs so I had to take Robin to a locksmith. It wasn't in vain though because Eric wrote a whole show around the incident.'

On 14 September 1961 Hattie recorded an episode of *Desert Island Discs* which was broadcast a month later. She was interviewed by the creator of the show, Roy Plomley. Although the melodic strains of Eric Coates' *By the Sleepy Lagoon* were familiar, what followed was much more scripted than the contemporary show that continues to be broadcast after its debut in 1942. The attempts at humour are rather feeble and it is all rather stilted.

What is interesting, however, is that Hattie's choice of music and her explanation for their inclusion are clear signposts to her personality; she admitted that it would be very lonely and far too quiet on the island for someone of her extrovert nature. Hattie wants 'big' music, lots of noise and 'some exciting arrangements'.

Hattie starts with a rousing choral piece, the fourth movement from Beethoven's Ninth Symphony, followed by *Hello Little Girl* by Duke Ellington and his Orchestra. Pieces by Handel (sung by Joan Sutherland) and Bach are mixed with tracks from Tommy Dorsey (*On the Sunny Side of the Street*) and a version of *God Rest Ye Merry Gentlemen* by The Modern Jazz Quartet. Hattie then chooses a piece, entitled *Lord Badminton's Memoirs* by her friend Peter Sellers from the album *Songs for Swingin' Sellers* and finishes with her favourite performer, Judy Garland, singing *The Red Balloon*.

Plomley states that he doesn't know whether to introduce her as 'a comedy performer, comedy actress or comedian' and asks what she really likes to be called, to which Hattie replies, 'Mummy'. In response Plomley initially refers to her as 'Mummy' before being corrected by Hattie, 'Wait a bit, this is for *my* children! . . . It's by my children that I like to be called 'Mummy' most.'

Hattie admits that she finds the thought of being a castaway horrifying but would be happy not to have to pay any more income tax! They discuss Hattie's work and she says, 'I hope somebody is going to offer me a job in the theatre. That would be nice. I think of all three mediums, I would rather be in the theatre with a good script. But I would rather be in television or films with a good script than in the theatre with a bad script. I would like to broaden my horizons. I would like to think that I won't always be stuck with the sort of fat girl part, that I could play something a little different.' Hattie says that, although she wouldn't enjoy the castaway experience, in a practical sense, she would cope quite well. She says she could build a hut and her cooking skills would serve her well, 'I'm quite good at sort of getting a lot of funny old things together, and making a decent meal out of it.'

When asked if she could build a boat or a raft, Hattie replies, 'It would be, I am sure, foremost in my mind to get away. I'd do everything in my power to get away from the island, but I don't think I'd have the courage to sail that craft on the Pacific Ocean! I'd just build fires, I think and put the responsibility on someone else.'

Hattie plays tribute to her last choice, Judy Garland, 'I think she is just so wonderful, that every time I see her, I come out of the theatre thinking, what do I think I'm doing in the profession? I think she's just the greatest thing that ever happened. Performers like this come once in a lifetime, and I'm just so pleased that it happened to be in my lifetime.'

Hattie chooses the Bach fugue as her one piece of music she would have to have on the island, 'I would never get tired of it' and she seems to be allowed two luxuries, a photograph of the family and a tape recording of Robin and Kim chatting as they play together. Hattie's book choice is *The Oxford Book of Quotations*.

The same year, 1961, also saw the release of a couple more films featuring Hattie. In *In The Doghouse* (starring Leslie Phillips), in which she plays the part of Primrose Gudgeon, a warm-hearted RSPCA Inspector, she is seen astride a horse. Fortunately, for all concerned, this scene was performed by a stunt rider. Hattie has a small role (Miss Richards) in *She'll Have to Go*, a farce starring Bob Monkhouse and Alfred Marks about two brothers who are torn between marrying a Corsican cousin (Anna Karina) or murdering her for her money.

Hattie's principal television commitment was with Eric Sykes but she managed to appear in an episode of the *Sally Ann Howes* variety show with Dick Emery, Jeremy Lloyd, Robert Beatty and Ronnie Carrol. She also made several appearances on the panel of *Juke Box Jury,* and one invitation to attend was accompanied by the intriguing note, *'Please bring two dresses as we have experienced a little trouble in that studio'*. This advice might have been more useful when, in December 1961, Hattie featured in a Billy Cotton television show.

Left: Hattie's theatrical inspiration: mother Mary treading the boards in Germany.

Above: Hattie's father, the 'dashing' RR Jaques, shortly before his untimely death.

Above: Dressing-up time.
'Josie' and older brother,
Robin, Chelsea 1926.

Opposite: 'Let's stop and
see the pictures,' an early
duet with American
performer Bob Nicholls at
The Players' Theatre.

Above: 'Carry on, Nurse'.
Hattie in Red Cross
uniform, aged 20.

Right: 'My heart is in a
whirl', Major Charles
Randall Kearney, US Ist
Army.

Above: Tommy Handley
adjusting Lind Joyce's
earring while Hattie (seated)
and other members of the
ITMA cast look on.

Left: 'A comedy with magic and music'. Hattie and a youthful Rupert Davies in the Young Vic production of *King Stag*, 1947.

Above: Art imitating life. Hattie as 'Alice' in *Chance of a Lifetime*, 1950.

Left: Spreading a little magic. As The Fairy Queen Antedota in *The Sleeping Beauty In The Wood*.

Opposite: Hattie, Daphne Anderson, John Hewer and Erik Chitty in the Players' panto *Ali Baba and the Thirty-nine Thieves*, December 1950.

Above: 'A Little Of What
You Fancy does You Good'.
Hattie in Marie Lloyd pose.

Above: The bride wore brown. Hattie and John's wedding day, Kensington Register Office, November 1949.

Left: Good friends. John Le Mesurier with Hattie's brother, Robin.

Above: Charity begins in East London. Hattie and John with a group of disabled children.

Right: On the set of *Happy Holidays*, summer 1954. Just before the tea party...

Opposite: 'Stone me, what a racket!' Hattie, Sid and the lad himself in *Hancock's Half Hour*. BBC

Above: Hattie as the
formidable Nanette Parry in
Make Mine Mink, 1960.

Right: At home in Eardley
Crescent with youngest son,
Kim, 1962.

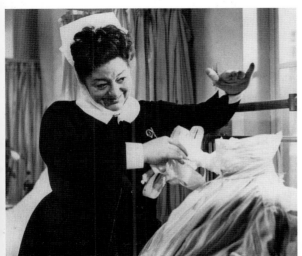

Above: Messrs Hawtrey and Williams, Hattie, Sid James, Joan Sims, Jim Dale and Barbara Windsor in a *Carry On* publicity shot.

Left: 'At least his rash has gone'. As Matron in *Carry On Doctor*, 1967.

Above: A contemplative Hattie during rehearsals for *Sykes and A....*

Right: The sweet smell of success. Hattie in Mary's Margate garden.

Above: A sketch from Spain. Hattie and Eric Sykes go Flamenco.

Left: 'Oh Eric!' A typical Sebastopol Terrace adventure...

Above: In Hong Kong with members of the *Hatful of Sykes* team, featuring Martin Christopherson (far left) and his infamous 'syrup'.

Left: Robin Le Mesurier on tour with Johnny Halliday.

While rehearsing the Christmas show with Eric Sykes at the BBC, Hattie, dressed as a fairy queen in yards and yards of tulle with a huge skirt, a pair of wings and an ornate ringlet wig, was standing in front of a flash box (a stage device which sends up a flash of light with a puff of smoke). It had somehow slipped the fairy queen's mind that her very full bouffant skirt extended way back behind her and was actually resting on top of the box, 'When it flashed I almost went up in smoke too. The tulle caught fire and the next thing I knew I was being rolled on the floor and being pummelled vigorously.' Eric Sykes had been aware that Hattie's frock was on fire and so rushed forward and began to beat out the flames, burning both hands in the process. Hattie was extremely grateful to her co-star. 'It was very frightening. I wasn't hurt but the dress was burned and the ringlets of the wig I was wearing were scorched by the flames. All that day we had rehearsed in front of the flash box but I was wearing my own clothes and no-one had appreciated the possible danger. The back of the dress was ruined beyond repair and there was no time to make another one before the transmission. I went before the cameras with the remnants of the dress pinned together at the back. I had to move in such a way as to keep the charred material out of the sight of the viewers.'

Eric Sykes described the event in his autobiography, although he actually reports it as having occurred while they were making *Pantomania*, several years earlier, 'Luckily I was only a yard away when it happened, and so I was able to beat out the flames and this is when my admiration for her went up into the premier league. During all the time I was beating out the flames like a demented washerwoman, she didn't panic; she stood perfectly still until the flames were just wisps of smoke. Then she smiled and, looking down at me, she giggled and said, "How's that for an entrance?" What a lady!'

The BBC personal injuries report form described the nature of the injury as a *small amount of shock caused from dress being ignited*. Fortunately, Hattie didn't need treatment other than *a short rest off stage*.

Between engagements, Hattie continued to devote herself to her charitable endeavours. A letter to the East London Spastics Society in February 1962 from WJ Ponsford, BBC Accounts stated, 'Hattie Jacques took part in a programme "Compact" on the 11th January 1962 and she has waived all rights to a fee in respect of this appearance in the knowledge that the BBC, at its absolute discretion, may make a suitable donation to charity. I have the pleasure in enclosing the Corporation's cheque for £26.5.0d. as a contribution to your funds.'

As mentioned previously, Hattie was also heavily involved with the Leukaemia Research Fund. As Hattie couldn't drive, the charity always sent a driver to take her to various events. It was usually the same elderly man who would call for her regularly and who she had got to know over the years. Shortly before she was to be collected for one such engagement in 1962, Hattie received a telephone call, informing her that her normal driver was unavailable and that the Fund would be sending Hattie someone else. They hoped she wouldn't be too disconcerted. Hattie was positively flustered when she saw the new driver. John Schofield was a devastatingly handsome, charismatic East Ender to whom she was immediately attracted. He was articulate, charming and funny and flattered Hattie shamelessly. After Hattie's charity appearance that afternoon, they spent the evening together and ended up in bed at Eardley Crescent.

John Schofield was married but was separated from his wife and had two children, one of whom, also called John, had suffered from leukaemia and had recently passed away. Consequently Schofield had volunteered his services as a driver. (Bruce Copp confirmed that Schofield was a very adept and quick at driving and said he wouldn't have been surprised if he hadn't been 'a getaway' driver at some stage!) Schofield described himself an entrepreneur, although John Le Mesurier's description of Schofield was less grand: 'A fast talking cockney who made a living, selling cars.'

This dangerous liaison was not destined to be just a passionate one-night stand. The two of them began to see each other as much as possible, and a number of fictional charity events materialised to allow them time together. Joan Le Mesurier described Schofield as, 'a very handsome man with lots of charm. He gave Hattie the undivided attention and support that John, working away from home so frequently, was unable to do. Schofield was earthy, sexy and rough and made her feel young again.' Although Hattie and Le Mesurier were attracted to each other, there had never been a sexual chemistry. Hattie had also confided that Le Mesurier had been rather a selfish lover while Schofield was apparently quite the opposite. . .

Le Mesurier's film career was beginning to take off and he was away on location more often from Eardley Crescent. But even when Le Mesurier was around, he didn't seem to be aware of what was happening behind his back. When Hattie offered Schofield a sofa to sleep on from time to time, this wasn't a particularly unusual occurrence, as there were always friends and acquaintances who had been invited to 'crash' at the house in spare rooms or on various couches or settees.

Hattie quickly became besotted with Schofield and, being so unconfident about her own looks, couldn't believe that someone so stunningly attractive could find her equally seductive. Her friends were concerned about John Le Mesurier and shocked at the apparent fragility of Hattie's marriage, which was believed to be one of the most secure in show business. They were suspicious of Schofield's motives and anxious about her obsession with him, which had manifested overnight. Robin and Kim took an immediate liking to this character who played football with them, took them on outings and was much more outgoing than their dad who they adored but who was much less physically demonstrative. The boys were used to Eardley Crescent being full of their parents' friends and companions, and so another 'lodger' was completely in keeping with the chaotic lifestyle. They naturally didn't have a clue about what was really going on.

Unfortunately, neither did their father for a while. It was only during the filming of *The Moonspinners* with Eli Wallach and

Hayley Mills at Pinewood in 1963 that Le Mesurier first realised that something was 'going badly wrong at home'. This time his 'vague act' wasn't an act – he really had been oblivious to what had been going on under his nose for some time. He describes the situation in his autobiography and attributed it to Hattie's desire to be wanted. 'So much was clear to me when I returned from a few weeks on location to find that Schofield was well on the way to acting the part of a surrogate father. Certainly, the children enjoyed his happy go lucky ways and pestered him to taken them bowling or on other exciting treats. Hattie tried to make light of the latest change in our domestic routine. After all, we ran an open house with friends popping in unannounced and not infrequently staying with us for days or weeks on end. But it would have been foolish not to know that this was different. I could have walked out, but whatever my failings, I loved Hattie and the children and I was certain – I had to be certain – that we could repair the damage.'

Le Mesurier spoke of the 'devotion lavished on Hattie by some of her friends'. He admitted that a marriage between actors was naturally subject to additional pressure. Apart from media focus, both had separate careers to pursue and 'we worked in an environment where it was easy to wander the thin line between affection and love'. Le Mesurier loved Hattie dearly and was in awe of her warmth, enthusiasm and generosity which she bestowed on all who knew her. He recalled that he should have been more concerned but 'jealousy is not in my character and I held firmly to the belief that Hattie was in control of her emotions'.

It was ironically during this turbulent time in the couple's life that Hattie was selected as the subject of *This Is Your Life*. The show was recorded on 12 February 1963 at the BBC television studios in Shepherds Bush where Hattie had been rehearsing *Sykes And A* . . . Eamonn Andrews was hiding behind a newspaper in the darkened studio and then approached Hattie and Eric Sykes. The lights went up and Hattie's response was, 'You're kidding!' She really seemed visibly shaken and she remained rather uncomfortable throughout.

Eric Sykes was interviewed first and told the audience that he had been hospitalised recently and couldn't work out why, for the first few days of his admission, Hattie hadn't been to see him. When Hattie did visit and he asked her why she hadn't been before, he discovered that she had been in hospital herself, but didn't tell Eric as she didn't want to worry him. 'That's the sort of person that she is.' Sykes attempted to amuse the audience, but he needed a better straight man than Eamonn Andrews, the holder of 'The Red Book.'

The next guest was her Red Cross Divisional Commander, followed by husband John Le Mesurier. He opened by saying that he had been surprised that Hattie was on time for their wedding, 'I must confess I'm inclined to be surprised when Hattie turns up for anything. It's a standing joke in the family. I always get to appointments half an hour early. Hattie, on the other hand, makes every moment count.' He went on to describe his wife's housewifely skills, 'So many things to be done. Dreary mundane things like shopping, a cupboard might need to be turned out at the last moment. She's like a whirlwind. How she manages I really wouldn't know.'

Eamonn responds by asking, unwittingly, 'Never a dull moment with Hattie? Le Mesurier wistfully replies, 'I'm eternally grateful to the way she runs the home, looking after the children, looking after me.' He then adds rather pointedly, 'The home comes first, if you don't mind me saying.'

There is a nervous giggle from Hattie as John continues, 'For someone who is so busy, and in the public eye, to do all those things is a jolly neat trick.' John obviously felt that he wasn't able to say what was really going on, but decided to be a little obscure. Hattie, who would probably have been unsettled by this attention at the best of times, was particularly and understandably disquieted during this section. The studio audience and viewing public had no idea that she and John were in the middle of a marital crisis and that John Schofield had moved in to the family home.

Rodney Conroy, accompanied by eight sailors from *HMS Victorious,* were next and he explained how Hattie had adopted their squadron. Hattie was genuinely pleased to see them. The presence of members of the Senior Service must have come as a welcome distraction from listening to her cuckolded husband. On came Leslie Phillips, 'I enjoyed working with Hattie. She was a very popular girl. In fact, I was a bit jealous of her popularity. In the film we were acting with a pretty little chimpanzee – but the chimp wasn't interested in me. Only had eyes for Hattie.' Rosie the chimpanzee was introduced to the audience, took centre stage and immediately hugged Hattie!

The next two guests were a woman from the East London Spastics Society whose daughter Hattie had visited in hospital and given a bracelet and the Canadian jazz musician Victor Booker with whom Hattie had co-authored a song (Hattie wrote the lyrics) *Don't ask me why I'm crying.* According to Booker, Hattie was the band's mascot and all of them had stayed at Eardley Crescent. Presumably he was talking about a quintet rather than a big band, although with Hattie one never knew . . .

Finally Eamonn Andrews announced, 'Behind this public image is a family girl.' On walked her brother Robin, embarrassed-looking sons, Robin and Kim, mother Mary and grandmother Adelaide, and bringing up the rear was John Le Mesurier. The only crucial person missing from this grand finale was John Schofield.

Hattie and her two Johns were by now to all intents and purposes living in a *ménage à trois.* Le Mesurier decided he could no longer take the pressure of the arrangement, 'To give us all time to think, I set myself apart from Hattie, mostly keeping to my own room but had I been thinking more clearly, this arrangement served only to aggravate everyone.' Neither Robin nor Kim had the slightest idea what was going on.

Hattie's domestic complexities didn't prevent her from working, however. She made a guest appearance in the satirical *That Was the Week that Was* on 1 December 1962 and was also asked to perform in *Christmas Night with the Stars* at the end of the month. She was also cast as Dolly Zarathusa, a fortune-teller, alongside the discommoded Le Mesurier in *The Punch and Judy Man*. The film, set in the dismal seaside town of Piltdown, tells the story of Wally Pinner (Tony Hancock) who is the Punch and Judy showman on the beach. His wife Delia (Sylvia Sims) runs a china shop. Charles Ford (John Le Mesurier) makes a living by creating sand sculptures of historical events and then lecturing about them. Pinner is asked to participate in the municipal gala celebrations and although he despises the mayor, his social-climbing wife accepts on his behalf, which he goes along with in order to save his marriage. The function ends in disaster for both of them but their marriage seems somehow likely to survive.

Although amusing in parts, the film was considered something of a failure and was apparently a rather difficult production. In addition, Hancock had very unwisely dumped Galton and Simpson and had just moved from the BBC to ITV in an attempt to broaden his audience.

Filming on *Carry On Cabby* began in January 1963. The script was solely by Talbot Rothwell and it was quite clear that this writer (later to pen Frankie Howerd's *Up Pompeii*) wanted to make the script a little more risqué than previous *Carry On* outings. The plot revolves around Charlie Hawkins (Sid James) the owner of a taxi firm who is happily obsessed with his work, thereby neglecting his devoted wife Peggy (Hattie). In order to gain his attention, Peggy sets up a rival firm, 'Glam Cabs', an all-female cab company.

The film wasn't going to be part of the *Carry On* series. It was originally entitled, *Call Me a Cab*, based on a story by comedy scriptwriters Sid Green and Dick Hills. There were a couple of minor difficulties during filming in that Charles Hawtrey had only passed his driving test the week before filming, and Hattie couldn't drive at all. She took her driving test once but failed and never attempted it again, relying on the kindness of strangers, real cabbies, lovers and friends to chauffeur her around.

Carry On Cabby was Hattie's favourite in the series because she had a slightly softer role and felt that there was a stronger storyline. Hattie is seldom off the screen and is sparkling in a role that gives her the opportunity to be much more appealing than her other harridan roles. It is no coincidence that Hattie shines: her affair with John Schofield was new and exciting, she had lost a lot of weight and she exudes new-found confidence in this performance.

Le Mesurier was finding it harder and harder to cope with the situation at Eardley Crescent and decided to take a break. He flew to Tangiers but had barely arrived when he became ill and decided to return home. Unfortunately, his condition deteriorated and he was admitted to hospital in Gibraltar on his way back to London. He was diagnosed as having a collapsed lung, pneumonia and jaundice, amongst various ailments.

Hattie received an urgent request from the hospital authorities to come to Gibraltar. She responded immediately and left with Schofield and John Bailey. Hattie stayed for a week in Gibraltar with Le Mesurier and then returned to Pinewood, but Le Mesurier remained for a month. He later recalled, 'I don't remember talking very much to Hattie because I was rather weak, but her presence and comfort were memorable.' On his return to Eardley Crescent, Le Mesurier found himself in an extremely uncomfortable situation, 'It was a curious sort of homecoming when I was not altogether certain of a home to come back to. I knew that only a miracle could save my marriage, but I also knew Hattie would not throw me out of the house. Being there was the only chance of showing her that we still had a chance together. The atmosphere was heavy to say the least . . . From the moment of my reappearance, John Schofield made clear his opinion that I should do the decent thing and quietly disappear.'

Le Mesurier, however, decided to do the opposite, blithely hoping that the situation would resolve itself. Hattie was susceptible to male attention, she needed to be loved and be found attractive, and it was his belief that this infatuation would eventually subside and Hattie would see sense. In fact the opposite happened, as Hattie and Schofield spent more time together and grew closer. The genial Le Mesurier simply couldn't compete with Schofield's cocky persona; he became more withdrawn and deeply unhappy, finally realising that his marriage was in real trouble. The final straw came when, according to Joan Le Mesurier, 'Hattie openly, and in Schofield's presence, declared her love for his rival'. Soon after, Schofield moved into the master bedroom at Eardley Crescent and Le Mesurier discovered that his belongings had been removed to a bed-sitting room in the attic.

By day, Joan Malin (now Joan Le Mesurier) was employed as a clerk at Marylebone labour exchange. By night, to supplement her income, she worked behind the bar at the Queens Theatre in Shaftesbury Avenue. One night in 1963 Joan and a friend of hers from the theatre went for a drink at the Fifty Club in Frith Street, Soho, a venue that was famous among the acting profession. They got into a conversation with former Players' dancer and chore-ographer Johnny Heawood, who suggested moving on to the Establishment Club. The Establishment, owned by Peter Cook and his friend and business partner Nicholas Luard, was the 'in place' for satirical humour and was managed by Bruce Copp, who had since moved out of Eardley Crescent and was now living in a flat in Chelsea.

Joan was introduced to Bruce, who informed her that amongst other stars, John Le Mesurier was in the house. Joan didn't know Le Mesurier by name, although she recognised him when Johnny Heawood called him over.

Le Mesurier took an instant liking to the very winsome Joan Malin, and they soon discovered a mutual love for music. He asked her for a date straightaway, 'Perhaps when someone special comes to Ronnie Scott's Club you might like to come with me, my little friend.' The two started to see each other, encouraged by Bruce Copp who, realising that Le Mesurier's marriage to Hattie was as good as over, wanted to see his friend happy again. Hattie was also keen for John to leave Eardley Crescent, but couldn't bring herself to throw him out. If husband John found someone he could be happy with, then so much the better, and any residual guilt might be assuaged. As soon as Hattie heard from Bruce Copp about Le Mesurier's meeting with Joan, she invited Joan to a party at Eardley Crescent in an attempt to further progress the relationship.

In Joan Le Mesurier's book, *Dear John*, she describes her meeting with Hattie; 'I really took to her. Her big heart and generosity of spirit were impossible to resist and I became one of the many who felt at ease, indeed welcomed and cherished, in her large and untidy house. She exuded kindness and received devoted affection from others in return . . . Hattie was splendidly emblematic of the fact that her love does not have to be rationed, that giving to one does not necessarily mean depriving another: she always had enough for everyone.'

Hattie was completely open about how desperately in love she was with Schofield and admitted that his macho charm made her feel 'like a young and giddy girl'. Joan was equally drawn to his likeable manner, but also wondered, 'If he was little more than a chancer, exploiting Hattie's largesse.' By now, this unsatisfactory and damaging domestic situation had existed for nearly a year, with the trio all becoming more and more frustrated and unhappy but supposedly lacking the initiative to do anything about it.

Hattie still didn't have the heart to dump her husband. Le Mesurier himself didn't have the wherewithal to move on, and Schofield, despite all his bravado, was powerless. Robin and Kim, aged ten and eight, remained oblivious to the situation. Joan wrote that, 'As often happens in such strained marital situations, they were spoiled both by John and by Hattie as the parents attempted to compensate for the atmosphere and for the times they were working away. At least John was getting masses of work, some of which cheered him up when he was out of town, but little lifted his gloom when he was home.' Le Mesurier did have concerns about how the situation was affecting the boys and later said that he hoped that not too much psychological damage was done.

John and Joan began to see more of each other, Le Mesurier further confiding in her about his unhappiness. He was still not reconciled to the inevitability of divorce and was frightened of starting yet another relationship but accepted that he couldn't continue in this manner.

Joan was incredibly patient with her new lover's predicament but finally encouraged him to leave the family home. A flat was found in nearby Barons Court which was furnished by 'a relieved' Hattie with some suitable furniture from Eardley Crescent, and at Christmas 1964 John Le Mesurier left his beloved family surroundings and moved into his new abode. Hattie was so grateful that the situation had finally been resolved that she helped Joan to open accounts for John at a couple of London department stores: Derry and Toms, and Barkers, and even more pertinent for John Le Mesurier, at a well-known wine merchants called Norton and Langridge. Joan says that he only had to pick up a phone and everything was delivered. Hattie was also concerned about Joan's lifestyle, 'Hattie, seeing how little I had to do, did not let me be idle for long. She had rented two charity shops which sold second-hand clothes and bric-a-brac to raise money for leukaemia research, so I worked there with her for two or three days a week and we grew even closer with so much time to share.'

Joan was initially reluctant to give up her independence and cohabit with Le Mesurier, who, she confided to friends, wasn't her usual type. He was also somewhat older than her and she wasn't short of a number of younger suitors. Joan had also been married previously to actor Mark Eden and was wary of becoming too involved with another actor. (Her son from this marriage, David, was later to strike up a friendship with Hattie's two boys.)

However, John, in his vulnerable way, persuaded her to move in with him. At weekends, the two of them would drive to Ramsgate to see Joan's family. From here, John would pop down the coast to Margate to see Hattie's mother. Mary had been upset with Hattie about her affair with Schofield and was particularly unhappy that she and Le Mesurier had split up as she had always been very fond of John. Mary didn't like John Schofield at all and was always uncomfortable in his presence.

Meanwhile at Eardley Crescent, Hattie was joyfully happy. It continued to be a hive of activity, with Queen Bee Hattie ruling over her domain. She continued to entertain lavishly and her social life was as busy as ever. To ensure the happiness of her children following the divorce, she would encourage them to have friends over at every opportunity. Hattie would entertain them and even had an intercom system installed, with speakers in the boys' rooms so that she could communicate with Robin and Kim as to how many friends they had in the house and would then cook meals for all of them. She, herself, however, was more than aware that if she wanted to hang on to her new lover, she would have to take care of herself weightwise. She went on crash diets and lost several stone. Home movies of this time show a very handsome Schofield playing with the children whilst a remarkably slim looking Hattie looks on lovingly.

Musician, writer and producer Nick Lowe has fond memories of times spent at Eardley Crescent. His first foray into the music business was as a teenager in the band 'Kippington Lodge', who were based in Tunbridge Wells. At the start of the 1960s, they were playing in local village halls and schools, but soon started to get gigs further afield, 'We would go to Scotland for £12.' The band needed representation and Nick Lowe answered an advertisement in *Melody Maker* placed by a would-be manager. This man, described by Lowe as a 'likeable shark, an old style Variety agent', turned out to be none other than John Schofield, then living at Eardley Crescent.

Schofield drummed up work for the band, and, as the members were still living in Kent, a lot of travelling was involved, particularly if the band were playing up north. Schofield would invite the guys to stay over at Eardley Crescent the night before, in order to get an early start. Nick Lowe remembers Hattie as being extremely generous and totally unfazed by having a group of aspiring musicians foisted on her. Hattie would provide hearty breakfasts, packed lunches for the road (he particularly remembers her delicious bacon sandwiches) and she was always welcoming. The guys were all in awe of her because she was famous, 'But she didn't act like a star at all, she was funny, warm, sexy and kind.' Lowe also remembers a great atmosphere in the house and how happy Robin and Kim were in this lively, fun environment where spontaneity ruled.

In 1964, Hattie had been rewarded with her own television series – this time with ITV, and the very show that had provided her with some ammunition while her agent negotiated with the BBC over Sykes. In *Miss Adventure*, which also starred Tony Britton, Hattie was cast as Stacey Smith, who stumbled into international escapades as a confidential investigator for a private-eye company. The programme was presented as a series of multi-part stories: *Strangers in Paradise* (six parts); *The Velvet Touch* (four parts); and *Journey to Copenhagen* (three parts), and unlike her *Carry On* and *Sykes* roles Hattie played this one fairly straight.

Ernest Maxin, who had worked with Hattie in *Our House*, wanted to direct Hattie in something different, a Hollywood-type comedy thriller. Hattie wanted to do a sort of 'Pearl White' for television (Pearl White was the heroine in the silent movie serial, *The Perils of Pauline*). 'My character should make a mess of everything and bumble her way through all kinds of perils and predicaments.'

Strangers in Paradise was set on a Greek island, although filmed in Mevagissey in Cornwall, where the cobbled windy lanes were the closest they could get to Greek village streets. Shop and road signs were changed from 'Jones' to 'Theodorakis' and lighting effects and mirrors were used to provide the town with a sunnier climate (an idea for the Cornish Tourist Board, perhaps). Hattie enjoyed the making the show, 'We had great fun filming *Miss Adventure* – if the viewers laugh at our antics as much as we laughed making the series then we ought to be okay.' But unfortunately Hattie was ultimately disappointed by the results, wanting it to contain more suspense and had envisaged it to be more of a 'cliff-hanger'. It turned out, however, to be more of a comedy.

The writer of the show, Peter Yeldham, had been approached by his agent, Beryl Vertue of Associated London Scripts, to talk to producer Ernest Maxin about a show for Hattie Jacques. Yeldham's first reaction was, 'I'm not a comedy writer' and he was also unsure about being committed for a long-running series. However, he was persuaded to meet Maxin and after discussions with his wife Marjorie, they decided to write the show together. Yeldham takes up the story, 'So we went to see Hattie in Earls Court. Her husband, John, had been in several of my shows, but it was my first meeting with Hattie. It turned out she'd asked for me because John had shown her one of my scripts, and when I said I wanted to work with Marjorie because much of the story idea was hers, that was fine with Hattie. She was friendly and charming and also very beautiful. I kept thinking she reminded me of someone, and it was later that Bill Kerr provided the answer, "Look closely at her face," he said. "Never mind the figure. The face looks like Ava Gardner." And he was right. What's more the camera loved her . . . and so did the public.'

Peter Yeldham ascribes some of the lack of success of *Miss Adventure* to the fact that the British public had associated Hattie for so many years with the sister of Eric Sykes that her conversion to being a private detective was slightly confusing. 'Also there was a basic flaw, because what we ended up writing was a sort of comedy-thriller. Although we had a good cast, including Tony Britton, Maurice Kaufmann and Bill Kerr and the show looked polished, I think it was only a moderate success. I think Ernest wanted it lighter, Hattie wanted more drama. It hovered uneasily between.' Between May and August 1964, Hattie appeared in four episodes of *Housewife's Choice* and contributed a piece to *Woman's Hour* called 'What I Most Want for My Children'. John Schofield wasn't apparently mentioned . . .

On 17 August 1964 Hattie appeared in a Granada Television production of Noel Coward's *Blithe Spirit*. She was inevitably cast as medium Madame Arcati and paid tribute to one of her illustrious predecessors, 'Watching Margaret Rutherford in the play made a terrific impression on me that I have never forgotten.' The play, which also starred Griffith Jones and Helen Cherry, was introduced by 'The Master' himself, who Sheridan Morley described as being delighted with Hattie's performance, stating that finally someone had delivered a performance that wasn't overshadowed by Margaret Rutherford. In fact, Noel Coward thought that Hattie should have done classical theatre but as she discovered throughout her career, it always seemed impossible to persuade anyone to cast her in more serious roles.

The show was directed by Joan Kemp-Welch at a cracking pace, and a anonymous review was extremely flattering; 'Hattie Jacques is of course eccentric as Madame Arcati, but also amazingly balletic whilst Griffith Jones is simply marvellous in the master's role. I had to keep reminding myself that I was watching Griffith Jones, who does the role so much better than Rex Harrison. . . . for those brought up on the film version, this is a pleasant surprise. Quite stagy, but so well edited from the original play that it really is an improvement!'

Hattie, still having concerns about forever being known just as Sykes' sidekick, tried her hand at other projects: she appeared in a Bernard Cribbins sketch show (*Cribbins*) which aired in February 1965 and read five Mary Poppins stories for the BBC children's programme *Jackanory*. She recorded thirteen shows in a magazine radio series, *Souvenir* and appeared on the panel of the radio game show, *Twenty Questions*.

Hattie also filmed her first commercial – an advertisement for the washing powder Omo: 'Even when you're busy in show business, there are still times when you have to wash a few things. That's when I find Omo a real blessing.' The timing of this job was quite interesting because she was about to have her dirty linen washed in public.

John Le Mesurier was, by this time, keen to marry Joan Malin, who although separated, was still married to Mark Eden. The relationship between Hattie and Schofield was kept a closely guarded secret as there was a feeling that any disclosure might have harmed Hattie's public image as a much-loved comedienne and respected mother. So it was decided that the best way to handle the media was to admit Joan's affair with John Le Mesurier and let Hattie take proceedings against them, thereby ensuring that Hattie was cast in the role of victim. Hattie and Schofield were also eager to marry and 'a double divorce' was obtained on the same day. The legal representatives arranged that Hattie's case was heard first, followed by Joan's.

On 28 May 1965 a national newspaper reported that 'Hattie Jacques was granted a decree nisi in London Divorce court yesterday on the grounds of adultery by her husband, John Le Mesurier. Miss Jacques was granted custody of the two children. In the next case Mrs Joan Dorothy Malin was given a decree nisi after alleging that Mark Eden had deserted her.' The press duly branded Joan as a marriage breaker – something that she wasn't terribly happy about but which she took on the chin. Joan later recalled the events, 'We made the front page of the *Evening Standard* that night. Under the photo – in which, incidentally, I looked very chic in a suit and a hat – it said "The other woman" which we expected, and the story went on to dismiss my affair with John as being a nine-day wonder. Obviously in the eyes of the law we were antagonists; I was the younger woman who had wrecked Hattie's marriage, so we couldn't smile or acknowledge each other but as she left the courtroom staring straight ahead, she blew me a kiss.' Afterwards all four of them met up at Eardley Crescent and over several glasses of champagne toasted each other's futures. Joan regretted that the press weren't present to take some more photographs!

A court order, issued on 3 August 1965, instructed that 'the Respondent do pay to the children Robin Mark Le Mesurier Halliley (Le Mesurier's original name) and Kim Charles Le Mesurier Halliley as from the date hereof all monies payable for their school fees and one half of the monies necessary for their purchasing school uniforms and sports clothing until they shall respectively attain the age of 18 years and further order Petitioner's costs.'

The decree absolute (Number 1343) was issued in the High Court of Justice 31 August 1965 and declared that the marriage between Josephine Edwina Halliley then Jacques spinster (the Petitioner) and John Elton Le Mesurier Halliley (the Respondent) be dissolved by reason that the Respondent had been guilty of adultery with Joan Dorothy Malin upon whom the petitioner has been served. The said Marriage was thereby dissolved.

A letter from Hattie's solicitor ends with the sentence, 'You are, of course, as you will appreciate, now free to re-marry should you so desire.' It was very much Hattie's desire to marry John Schofield, whose name first appeared in the telephone directory at 67 Eardley Crescent that same year.

After the divorce Hattie said, 'John was and still is a gentle and very lovely man. We are still great friends . . . it doesn't matter how civilised people are about dissolving a marriage, it's still a wretched business. John and I are the greatest friends and still I love him and I think he loves me. There were never any recriminations. I wouldn't have been able to stand that, bad feelings between the parents of children. He's a lovely person, so sweet . . .'

When John Le Mesurier and Joan decided to marry in 1966, Hattie and the boys wrote to congratulate them. (Hattie signed herself as 'Jo', the name by which she was always known to her friends and family.)

Hattie Jacques
67 Eardley Crescent SW5

Dear Johnny

Thank you for telling me your news, I do feel I would like to tell you that truly and sincerely I wish for your happiness, for your peace of mind and for everything to be good in your future marriage. Joan is a lovely person and loves you and is much better for you than I could ever have been. We have all been through a pretty wretched time but out of it all I'm sure will come great happiness for all of us.

God bless and my love.

Jo

Dear Daddy and Joan

I am really glad that you are getting married, because I love you very much. I hope you are very happy together, I know Kim and I will like it a lot.

All my love, Robin

Dear Daddy and Joan,

I hope you have a happy marriage, it's a lovely idea.

I love you both a lot. Kim

All seemed blissful. Hattie admitted to never having been happier and Joan Le Mesurier said at the time, 'Hattie had her chap who made her vulnerable and girly. She was utterly dazed by him and was totally in love. And I had John – there was hope for the future.'

CHAPTER NINE

Oh I Did Want to be a Ballerina . . .

I'd just like to see a role for women where someone who isn't traditionally attractive is not portraying the best friend. You know, the character that only speaks in questions. 'Gee, are you gonna go out with him? Do you think I look fat?'

MARTHA PLIMPTON, ACTRESS

JOHN SCHOFIELD NEVER did marry our Hattie.

It's probably just as well – if there had been a wedding, it's likely that the reception would have lasted longer than the marriage. For a while, following the divorce, the co-habitation went reasonably well; Hattie happily played housewife and supported Schofield financially, funding his various entrepreneurial activities. She was the slimmest she had been for years and her lover was an enthusiastic 'stepfather' to Robin and Kim. Schofield took Hattie away for romantic weekends and longer holidays in between her work engagements, which still mainly revolved around the Sykes sitcom.

Schofield certainly enjoyed living at Eardley Crescent and mixing with Hattie's show business friends, who were divided in their opinions about him. Most of them found him charming, although they were suspicious that he was using her financially and was building up quite a list of contacts through Hattie. Bruce Copp confirmed that Hattie invested a lot of her savings into his schemes while they were together, none of which seemed very successful. Schofield was always generous, however, especially with the boys, who continued to enjoy his company.

A long-term friend of Hattie's from The Players', Violetta, wasn't convinced by the East End charm and didn't take to him at all. Although she understood that Schofield 'was genuinely very fond of Hattie and possessed an incredible sexual attraction for her,' she predicted that it was only a matter of time before he dumped Hattie. She felt that Schofield was always a bit of a rogue and was convinced that he would let Hattie down sooner or later. She also didn't think that he was that good-looking, unlike Barbara Windsor, who had met Schofield on the Pinewood set and described him as, 'stunning, a gorgeous bit of crumpet'.

Unfortunately for Hattie, most women who met Schofield agreed with Babs and this only increased his confidence. Schofield believed his own publicity and was convinced he could use his East End charm to devastating affect. Before long, he had attempted to seduce a number of women whom he met through Hattie – mainly her friends – and including Joan Le Mesurier. Bruce Copp describes Schofield as having 'a wonderful line with women, no-one was safe from his attentions, he tried it on with anyone that he could – including my own sister in law.' This was all done behind Hattie's back. She remained oblivious to Schofield's lascivious behaviour and devoted to him.

There is also some evidence that Schofield was occasionally violent to Hattie, perhaps most likely when she finally caught on to his miscreant behaviour. When Bruce Copp was running his Chelsea restaurant, The Hungry Horse, Hattie came to see him. She had a cut below her eye and was wearing a headscarf and dark glasses – which she never normally did. She subsequently admitted to Bruce that Schofield had hit her.

At another time, after their divorce, Hattie visited John Le Mesurier in hospital. 'Hattie arrived one morning with some mail and magazines, coupled with the good news that I was going to be let out in three days' time. She was wearing a pair of dark glasses.

She said that she had bumped into something and given herself a black eye. I knew better. The truth was that she had been in a fight with Schofield – he was jealous of Hattie's visits to me and felt threatened.' Whether Schofield really was still emotionally intimidated by Le Mesurier or there were other reasons to explain Hattie's injury is unclear. There is not sufficient evidence that Schofield was regularly violent to her, and Robin Le Mesurier is adamant that Schofield usually treated his mother well. There is no doubt that the unconfident Hattie, greatly lacking in self-esteem when it came to her appearance, was so grateful for Schofield's attention that she might well have tolerated occasional abuse.

In the middle of 1966, Hattie was contracted to appear in *The Bobo,* which was released the following year. Filming was to take place in Rome, and Hattie flew out, leaving Schofield at home and the children in the care of various au pairs and friends. She was cast as Trinity Martinez, housekeeper to Olimpia (Britt Ekland). This is a decent part in which Hattie is more than convincing with an excellent Spanish accent. The picture tells the story of an unsuccessful matador, Juan Bautista (Peter Sellers), who arrives in Barcelona to seek fame and fortune as a singer. He meets a famous theatre impresario and is offered a week's engagement providing he can seduce Olimpia, the most beautiful woman in Barcelona. There are some amusing moments and some very funny dialogue, as in Sellers' 'I'm not very good at bullfighting – I can't keep my feet still.'

The Bobo was initially a very positive experience for Hattie, 'Fascinating . . . one of the loveliest things I've worked on. It took five months to make in Rome and although I'd worked before with Peter, I admired him greatly. He was so inventive. He even did his role in a thick Spanish accent, which the rest of us did at a lesser grade. I'm also potty about Britt. We loved the film, but it never came to much. Before making it I went on the biggest diet I'd ever undertaken and lost five stone. But so few people saw it.'

Although Hattie described the experience in such positive

terms, there were problems on the set. Sellers' relationship with his then wife, Britt Ekland, was tempestuous to say the least. He was openly rude about her personally and particularly vociferous about her acting ability – or lack of it. He tried to have the director Robert Parrish sacked and attempted to organise a petition to this effect. He even made an effort to direct the odd scene behind Parrish's back. However, for Hattie this was the least of her worries. Schofield visited her on location and they had a huge argument when Hattie accused him seeing another woman. She later telephoned Joan Le Mesurier in floods of tears to say that Schofield had told her that he had fallen in love with an Italian heiress.

Following the film being wrapped, Hattie returned to Eardley Crescent. She was admitted briefly to hospital soon after for investigations about a kidney complaint. Robin Le Mesurier was only thirteen at the time but Hattie told him the story in later years; Schofield came to see Hattie in hospital and told her that their relationship was finished – he was leaving Hattie for the heiress. Robin explains, 'John was very rude to Hattie and told her that it "was all over". He tossed a medallion that she had given him (three fingers moulded together in gold and inscribed "I Love You") on the bed and stormed out.' Robin said he was surprised when he heard this from his mother as he felt it wasn't in Schofield's nature to behave in this manner. Robin believes that Schofield must have felt so guilty and upset about what he had done to Hattie that the only way he could cope was to be so brutally frank. Maybe.

Schofield left. He disappeared. He didn't return to Eardley Crescent to collect his belongings and, even more mysteriously, he didn't see Robin or Kim again to say goodbye. Perhaps that *was* guilt. In any case, he was never seen again by Hattie's family or friends and no-one, to this day, knows exactly where he went, although it is likely he returned to Italy and the heiress.

Hattie was heartbroken. Inconsolable. Copp said that he had never witnessed Hattie crying until she rang him up to tell him that Schofield had betrayed her and was now gone, 'Poor Hattie was sobbing, sobbing, sobbing on the phone.' Bruce was also upset because for all Schofield's machismo and occasional poor behaviour, he felt that he was 'a good man who did love Hattie in his own way'. Both Bruce and Joan Le Mesurier felt that Hattie was never quite the same again. Hattie confided in Patsy Rowlands that she couldn't come to terms with the fact that Schofield had gone: 'I sit on one side of the fireplace and there is no-one on the other side.' Barbara Windsor felt that Hattie lost a lot of her spirit after the break-up and never recovered from being deserted by Schofield.

Things were not exactly going smoothly for John and Joan Le Mesurier, whose relationship proved to be equally problematic. Within six months of their marriage Joan Le Mesurier had fallen in love with Tony Hancock and continued a volatile affair which only came to an end with the comedian's tragic overdose in Australia in 1968. Le Mesurier was again aware of his wife's infidelity. Joan recalls, 'We never discussed divorce. The way patience and love and hope had just about sustained him during the darkest days of his marriage to Hattie was a strength he was able to muster again. Hattie was as usual a comfort: who better to understand what had happened to me. She was always there on the end of the phone to give me help and advice . . . I remember her saying, "Open hearts are easily invaded."'

Hattie protected herself from future hurt by surrounding herself with a coterie of gay men who would bestow love, friendship and patronage unconditionally. None of them could individually take Schofield's place, although Bruce Copp did say that if he had been straight, he would definitely have made Hattie an offer she couldn't refuse.

Ever since she had been at The Players', Hattie had felt an affinity for gay men. They were unthreatening and most of all, she could be herself. The feeling was mutual; homosexual men were attracted to her – she was a mother figure in whom they could confide and who gave advice and unreserved support.

Hattie had purchased another property at 54 Waterford Road, just off the Kings Road. She bought this not just as an investment but also as a home for her mother, who had now left Margate because she wanted to be nearer to Hattie and her grandsons. Hattie later rented 54 Waterford Road to her brother, Robin, and his girlfriend, Anne Valery. Although Robin wasn't as family-orientated as his sister and they held different political views, the two of them maintained a close relationship.

Martin Christopherson lived next door in Waterford Road and was a window dresser at the department store, Simpsons of Piccadilly. His lover had been killed in a motor-cycle accident at the same time that Schofield had left Hattie. Both Hattie and Martin were despondent and needed mutual support. Hattie also required help with her day-to-day business and so employed Martin on a part-time basis, although he initially continued to work at Simpsons. In time, Martin's responsibilities expanded and apart from his secretarial work he ended up doing lots of odd jobs for Hattie, including interior design, decorating and her sewing. All Hattie's friends have remarked on the fact that he cut a rather an amusing figure: he had a girlish, pretty face but wore a terrible, lopsided wig, a brown, curly, ersatz Shirley Temple affair, that gave him a slightly ridiculous appearance. Hattie was the only person who was allowed to see him without the wig. She bought him an expensive replacement which he never wore. Martin was a great support to Hattie, whom he adored. She was, in turn, very fond of him. One friend described them as being like a married couple without the sex.

Hattie threw herself into her work and a myriad charitable events as a way of coping with her heartbreak. Work wasn't merely a distraction, however. Hattie was always professional and never turned in a performance that wasn't her best. She also found solace in regular contact with her colleagues. 'The nicest part of this business is the people. Rehearsals would be lovely if it was possible just to meet all one's old friends and not to have to worry about learning lines and zigzagging across the studio.'

Hattie appeared in *The Plank* as 'Woman with a rose in her mouth'. This was a comedy, mainly using mime and slapstick, for television, written by Eric Sykes and a variation of the film which had originally been broadcast in 1964 when Hattie played Sykes' principal assistant. (There was yet another version in 1979 with Arthur Lowe and Frankie Howerd.) The plot consisted of Sykes and his assistant facing unusual difficulties in procuring the last plank that they need to complete construction of a floor.

Hattie was cast as Miss Popinjay in a children's television series, *Knock Three Times*, which also featured Jack Wild, and she also joined her old friend Spike Milligan in the first series of *The World Of Beachcomber*, unsurprisingly, a somewhat surreal comedy show. She was a guest on *That Was The Week That Was*, *The Lulu Series* and *Howerd's Hour*, a television special for ITV starring Frankie Howerd and written by Eric Sykes.

Despite keeping herself busy with these various commitments, ensuring the children were happy and organising social gatherings, there were times when Hattie was left alone – something she hated at the best of times. Apart from one or two very close friends with whom she confided, she was not one to play the martyr. Instead, when she was truly miserable, Hattie sought refuge in food.

From being her least heavy while with Schofield, Hattie now started to put on weight rapidly. She herself admitted, 'I like every food except tapioca pudding and boiled fish . . . my trouble is comfort eating – when I get upset I eat all the time. I enjoy giving dinner parties for my friends and I usually do that once a week. Having my friends about me is very important as I get older. I work really hard at keeping them.'

Hattie's size had been an issue for her ever since she was a young child, and throughout her life it was something with which she never came to terms. Although she loved swimming, she hated going to the seaside and being seen in a swimsuit. Joan Le Mesurier remembers that once when Hattie was on the beach with the boys, other holidaymakers openly made rude comments about her as she relaxed in the sand. She walked away, waded into the sea and wept. Bruce Copp also recalls a holiday spent on the Rhine with Hattie and John Schofield. Wherever they went, the Germans would point and laugh at Hattie. Hattie was convinced it was because of her size and the implication that because she was with two men and wearing make up that she must be a prostitute.

Hattie often spoke about being shy and said, 'I've always been a big girl, but I get terribly embarrassed sometimes, I'm a very sensitive person. I suppose I'm pathologically shy. I can't help it – even at parties among my chums I have to take a deep breath before I go into a crowded room.' It is true that even with friends Hattie was deeply self-conscious and, depending on her mood, would sometimes have to summon up courage to join a group of familiar people.

Robin Le Mesurier said that his mother had once said to him, 'I can't wait to get rid of my body. I want to be free of it once and for all.'

Hattie wore clothes that suited her build, 'I don't know my vital statistics – my dressmaker is very kind . . . I tell her what I like and she gets on and makes it and doesn't show me the tape measure . . .' Hattie didn't like tweeds or tailored suits, 'too often big people go in for mannish clothes . . . I've got a royal blue velvet cocktail dress for personal appearances and my favourite frock is purple.' She was frustrated by the fact that she couldn't walk into a shop and buy clothes off the peg. 'They always offer me plum coloured, button through dresses for matrons so I collect stoles instead. It doesn't matter what your shape is for them.' (She did eventually find a shop in New York that catered for 'outsize ladies' where she used to shop regularly.)

Hattie apparently received a regular flow of letters from women asking to buy her old clothes because they had the same 'figure problem'. Her response was, 'My Goodness, after they have been dry cleaned six times to get the stage make up off they are not fit for anything.' Hattie stated that 'I must feel feminine and happy in what I wear so I go for full skirts which are kinder to one's legs . . . don't dress quietly, just to minimize your size. If you are big, you are going to look big anyway. And if you have a colourful personality, then for heaven's sake play up to it.'

Poor Hattie. It wasn't just the size of her own body that she was battling. She was also competing with the fashion zeitgeist. It was, let us not forget, the same era that Jean Shrimpton shocked the world in the miniest of mini skirts and Twiggy, one of the first waif supermodels, epitomised the age and was named as 'The Face of '66' by the *Daily Express*.

Hattie was constantly beset by people making comments about her weight. She was once in a cab when the driver looked at her in his rearview mirror and proclaimed, 'You look very much like Hattie Jacques.' Hattie replied, 'I'm often mistaken for her.' The taxi driver smiled and said, 'Of course you're much thinner.' Jokes such as 'Pull up a couple of chairs and sit down', were constantly trotted out and infuriated Hattie. 'Over the years I've learned to build a sort of invisible wall around me against such 'funnies' but I still say to myself, Oh God! Not again! You see people think they're cracking a fat girl joke for the first time – I'm hearing it for the umpteen hundredth permutation.'

Publicly, Hattie faced the subject head-on, although her stance changed – presumably depending on who was interviewing her and how she was feeling at the time. She either adopted an 'I don't care what they think' attitude – 'If you're fat, everyone expects you to be funny . . . I've got used to it now and I make the most of my weight . . . the truth is that size just doesn't worry me at all' – or she admitted to how much she was hurt: 'I hate being the size I am with all my heart and soul. I hate it simply because I'm a woman. And it's difficult to be fat and feminine at the same time.'

In fact Hattie didn't really like doing interviews, although she always agreed to such requests. In the television interviews that still exist, she does look extremely uncomfortable. She also detested having photographs taken, which she likened to going to the dentist. Of course, putting herself in the public eye was part of the game she had to play and although she did protest occasionally about being 'public property', there was no doubt that Hattie did like the limelight and, like all her fellow artistes, missed the attention when it wasn't there.

The press of course were merciless and never missed an opportunity to pun headlines that referred to Hattie's size. Articles with titles such as; 'A fat girl has fun', 'Hattie talks about broad comedy', 'Hattie's weight keeps us laughing', 'Television's favourite fat girl', 'Hattie weighs in with the Carry On lot', 'Hattie plumps for home' etc. . . . etc. . . . She was described as 'a substantial comedienne', 'Ten gallon Hat', 'an absolute darling with a little girl voice that belies her gentle bulk'. A particularly vitriolic piece in a South African magazine in 1979 read, 'Hattie Jacques waddled across her hotel room and plumped her 127 kilogram frame down on the couch . . . Hattie dresses in what can only be described as "patterned tents", despite it being a sweltering hot day.' (By then, Hattie, who did like to cover her legs anyway, was suffering from very nasty ulcerated legs which she didn't want anyone to see.)

An article in the magazine *Good Housekeeping* in 1961 began, 'I called upon this outsize and lovable lump of London town at 3.30 pm to be offered a bottle of wine, a punnet of strawberries and a great deal of warm and worldly wisdom.' Hattie was, inevitably, prompted to talk about her size, 'Now, I'm a big girl – a very big one. There are two ways in which big girls get laughs; they can be laughed at – which I don't believe in because outsize is a form of deformity and laughter at deformity is not a good idea. On the other hand they can laugh contentedly at themselves and that's quite a different matter.' Hattie went on to talk about how being fat helped her in her professional work. She admitted that, 'It forced limitations on me and has given me jobs that thin girls would never have got. It saved me an awful lot of heartache about wanting to be Cleopatra and Juliet which never come into one's thoughts at all. That's such a relief.'

This typecasting wasn't a relief to Hattie at all. She was constantly frustrated at having to play a lovable large lady or demented harridan and was very seldom given the opportunity to stretch her acting skills. In the same interview, she stated, 'I hope what success I have is not solely because I'm large. It does occur to me that that I might have had enough talent to get somewhere without quite as much flesh. The only woman I can think of who is large without losing her dignity is Margaret Dumont who used to be with the Marx Brothers.' This is probably because, as has been well documented, Miss Dumont was in a perpetual state of bewilderment, not having the faintest idea about what was going around her and barely understanding a word Groucho was saying.

Dissatisfaction in the acting profession is hardly rare, and it's true of performers that they tend to covet work that they either are being denied or haven't been given the opportunity to explore. Comedians are desperate to do straight work, and serious actors want the chance to be funny. Hattie was in constant demand and British audiences adored her. It must have crossed her mind that if she was unsuccessfully cast in other roles, not only would her professional life suffer but she might lose some public popularity. An actress cannot play Juliet if she's built like the Nurse. But what irked Hattie the most was that the only nurse she was asked to play was in the *Carry On* films. It all comes to philosophy of acceptance. Perhaps the wisest performers don't moan about what they're not and just enjoy their fame for who they are.

In a BBC television interview in 1975 with Terry Wogan (*Wogan's World*) Hattie was extremely frank. 'If you're a fat girl like I have always been, you can't be a normal character in a play, you can't fall in love . . . or get married or have children . . . if you're large, you're not allowed to play anything else but comedy. Not that I'm complaining, I love playing comedy, but at the same time I've never had the opportunity to play something a little straighter . . . I haven't had the opportunity to extend myself, if you'll pardon the expression . . . as a matter of fact most of my comedy is straight. I'm not a broad comedienne. I don't enjoy doing the Union Jack drawers type of comedy, you know, slipping over and there you are with a large pair of Union Jack directoire knickers. I don't enjoy doing it and I don't enjoy watching it.'

Wogan continued, 'Your big ambition was to be a ballet dancer.' (There was a nervous titter from the audience.) Hattie laughed, 'Well, of course. And still is! Oh I did want to be a ballet dancer. Terribly badly. But there were reasons why I couldn't. Well, one big reason why I couldn't.' (Big guffaw from the audience.) It's all rather poignant and made even more upsetting by the fact that the audience were still laughing at her size while she was, in a small way, publicly baring her soul.

Obese people have always been the target of humour and cruel jibes. In the world of films and television, they have been absolute sitting ducks. Fatty Arbuckle, in the days of the silent movies, was a tragic figure, but considered hilarious because of his girth. Even today, despite the fact that racist and sexist jokes, and jokes about the disabled are quite rightly discouraged, humorous insults about fat women are somehow acceptable. Negative images and stereotypes of fat women continue to permeate television and films. Hattie would not have been a great fan of *Little Britain,* and I can only imagine what she would have thought of the appallingly offensive Eddie Murphy film *Norbit.* The role of supporting actress in which Hattie often found herself has its own occupational hazards; when the late Vivian Vance played Ethel Mertz in *I Love Lucy,* her contract stated that she had to remain twenty pounds overweight so that she would look older and frumpier than Lucille Ball.

Throughout her working life, Hattie was expected to undertake the demeaning role; in a clip from the 1955 series *Our House,* Hattie is trying to buy a blouse and, in a series of questions, asks the sales assistant for different types, styles and colours to which the assistant replies, 'Not in your size, Madam.' Finally the exasperated Hattie asks, 'Got a handkerchief?'

In *Carry On Cabby,* Hattie is in her bathroom, wearing just a towel. She steps on the scales, raises her eyes to the heavens and says, 'Who would have thought a towel would have made that difference?'

There are many other examples, and in *Heroes of Comedy*, a Thames Television documentary about Hattie, a number of her fellow artistes paid tribute to her work, while recognising the limits that were placed up on her. The actress Angela Douglas, a friend for many years, read a letter from Hattie, '*They've asked me to go to The National Theatre – of course it's "a fat part". Coincidentally, there's a song on the wireless at the moment called, "But you don't know me", enough said . . . much love, Hattie.*'

The dichotomy for Hattie was that her size also helped her enormously in regard to her professional career. In *Heroes of Comedy*, Bob Monkhouse commented, 'She was a great big roly poly and roly polys are funny. She was such a great comedienne – everyone wanted her, but the movers and shakers of entertainment didn't perceive her as anything other than a fat lady. . . I never liked jokes about Hattie being overweight . . . size was never referred to in Sykes.'

This isn't absolutely true as there was one episode when Hattie had submitted a lonely hearts advertisement and described herself as being of 'medium size' to which Eric Sykes reacted with a doubtful look. Still, it is very mild and Hattie was always grateful that Sykes, 'hardly ever made jokes about my size which was a refreshing change. I used to be terrified of television. Now with scripts written by Eric I love it.'

Actress Miriam Margolyes once said of her own shape, 'Fatness is not a state of mind and mustn't be allowed to become so. I've been fat all my life and I expect to die fat. But I'm not fat inside. I'm a little darting thing with quick movements to match my quick mind and when I realised I was fat, which was probably when I was eleven, I decided to use it to my advantage.' Miss Margolyes is a great fan of Hattie's, 'She was so incredibly loved . . . unusual, amazing for a fat lady. You wouldn't expect it.'

Hattie did attempt to lose weight from time to time and put herself through some very strict regimes, including such things as 'the lettuce leaf' diet, 'Once, I lost five stone at a go through sheer starvation. My doctor scared me with talk of a possible coronary and gave me vitamin injections to keep me going. I looked very ill and haggard.' Joan Sims once persuaded her to spend time at Grayshott Hall, a health farm in Surrey, where Hattie was treated to massages, enjoyed the use of a swimming pool and suffered a regimen of healthy eating. Hattie couldn't stand it and went home after a couple of days.

The trouble was that when Hattie did undergo these slimming disasters, they usually went unnoticed. The weight loss just wasn't obvious enough. Hattie went on a very radical diet, losing three stone, before filming one of the *Carry On* series, but on the set, on the first day of shooting, not one person noticed or commented on her looks. This was totally demotivating for Hattie, who wasn't particularly greedy but did love her grub. Compulsive eating has been described as a kind of eating disorder and, unlike bulimia, there is no attempt to rid the body of what has been eaten. Hattie may have felt some degree of powerlessness in being unable to control her comfort eating and this activity ultimately added to her poor self-image. There is no doubt that much of her life did revolve around food and she was somewhat obsessed by it, but there is no evidence of Hattie going on food binges.

Hattie wasn't one for exercising. She had incredible energy and her ability to keep up the pace at her legendary parties was due to 'purple hearts' (a combination of amphetamines and barbiturates which were popular in the early 1960s), which she used to pop occasionally, handing them out in liberal quantities to her party guests. It was no wonder that she sometimes had the stamina to take breakfast orders from her guests at four in the morning and dish out copious amounts of bacon and eggs to the 'diehards' who remained.

Hattie said she lit up a cigarette only once a day, although of course this one match was responsible for igniting at least sixty a day. Hattie was, by her own admission, a chain-smoker, although her claim that she didn't inhale is a little unlikely. She sometimes had several cigarettes, glowing in various ashtrays at a time. Hattie enjoyed smoking and didn't ever really want to stop. She did once, however, attend a hypnotist to help her kick the habit. He began the session by telling her, 'Relax, just imagine that you are sitting peacefully in the warm sunshine on a deck chair on the beach.' Hattie maintained that this was the worst suggestion he could have made, 'There is no situation I dislike more than being on a beach. I pretended to be hypnotised so as not to hurt his feelings, but it was no good.'

In a magazine interview she admitted to her addiction, 'I smoke too much, somewhere around sixty a day . . . the telephone rings and if I haven't got a cigarette lit I reach for the packet. I can't talk on the phone without a fag. By the time I get the cigarettes, and light one up, as often or not the caller has given up and hung up.' Hattie was not a great drinker, although she enjoyed the occasional glass of wine or champagne, particularly at Christmas.

Hattie's son Robin confirmed that she was always at her happiest at Christmas. Planning for the festivities usually began in November, when she and Martin Christopherson decided on a yuletide theme. One year, a pink Arabian tent, another, a winter snow scene. It was more than likely that Simpsons provided not only the design facilities but also the materials that embellished Hattie's seasonal celebrations. Hattie loved to make lists: food, drink, presents and almost as important, she prepared cassette tapes for the musical quizzes and subjects for 'The Game', a variation on Charades. Of course, there wasn't just one winner of these different competitions – prizes were given to at least four runners up. Games of canasta and scrabble were played with great enthusiasm, particularly by the hostess. Presents were carefully selected and Hattie even opened the Christmas crackers, discarded the cheap plastic gifts and inserted more interesting presents such as silk scarves and expensive watches.

Joan Le Mesurier described the Christmas shindig as 'at least a three-day event, in which the menus were always prepared in advance. There was always a choice of starters and puddings and huge amounts of food and wine were consumed by Hattie's guests. Those were her favourite times and all her mates were there.'

Christmas Day itself would be welcomed in by the arrival of Bruce Copp at 7am, bearing six oysters and a half a bottle of champagne which he and Hattie savoured before the actual cooking began. There were three kitchens in the house, each containing an oven, and so three large turkeys could be roasted simultaneously. There were always about twenty people for the meal, and Hattie had a special table made so that everyone could be seated comfortably. The three turkeys would be served with several types of stuffing that Hattie had concocted, a selection of vegetables, variations of potatoes, sausages and bacon, and all topped by Hattie's famous gravy (which, according to Anne Valery, probably contained a hint of cigarette ash which the 'chef de la maison' had inadvertently added whilst stirring).

The Christmas cast list obviously differed depending on the era but, apart from the obvious family members, included brother Robin (who sometimes found the event a little too excessive) and Anne Valery, Bruce Copp, Peter Greenwell, singer David Kernan, various associates of the *Carry On* company and in later years cast members of the stage show *A Hatful of Sykes*. Kenneth Williams and Joan Sims never missed the event and also in attendance was Joan's mother, Gladys. Gladys was not the most popular of guests. Apart from the fact that she was very conventional and never stopped talking, she was constantly critical of her successful daughter and for some reason Miss Sims was completely subjugated by her domineering mother and never able to stand up to her.

After the table-creaking Christmas lunch, Kenneth Williams and Joan Sims, in an impromptu double act, would dispense the presents which were stacked in a large mound around a beautifully dressed tree that normally reached the ceiling. Williams recalled one such extravaganza in 1972:

I had another happy reunion on Christmas day when I went to Hattie Jacques's house. She had a lot of friends round a groaning table and presided over the meal with that special warmth and affection which so endeared her to everyone. We all got a present – some even got two – but Hattie was given so many you couldn't count them. Joan Sims did the distributing, playing the Fairy of the Christmas Tree and calling out the names and good wishes, coupled with rude asides; as Hattie's pile of gifts mounted in front of her on the table, her face was gradually hidden by the parcels, and everyone was giggling as she protested, 'It's getting dark behind here.' But Joan went on producing the packages and eventually cried, 'And yet another tribute to the over-endowed Miss Jacques,' Joan handed yet another huge parcel to her, saying with a bitter smile 'Here's *another* bleedin' present for you Hattie! And it couldn't happen to a nicer person . . .', by which time everyone was laughing hysterically! My face actually ached with the pain of laughter. First Christmas day that I've ever known such hilarity.

It was at this particular celebration that Hattie's present of the Noel Coward record to Williams, described in this book's prologue, was made. This was a typical generous act by Hattie. So many people depended on her in so many different ways. According to Joan Le Mesurier, 'She possessed an extraordinary emotional empathy, she always had a wise answer and provided solid support, both in practical and emotional ways.' If any of her friends happened to mention they needed something she would go out of her way to obtain it – apart from Charles Hawtrey whose personal requests were something that even Hattie wouldn't procure . . .

Hattie was a firm and stalwart friend and confidante to Joan Sims who was extremely fragile, had a serious drinking problem and became reclusive in later years. Hattie rescued Joan on many occasions from various emotional entanglements and was even called in to retrieve Joan's dinner parties when the hostess became too smashed to cook! In her autobiography, *'High Spirits'*, Joan Sims wrote of Hattie, 'Her household had become like a second home to me, but at a price: looking on at the sheer normality of ordinary family life, seeing one or other of her sons popping in and out, would sometimes bring home to me acutely what my own life had lacked, and that feeling cut through me like a knife.'

Sims was never able to reciprocate the support and this wasn't just because of her own frailties, 'Hat went through a terrific amount of heartache: although she didn't exactly cry on my shoulder at the time I knew she was deeply wounded . . . she was very private . . . most of her feelings locked up inside her.'

CHAPTER TEN

Carry on Hattie

Our comedies are not to be laughed at.

SAM GOLDWYN

FOR THE NEXT decade, although she suffered from health problems and struggled to come to terms with the loss of John Schofield, Hattie worked tirelessly. In fact she had never been busier.

Hattie appeared in another Eric Sykes project, *Sykes Versus ITV* which was broadcast in 1967. This was a 'one-off special' which took the form of a courtroom trial: in the dock was Sykes, who had to provide evidence as to why he should be given the opportunity to do the show. He was 'defended' by Hattie Jacques and the prosecutor was none other than Tommy Cooper.

During the first day of rehearsals Tommy Cooper told Hattie that he was going to buy a cine camera. Cooper explained that he wanted to film himself while working in order to see what his performance looked like. Hattie was slightly bemused at how this was going to work but the comedian was so keen that she didn't want to dampen his enthusiasm. The following day, Cooper buttonholed Hattie again, 'Don't you think it's a great idea? I think I've decided which camera to buy.' The third day, the manic magician told her that he was very close to actually purchasing the said camera and was beside himself with excitement. With each conversation, he became more and more enthusiastic. On the last day of rehearsals Cooper called Hattie over, 'You know what I've been telling you about the camera?' Hattie nodded wearily. Tommy looked triumphant, 'Well, I've got a better idea – I'm going to get myself a mirror!'

Hattie followed up *Sykes Versus ITV* with an appearance in *Titi-Pu*, an imaginative version of *The Mikado* which was the first-ever colour musical specially produced for television. The co-stars were John Inman, Harry Worth and Richard Wattis. A more serious project in which Hattie featured in the same year was *The Memorandum*, written by Vaclav Havel, a Theatre 625 production for BBC 2.

Hattie ended 1967 by appearing in another of the *Carry On* series, *Carry On Doctor*. Jim Dale is Dr Kilmore, a friendly, hardworking and popular doctor, who all the patients adore. He is, however, not trusted by Dr Tinkle (Kenneth Williams) and Matron (Hattie), who can't wait for him to make a mistake. Strangely enough, Peter Rogers had written to Joan Sims in August asking her if she would, 'Please read the enclosed with the idea of playing the part of the Matron.' This is difficult to comprehend, as Hattie was so linked to the character. However, for whatever reason, Sims wasn't cast and Hattie was given the part of the sexually voracious battleaxe.

Kenneth Williams noted

Delightful to be back with all the old chums. The first day involved Barbara Windsor, Jim Dale and the adorable Hattie Jacques . . . when I saw her she was peering into the make-up mirror asking rhetorically how anyone could be funny at eight o'clock in the morning. Hattie was used to theatre hours and we never really adapted to rising at 6am, journeying out to Buckinghamshire and getting made up and costumed by 8am. Worse for Hattie because she had to have her hair done as well. A lot of my scenes were with Hattie. She had to chase me around the bedroom and roll me on the bed in passionate embraces. And we used to giggle a lot in the process. I had to scramble out of her arms saying, 'No, no, matron I was once a weak man.'

As she grabbed me again, her reply was 'Once a week's enough for any man.'

Although released in 1969, *Carry On Camping*, the fifteenth in the series was filmed in the Autumn of 1968 and set on a camp site where a group of girls from a school called 'Chayste Place' are accompanied by their headmaster Kenneth Williams and the Matron, Miss Haggard. Hattie had the name of the school written on her top – thus 'Chayste Place' was emblazoned across her bosom. The weather was cold and wet, and Barbara Windsor recalled her time on location, 'The rain started after a few days. To maintain the continuity, the tree leaves had to be stuck in and sprayed green, and the grass which had become mud got the same treatment. When we got home after filming each day, we had green ankle socks.' Between shots Hattie completed *The Times* crossword with Bernie Bresslaw, Sid played poker, and Barbara hung out with Kenny Williams. Babs always thought that the best bits in *Carry On Camping* were not her own naked boobs but actually the scenes with Hattie. She described Hattie's performance as, 'fabulous – her flirting with Kenny was incongruous but it always worked.' Barbara characterised Hattie as 'a most glorious lady, sexy, full of fun and the "Mother Courage" of the cast.' She also recalled Joan Sims referring to Hattie as, 'a bit of a goer – that one.'

Another actor who is full of praise for Hattie is Graham Stark, who worked with her on a number of occasions. He first saw Hattie on stage at The Players', 'Hattie was unforgettable because she was so good and she had marvellous timing. One of the great British comediennes – a lovely lady.' Stark was in two of Eric Sykes short films, *The Plank* and *Rhubarb Rhubarb* and also starred with Hattie in *Inside George Webley*, a 1968 Yorkshire Television series with Roy Kinnear.

Both Graham and Hattie featured in *The Magic Christian* with Stark's great friend Peter Sellers. Production on the film began in February 1969. It is a comedy about the world's richest man, Sir

Guy Grand (Sellers), who adopts 'a drop out' (Ringo Starr) as his son and heir, and spreads his money in a variety of eccentric ways to prove that money corrupts – everyone has his or her price. Hattie has a cameo role as Ginger Horton, an upper-class eccentric, a vision in pink, wrapped in what appears to be a silver fox stole and sporting a ginger wig. Throughout the scene, which is set aboard a train, 'Ginger' clutches a pet Pekinese dog under her arm and affirms her obsession with reading about Nazi wartime atrocities. It is a lovely quirky performance – albeit too brief.

The Magic Christian, adapted from the novel by Terry Southern but relocated to England, is a satire on wealth and is very much of its time; there is much psychedelia, and the narrative is interspersed by newsreel footage hammering home the political directive. It attempts to capture the swinging sixties London scene, but the film's desperation to be 'wacky' results in a somewhat muddled effort, containing a series of Pythonesque sketches – not that surprising in view of the fact that John Cleese and Graham Chapman were two of the credited writers. Despite its sympathetic message, the film looks dated now. Also in the cast were John Le Mesurier and Clive Dunn.

Hattie had a small part in the comedy *Crooks and Coronets* before reprising her role as Matron in *Carry On Again Doctor.* She collaborated with Jim Dale again in his own TV series and also appeared in a television production of *Pickwick* in which she was cast as Mrs Bardell. In the comedy, *Monte Carlo Or Bust,* starring Terry-Thomas, Peter Cook, Tony Curtis and Dudley Moore, Hattie played 'a lady journalist'. Christmas 1969 saw her feature in *Carry On Christmas,* which was the team's first venture into television and proved to be the biggest ratings winner that Christmas.

During the late 1960s and early 1970s the *Carry On* company put out two movies a year, and a Christmas special. In *Carry On Loving,* Sid James and Hattie run the Wedded Bliss Marital Agency. The whole operation is a sham, however, including the fact that Sid and Hattie aren't actually married; they have an agreement that Sid keeps all the best-looking girls on the books for himself. The first day of filming for Hattie was on 6 April 1970 and apparently her costumes were the most expensive in the budget, with her various outfits amounting to almost £100!

'*Loving*' was closely followed by *Carry On At Your Convenience* set in the factory of W.C. Boggs (played by Kenneth Williams), makers of lavatory and bathroom equipment and beset by trouble with the bolshie workforce. Sid James and Hattie are again husband and wife (Sid and Beattie Plummer).

Sandwiched in between the films was *Charley's Grants*, a strange TV sitcom about the arts grants scheme, created by John Wells and John Fortune and playwright NF Simpson. The basic premise is that of a down-at-heel aristocrat, (Willoughby Goddard) who attempts to solve his financial difficulties by scrounging grants from Miss Manger (Hattie) of the Heritage Trust. Unsurprisingly, the show didn't run to a second series. Hattie was a panel member on the Radio 4 programme *Sounds Familiar* and she also appeared on the record of a musical version of *The Owl and the Pussycat* with Roy Castle, narrated by Harry Secombe. Another children's show in which Hattie featured in 1970 was an appearance in an episode of *Catweazle*.

The following year Hattie teamed up again with Eric Sykes in *Sykes and a Big Big Show*, a six-episode music and sketch show based on the production of a variety show. Opera singer Ian Wallace also featured, as Sykes faces a number of difficulties in attempting to reach the Albert Hall, where he is supposed to conduct a Prom Concert. Hattie appeared in sketch shows with Harry Secombe and Frankie Howerd and in an episode of *Doctor At Large* (Mrs Askey). She featured as Miss Keen in a short film for children *Danger Point* in which three teenagers steal a local yacht and set out to sea, encountering a number of perils including a dangerously drifting mine. *Danger Point* was filmed on location in the Isle of Man.

John Le Mesurier was now working consistently in films and television and had appeared in a Dennis Potter play, *Traitor*. Set during the Cold War, Le Mesurier played the part of a British defector, living in a state of drunken reverie in a run-down Moscow flat. His performance was so strong that he was nominated for a BAFTA best actor award.

Hattie was at home with her son Robin watching the ceremony and although delighted that her ex-husband was finally being recognised by his peers for his acting talent, she was also upset that she wasn't with him and part of the celebrations. She was reduced to tears when his name was announced as the winner and admitted to Robin that she had wanted so much to be there with John. Hattie wasn't crying out of professional resentment or even envy about Joan Le Mesurier, who was at John's side, but from an unhappiness that, through her own actions, she had lost John or there was now no-one with whom to share her life.

Hattie always remained supportive of her ex-husband, and some years later when John became ill, Hattie sent him a case of the only wine he was supposed to drink: non-alcoholic. In fact, after being advised to give up alcohol on medical grounds (advice he wasn't always inclined to follow) Le Mesurier wrote in his autobiography that he took up 'extra strong cigarettes'. Of course, the household at 67 Eardley Crescent hadn't been strangers to marijuana since the 1960s and John was supposedly a little stoned when presented by Princess Anne with the BAFTA award!

Hattie returned to Pinewood in *Carry On Matron* in which she had the title role. She was up against Sid Carter (Sid James) and his gang of unlikely mobsters as they attempted to steal birth-control pills stocked by Finisham Maternity Hospital in order to sell them to the third world.

The film was notable, not only for Hattie's authoritative performance but also for the fact that her health was beginning to concern the production team. Robert Ross explained that the on-set *Carry On* physician, Dr Black, noted 'since my last examination on 24 March 1970 there has been an impressive drop in blood pressure 170/130 to 150/110 and she is receiving hypertensive drugs from her own doctor. A fall of this magnitude must, I think, imply an improved prognosis even though her weight has increased from 18st 10 lbs to 19st 7lbs.' Kenneth Williams refers to filming in his diaries:

My next scene was with Hattie Jacques so I was home and dry. We had a kind of rapport that made work a pleasure. Unlike me, she was very deft with all the props and the scene went smoothly in one take.' I said 'Very different from that night at Joan Sim's party when your flamboyant gesture knocked her vase off the mantelpiece. 'Oh yes,' laughed Hattie ruefully. 'Joan said it was a family heirloom that had been handed down!' 'That night it was knocked down!' Hattie later referred to this particular production as, 'The vulgar with a bit of oo la la . . . it sort of sums up the *Carry Ons*, doesn't it?'

Concerns about Hattie's health caused major difficulties in Peter Rogers' next production, *Carry On Abroad*. Hattie had originally been given a major part in the film and was due to be fifth on the billing, but her role was drastically reduced to just one week's work and she ended up eleventh on the bill. Although she and Peter Butterworth combined well as inept hoteliers Floella and Pepe, this wasn't what was first envisaged for Hattie. Immediately after filming was completed, Peter Rogers was informed by Lloyd's, the insurers, that owing to Hattie Jacques' ballooning weight and blood-pressure problems, 'no cover whatsoever can be given in respect of her for any future film'.

This was the last in the series to feature 'the full team' and the swan song of Charles Hawtrey, who played Eustace Tuttle in his last *Carry On* role before falling out with the production team. *Carry On Christmas*, a special for Thames Television was broadcast on 14 December 1972 and Hattie was cast in various parts, including a Fairy Godmother. With both Sid James and Kenneth Williams missing from the cast, Hawtrey naturally assumed that he would get top billing. When he discovered that his name was to appear below Hattie's, he refused to appear. Peter Rogers and

Gerald Thomas, mindful of Hattie's television success with Eric Sykes, were determined that Hattie was to be awarded top billing on the show. Barbara Windsor recalled the events:

> Charlie threw a moody. He went off to Bourne and Hollingsworth to have something to eat and he said, 'If they want to talk to me I'll be having Brown Windsor at the restaurant!' Gerald Thomas telephoned the department store's restaurant and gave Hawtrey an ultimatum: accept second billing or nothing. Hawtrey refused and hung up. He let Gerald Thomas down badly just two days before filming and so he was never used again.

During 1973, Hattie's health deteriorated further: an extract from Kenneth Williams' diaries on 9 September 1973 notes, 'Hattie was looking rather drawn and apparently she's been in hospital and they've discovered arthritis but everyone at the party was hinting at worse disorders.' In November Hattie was admitted to hospital again – this time with an obstruction in one of her fallopian tubes which ended in her undergoing a hysterectomy. She remained in hospital for two weeks and then returned home to convalesce. Hattie bounced back to enjoy her Christmas festivities as usual and even hosted a New Year's Eve party. She rang Kenneth Williams to invite him but for fear of offending her he told her he was going elsewhere, 'whereas in fact, I am going nowhere. If I attend *one* more party I shall go stark raving mad.'

Filming on *Carry On Dick* started on 9 March 1974 and was to be Hattie's last appearance in the film series. Hattie is Martha Hoggett, the Reverend Flasher's (Sid James) faithful housekeeper who is oblivious to Flasher's double life as Dick Turpin. The film was also significant in that not only was it Hattie's final outing but it was also the last *Carry On* appearance of Sid James. Kenneth Williams did not enjoy himself during the filming and it was only Hattie who kept him going, 'Day redeemed by presence of Hattie: she is a constant joy, and dear Bernard . . . we all lunched together.'

Hattie and Bernard Bresslaw were once invited to the Cork film festival and stayed at an extremely plush hotel. While studying the dinner menu, one evening, Hattie asked the waiter what he could recommend. He was unequivocal, 'Ahh . . . well . . . you'll be wanting the lobster . . . oh, yes the lobster. It's fantastic! In fact, it's not only the best in the County, oh no, it's the best in Ireland. You know, people come from all over the world for our lobster.' Hattie's eyes lit up and returning the menu with a flourish announced, 'That's perfect – that's exactly what I shall have!' The waiter took the menu and shook his head sadly, 'I'm very sorry. You can't. We haven't got any. The lobster's out of season.'

Hattie appeared in one episode of *Carry On Laughing*, another television series, in which she appeared as Queen Elizabeth in *Orgy and Bess* and which was first broadcast in January 1975. But, sadly, Hattie's *Carry On* days were now definitely over. Lloyd's wouldn't insure her again and although Peter Rogers had taken a chance by not insuring her during the filming of the last two projects, the risk to continue in this manner was just too great.

In the 1980 Tony Bilbow television interview, the presenter asked Hattie why she made so many *Carry On* films. Hattie replied, 'For fun. Not for the money. No, that's not quite fair. But it was for fun. It was like a shot in the arm. All those chums – we've grown up together. Good chums. It was like belonging to a club. We used to have lots of laughs.' Although Hattie always tried to be fair to her employer, it certainly wasn't for the money: Peter Rogers himself admitted, 'I'll do anything for my actors except pay them.'

At the peak of the *Carry On* series, Barbara Windsor, Joan Sims and Hattie were earning £2,500 per film – the very same fee that that they had earned in 1959 and was reported to be half that which the men earned. Peter Rogers wouldn't budge in terms of negotiation, although he has always maintained that the cast were offered a percentage of the films' profits – an offer which their agents always refused. This has always been denied by most of the actors. None of the cast ever benefited from the continuous television re-runs of the films or the worldwide broadcasts of the television compilations.

Russell Davies, editor of *The Kenneth Williams Diaries*, reported that, 'None of them made much money out of the Carry Ons . . . as explained by the production team, the idea was that instead of paying out big money to a star, they would share a sum among the team in which no member predominated. It is not a particularly persuasive notion (even on a big-name picture, the support players have to be realistically paid); but the work was regular and nobody in the cast carried individual responsibility for a flop.'

The notion of a regular ensemble of comedy actors appealed to the cast. This was the main attraction to Hattie, who maintained, 'There was no question of you not knowing what you were to do, and you were in the deep end from the first day. But working with people you had sort of grown up with in the business made it all that much easier. All the cast were so likeable and understanding – they helped each other like members of a repertory company.'

Peter Rogers described Hattie as the Mother Confessor. 'She had such a presence that you always wanted to be in her company. All the cast loved her.' They all gathered around her and actress Dilys Laye, who appeared in several *Carry On* films, confirmed that 'If you had any problems or had any difficulties, you'd go to Hattie. The films were made very quickly and if you didn't know your lines they were cut. But Hattie always had time to talk to you on set.' Jim Dale wrote that, 'On the set she was always full of fun and a very generous person.' Angela Douglas remembered Hattie's sense of fun, 'I took Hattie to my mother's for tea once. She bred budgies and Hattie saw the sign on the gate, which read, "Young cocks, ginger, tamed, fifteen shillings." Hattie's response was, 'Don't know about you girl, but that's good enough for me.'

Hattie loved Kenneth Williams both professionally and as a friend; not only was he extraordinarily entertaining but she found him to be incredibly erudite. She once said that, when she was on set, if ever she wanted to find out about a subject or learn something new she would always ask him for the answer. Like all his fellow actors, Hattie was intrigued by Williams' enigmatic private life. She, Joan Sims and Kenneth once shared a car home from Pinewood. When they arrived outside his flat near Great Portland Street, Williams wanted to disappear quickly into his sanctuary but Joanie and Hattie were having none of it and insisted that they were coming in for a cup of tea. Williams was horrified and asserted that no-one, other than his mother, entered his flat. Hattie was equally adamant and told him,' We're coming in . . . no arguments.'

The story is continued in Joan Sims' autobiography, *High Spirits*:

> Unsurprisingly the combined weight of Hattie and myself prevailed and Kenny reluctantly led the way up to his little flat. It was furnished in an extraordinary way. The sitting room was totally bare: there was no television and just about the only item of furniture was a lectern in the middle of the room. The walls were lined with hundreds of books but there were no other personal items of any sort: no pictures, no ornaments. It was almost like a hospital ward, so clinical was its mood, but to Kenny it was a haven, and while I hardly ever saw him quiet in public, I could imagine that this was where he found his peace. One area of his flat remained resolutely out of bounds: 'You can't use my lavatory!' he insisted and we could only reply with; 'We don't want to use your bloody lavatory.'
>
> We'd got behind the outer barrier, and that was enough.

Hattie's agent Felix de Wolfe is quoted as saying that her work in the *Carry On* films didn't appeal to Hattie at all and that, 'she stayed with it because it was a job and she had an obligation to the rest of the team'. It was true that she grew tired of playing characters in uniform and 'sexless, mannish characters and wanted a genuine role for a change'. She also stated that she didn't like farce or broad comedy although she admitted that, 'I can't in all conscience say the *Carry On* films were not broad but in any case I think they've had their day now anyway. I don't like playing nagging wives or butch battleaxes. It's appearing unfeminine that I worry about. I'm playing very much against my looks, but I want to be protected, to feel like a woman. I'm not cut out for low comedy.' In all honesty, Hattie was not a prude and had no objection to vulgarity – she did, after all, learn her trade in the music hall tradition of The Players'. The difficulty sometimes for Hattie was being typecast and the lack of subtlety in the scripts. John Le Mesurier was not a fan of the *Carry On* films and laid the blame firmly on the production team, who he felt always adopted a sledgehammer approach when occasionally 'a light touch' might have been more interesting. I'm not sure that the legion of *Carry On* fans would agree with that . . .

Apart from the *Carry On* films and various other projects, Hattie had also returned to television screens with her old partner, Eric Sykes. His new sitcom made a welcome comeback in 1972 and this time the show was broadcast in colour. The title was simply *Sykes* but many of the episodes were heavily reliant on the earlier scripts and stories. Eric and Hattie were still brother and sister and the setting was still Sebastopol Terrace, although the two of them now lived in a different house. Also returning to the fold was Richard Wattis as Mr Brown. At its peak, *Sykes* brought in seventeen million viewers.

Sadly, on 1 February 1975, following the completion of the third series, Richard Wattis died aged 62. The profession and his many friends suffered a great loss with his death. He was much loved and, like Hattie, was also a great gourmet. Although much too young, he passed away replete in a Kensington restaurant whilst tucking to one of his favourite meals. Hattie was very fond of Wattis and they socialised regularly. The two of them, in the company of Bruce Copp and Joan Sims, went on the cross-channel ferry on a day trip to France. Unfortunately the weather was inclement and the sea was very rough resulting in seasickness amongst the passengers. Wattis announced, in true form, that the only remedy for such queasiness was several glasses of champagne. Needless to say Hattie, Joan and Bruce didn't need to be convinced and they spent the rest of the trip getting slowly smashed. When it was time to disembark in Boulogne, there was no sign of Miss Sims and it was only after a thorough search of the boat that she was found semi-conscious . . . in the gentlemen's toilet.

Despite her previous misgivings, Hattie was pleased to be working again with Eric Sykes and to be back on television regularly. Joan Sims was cast occasionally in the series, and in one famous episode, which she later described as one of her very favourites, old friend Peter Sellers made an unforgettable cameo appearance: as 'Little Tommy Grando', an East End villain, who initially pretends to be an ex-school friend of Eric's who has run away to sea. Sellers looks hideous with a terrible cropped wig, painted eyebrows and buck teeth. He then tries to convince Eric that he is actually an old flame of Hattie's and leaps on her with such passion that, much to Hattie's surprise, he actually bites off one of her earrings by mistake. Next, he attempts to beat up Sykes, assuming him to be Hattie's husband. Of course, Sellers is neither an old flame nor an old friend but an escaped convict who wants to use the house as a hide out. He ends up disguising himself in one of Hattie's frocks and makes good his escape from the police. The three of them have a lot of fun and there is much corpsing and mugging.

Hattie had reason to remember a couple of episodes in particular. In one, she was perched on a rooftop, floating on a fast current down the River Avon – the script called for them to be stranded on the roof after a gale had blown their holiday home into the river. In a magazine interview, Hattie stated, 'It was freezing out on that water – the trouble with Eric is that I just don't know what antics he will dream up for me next.' Hattie occasionally used a stand-in, Joe Murphy, a stunt man from Harlesden, who was bewigged and dressed to look like Hattie and also admitted to needing some padding to complete the charade. There was, however, one stunt that Hattie did without the help of

Mr Murphy 'One of the funniest stunts Eric asked me to do was in a circus scene. I had to lie down and let an elephant walk over me. I just lay there and hoped the elephant wouldn't find me too big to step over. Eric was terrified and he was only watching!'

In another script, Eric had to teach Hattie how to drive and had to pretend to be nervous during their outings. In fact, there wasn't actually much acting involved as Hattie had never passed her test and really did have to steer a car in traffic. Hattie had owned several cars over the years but never obtained a driving licence. In fact, she rather enjoyed being driven around and once said that she bought cars for other people to drive.

Years ago I was playing at Gloucester and bought an old car for £45 which then represented two weeks salary. I wasn't bothered by the fact that I didn't know the first thing about cars – I simply fell in love with it. But it became a problem when the day came to return to London. How was I to get there? Kenneth More was there at the time and I asked him to drive it home. I'm sure he always regretted volunteering. My beautiful little car would not keep running for more than a few miles. It took us ages, alternatively pushing the thing for what seemed like miles then jumping in it as it started to get to London.

Hattie graduated from a Morris Minor to a Volvo, which she let sons Robin and Jake drive. Unfortunately, Jake once forgot to put oil in the car and the engine seized up, resulting in it being written-off.

In the autumn of 1974, half way through filming the eight episodes of the third *Sykes* series, Hattie suffered another cancer scare. She shed weight at a dramatic rate and was in terrible pain. She had been ill for three months and had undergone a number of tests. The doctors were unable to find the cause of her illness and suggested she go into hospital for an exploratory operation. Hattie refused any surgery and insisted that she battle on until the end of the series. She ate very little and didn't even smoke. The sight of Hattie without a cigarette in her hand was enough to convince family and friends that she was indeed extremely sick. Hattie's state of health was kept from the press, although she had to remain seated throughout the rehearsals and the only time she was well enough to stand was during the actual recording of each episode. Immediately after recording the final episode on 5 December, Hattie was admitted to Charing Cross Hospital. She underwent surgery without delay and was found to have tumours on both her kidneys . . . fortunately benign. Hattie later commented, 'Of course, I know the adage that "the show must go on". It wasn't that so much that – I just felt I couldn't let Eric and the other actors down.'

This was not the greatest year for Hattie. She had endured another extremely difficult time earlier when a domestic crisis involving her two sons caused major problems in the Jacques household. Although neither parent pushed him into the acting business, Robin Le Mesurier had a screen test for a Disney film, *Horse Without a Head* (1963) which he didn't get. Robin wasn't disappointed – acting really wasn't for him. He did, however, have a great interest in music and started to play guitar at the age of nine, teaching himself to play on an instrument bought by John and Hattie. Robin left school at sixteen and was offered a place at the Royal College of Music, but at the same time was offered a contract with EMI and recorded a single at Abbey Road, co-written with Jim Relf from the Yardbirds.

In fact, by 1974, both Robin and aspiring drummer, Kim, now known as Jake, were beginning to make names for themselves in the music world and consequently musicians and hangers on regularly visited and stayed in the house. Jake was a regular smoker of cannabis and occasionally supplied his friends with dope. A roadie, by the name of Christopher Walker, had bought some cannabis from Jake and happened to be stopped by the police still in possession of the cannabis. He must have told the officers where he scored the drugs because within hours the house was full of the Met's finest. They were apparently extremely heavy-handed as they searched the premises, breaking furniture, stripping carpets from the floors and even digging up the garden. The most improbable part of the raid was that a police woman insisted on strip-searching Hattie – an experience that was clearly draconian and, for the self-conscious Hattie, a thoroughly humiliating event.

Robin returned home in the middle of the search, which resulted in the police uncovering a massive drugs haul of one joint, containing a small amount of Acapulco Gold. Robin and Jake were distraught, particularly as their mother had been dragged into the whole event. Hattie was indeed shattered, although she was not without some responsibility: she certainly knew that her sons were smoking dope. The family home at 67 Eardley Crescent, although hardly a drugs haven, was witness to regular medicinal stimulation over the years, although whether she knew Jake was dealing in a small way is doubtful. There was some criticism from family friends that Robin and Jake continued to be mothered, some might say indulged, by Hattie well into adulthood and that while she was around, the boys never really had to fend for themselves.

The Evening News of 25 May 1974 reported the events under the headline, 'Hattie's sons quizzed'. 'Actress Hattie Jacques' two sons have been questioned about substances police found at their home. Both boys, Robin, 21 (one of the Wombles) and Kim, 17, were questioned for several hours by police at Kensington yesterday. Earlier police had called with a search warrant. Miss Jacques and sons were present when substances were found. The boys were questioned and bailed to appear at the station in four weeks time. The substances were sent for a lab report.'

After the news had hit the newspapers, Bruce Copp and a distressed Hattie went for a drink at a nearby hotel and they overheard a woman at the next table saying, 'I do feel sorry for Hattie Jacques, those boys are so difficult.' Hattie was outraged and had to be calmed down by Bruce not to confront her.

On 26 June *The Times* reported the court case, 'The two sons of Hattie Jacques were each fined £20 for possession of drugs – they pleaded guilty to possessing cannabis.'

Although Robin pleaded guilty to 'possession', the joint belonged to Jake. The drugs offence had immediate implications for Robin who was by now guitarist with The Wombles. Robin thoroughly enjoyed earning some decent money while remaining anonymous in his rat outfit! Sadly the cannabis bust resulted in Robin having to leave the group, which was devastating at the time. Following his move to the United States in 1976 to play with Rod Stewart, Robin's application for a 'Green Card' was much delayed and even until recently he has encountered visa problems.

This period was quite eventful in the lives of the Le Mesurier family. Extraordinarily, in the very same week that Robin and Jake appeared in court, Hattie received a letter from the Cabinet Office stating that she was to be offered an OBE presumably in recognition not only of her successful show business career but also of her extensive charity work. Hattie thought long and hard about accepting the gong but, ever protective of her sons, agonisingly decided to turn it down. She was concerned at the adverse publicity it might bring Robin and Jake and wanted to keep them out of media attention.

During the mid-1970s Hattie also appeared as a security official in *Three For All* – a film with Leslie North, Adrienne Posta and Cheryl Hall about 'a pop band and their girlfriends who have fun in Spain' and in *Hattie's Music Hall* – an old time radio show for New Year's Eve in 1975 with Players' veteran Peter Greenwell. Another reunion with another Players' colleague was an appearance with Ian Carmichael on *Celebrity Squares* in 1976, the same year in which Sid James died.

Hattie was genuinely fond of Sid and she paid tribute to him soon after his death. 'Sid James was one of the most unselfish of actors, never deliberately upstaging anyone. He was a very kind man – yes and chivalrous – that old-fashioned word really applied to him. He cared for all his friends and they cared very much for him . . . Sid James the man belied everything that he appeared to be. The brashness wasn't in his nature at all. He was a gentle man in the truest sense.'

Sid may not have been brash but he was the sort of man who would be outraged and take suitable action if a woman of his acquaintance was the subject of unwanted attention from a male admirer. Once the woman was suitably grateful, he would make the same play himself. On one occasion, he rang my father early one morning and said, 'Eric, if the wife rings, I was with you last night.' Before my dad could comment , Sid put the phone down leaving him in a terrible quandary – not only was he unhappy about covering for Sid but if he did decide to help out Sid, he had no idea where they were or how they were meant to have spent the evening. There was no story to correlate. My father said he spent the day in dread fear of Sid's wife Valerie ringing. Fortunately she didn't telephone, and in any case, she was quite aware of Sid's affair with Barbara Windsor.

The term 'lovable rogue' was invented for Sid James.

Albert Camus is quoted as saying, 'Too many have dispensed with generosity in order to practice charity.' Hattie managed to combine both traits with great alacrity. She was generous to a fault and tireless in her philanthropy. Her commitment to charity work was always sincere but as she grew older and was unable to find happiness on a personal level, she reached new levels of beneficence.

There is a feeling amongst those who knew her best that her professional work never provided her with the appreciation she required and that she was driven by a huge insecurity to do good deeds. This was not for public praise – she tried to keep her philanthropic activities as quiet as possible, although she obviously did get publicity. She worked in charity shops long before she was famous. Robin, her son, also used to help with the collection of clothes for the shops. Hattie tried never to refuse a request for help – her agent Felix de Wolfe joked, 'Hattie would open an envelope if asked to.' The list of Hattie's 'good works' could fill a whole book on their own but the following gives some idea of her charitable enterprises.

Hattie paid for a group of children from Birmingham to enter the *Bristol Evening Post* exhibition and she was also in attendance to present prizes in a poster competition. She opened an exhibition of sculptures and art in aid of the Leukaemia Research Fund and also a charity golf tournament which raised money to purchase two televisions for the Radwinter Road hospital in Saffron Walden. Hattie appeared in adverts for Help The Aged and was forever knocking down piles of pennies in pubs for The Spastics Society. She donated a pair of cuff links to a charity sale of celebrities' possessions at St Andrews University with the words, 'I couldn't find a man to fit them'. (They fetched £1, while Bobby Charlton's tie fetched £1.60!)

Hattie remained close friends with her old Players' stalwarts Don Gemmell and Reginald Wooley and used to visit them regularly at their house in Sewards End, Hertfordshire. They held an annual fete to raise money for charitable purposes and enlisted the help of a number of celebrities. Needless to say, Hattie was always first on their list and she made an appearance every year for over a decade. Hattie was very taken with the hamlet: 'I adore the village. If ever the time comes when I can have a home outside London this is where I would like to be.' One can't really imagine Hattie living outside London but she was genuine in her fondness for Gemmell and Wooley and their surroundings.

Hattie signed her autograph five hundred times to raise money for the National Playing Fields Association at the Lincolnshire Traction Engine Rally. In fact everywhere she went, her signature was in demand and so she decided that whenever she was asked for her autograph, she would charge a small amount (before decimalisation it was usually half a crown), which she duly donated to one of her many charities. At the opening of every event where Hattie made an appearance, a queue would form.

On one such occasion, a woman at the front of the line handed over her half a crown to Hattie and enquired, 'Miss Jacques, I've always been a great admirer of yours. Can I have two autographs please?'

Hattie replied firmly, 'Then, I'm afraid you'll have to pay five shillings.' The woman looked a little crestfallen and responded, 'Actually the second one is for my husband – he's the one in a wheelchair.' So saying, she pointed in the direction of an elderly man.

Hattie smiled sweetly at him. He glared back and said, 'What do I want with her bleeding autograph?' The woman, suitably embarrassed replied, 'Then I'll give it to Doris.' Her husband, unabashed, snapped back, 'Doris? She won't want it either. Waste of bleeding money.'

John Le Mesurier felt that her

energy expended on social causes reflected a great need in Hattie as much as in those she was trying to help. She wanted desperately to be liked and respected for herself, something that she felt did not come easily in her own profession. She was a comedy star yes, but always the Aunt Sally, the faintly ludicrous figure of authority to be knocked over by other people's jokes. As a charity worker she was seen in an entirely different light. By giving her natural personality free rein, she was able to inspire love for the real Hattie and this, in turn, gave her the energy and exuberance to attempt yet more.

CHAPTER ELEVEN

A Hatful of Sykes

My only regret in the theatre is that I could never sit out front and watch me.

JOHN BARRYMORE

T HE GLORIOUS SUMMER of 1976 saw Hattie take up residence in Torquay, appearing with Eric Sykes in the summer season show *A Hatful of Sykes*. The two one-act plays were staged at the Torquay Pavilion and based on two episodes of *Sykes* but were filled with lots of 'ad libs' (some staged). If an audience member was late, the cast would start the show again with Eric and Hattie doing it in double time. The production opened to poor reviews – 'Tedious and predictable' – but they needn't have worried about the critics as the show broke all records between May to September.

The season was actually a very happy time for the cast although inordinately hard work. The show was twice nightly (5.30pm and 8pm) apart from Friday, when there was only one performance and the cast all used to go fishing together. Hattie really liked the sport, which she found extremely relaxing. She even caught a conger eel while angling aboard the Torquay deep-sea angling boat *Girl Alison*, 'It was a bit of a struggle to land the fish. I thought I'd hooked some sort of Loch Ness Monster.'

A photograph of Hattie and the eel was reproduced in the magazine, *Reveille* on 13 August with the all-too-predictable, 'What a whopper, Hattie!'

Hilary Gagan, Eric Sykes's personal secretary, accompanied the cast to Torquay and was another person captivated by Hattie's personality, 'Hattie possessed such an adventurous spirit – she was always up for some fun. She was always smart and I remember her being a great flirt. Hattie was incredibly approachable and particularly kind-hearted. This generosity of spirit also extended to the stage – she never begrudged anyone a laugh or a round. Hattie would give freely of her time to anyone who needed help.' Hilary's marriage was in trouble at the time and Hattie offered constant support, even sending postcards and letters to Hilary's children when she was away. Hilary felt she could genuinely contact her at any time of day and night for a chat.

Hattie, who had arthritis, had also developed varicose veins in recent years and was now suffering from ulcerated legs causing her constant pain. She never complained, but Hilary was more than aware how much Hattie's deteriorating health was affecting her.

Actor Nigel Hamilton recalled that Hattie had rented the most wonderful flat with a balcony overlooking the harbour and, attempting to emulate the atmosphere of Eardley Crescent as much as possible, ensured that there was a large dining table so that she could entertain as many people as possible. It was inevitably Hattie who arranged most of the social events, and Sunday lunch at her 'digs' soon became a regular event. This was Hattie's first traditional summer season and she made the most of it; lots of her friends visited and her temporary home became a seaside extension of her Earls Court home. She was soon surrounded by her band of gay men, who Nigel described as, 'all eager to dance attendance on her!' Son Robin, accompanied by various friends, was also a regular visitor at weekends, although Jake seldom went to see his mother.

Another key member of the cast was *Sykes* stalwart Deryck Guyler. He had first started in show business, performing a variety act – singing songs, telling jokes and playing a customised washboard (it came with added bells, horns and cymbals) around local pubs and clubs in Liverpool. Guyler would take his washboard with him everywhere he went – even on holiday, and even when flying wouldn't be parted from it, so that he wouldn't allow it to be stored in the aeroplane's hold. Both he and his wife, Paddy, who referred to Deryck as 'Daddy', were converts to Catholicism and extremely religious. Guyler suffered constantly from 'a dicky stomach' and so 'Daddy and Paddy' also travelled everywhere with a primus stove so that they could always cook plain English food on tour.

Nigel and Hattie spent a great deal of time together during the Torquay production and he looks back on that summer with absolute joy. Hattie was a total spendthrift; she liked eating out every night after the show and invariably picked up the bill for all the guests. Other artists appearing in Torquay that summer were Larry Grayson (one of Hattie's favourite comedians) accompanied by his 'friend' and pianist 'Wayne King' and the less camp Moira Anderson, who all gave up their time for a midnight matinee charity event. According to Nigel, Hattie looked 'a million dollars' in a very elegant evening dress. She always received tremendous applause as soon as she made her first appearance on stage. Eric Sykes often diverted from the script but Hattie was on his wavelength and never failed to respond quickly. Nigel recalled that by the end of the engagement, the script had radically changed.

After the Torquay summer season, Hattie and Nigel remained friends and he was, by now, a fully paid up member of 'The Hat Pack'. Nigel was also useful to Hattie in several ways; he enjoyed driving and would often chauffeur her around, and as he was good-looking, Hattie liked to have him as her escort. Later on, Nigel dealt with her correspondence and sorted out her bills, somewhat to the consternation of Martin Christopherson, who felt he had first call on her. According to Nigel, apart from the Sykes television shows, Hattie wasn't always in demand and was not earning a great deal. This didn't prevent her from keeping up the appearance of being financially secure and she remained as generous as ever with her friends and colleagues.

From 25 February to 5 March 1977, Hattie and Eric appeared

at the Hong Kong Sheraton during the Hong Kong arts festival, in which they performed another version of *A Hatful of Sykes*. It was basically the same show but reduced to one act. Nigel Hamilton stage-managed the show and hired local artisans to build the set. None of them could speak English and as there were no design plans, he had to use sign language and photographs. The stage and a revolve also had to be built, all within two weeks. Nigel even had to arrange someone to paint copies of the John Constable paintings which adorned the walls of the set.

Nigel had travelled to Hong Kong prior to the rest of the cast and had procured all the props and furniture. He occupied a top-floor room at the Sheraton with fabulous views and a full bar. When Eric Sykes arrived, he was allocated a suite on the fourth floor of the hotel without a view. When he visited Nigel for a drink, in his suite, Sykes took one look at the splendid surroundings and half jokingly said, 'Who's starring in this show?' Apart from stage-managing, Hamilton also reprised the parts he had played in Torquay: 'a Lord' and 'a policeman'. Hattie paid for Martin Christopherson, who by now had left Simpsons and was struggling to make a living as a freelance designer, to join her in Hong Kong as her assistant where he was also employed to work the lights. (Hattie tried to find work for him wherever possible, often footing his salary and paying him over the odds.)

The show ran for ten days and the production was a great success. The cast had a wonderful time and were able to participate in the spectacular New Year celebrations. Hattie found the heat uncomfortable and the city and its inhabitants too noisy for her liking. On one occasion several of the cast went for a walk to 'The Peak', Hattie included. She bumped into Eleanor Summerfield, with whom she had worked at The Players'! They had a very happy reunion in unlikely circumstances but unfortunately the walk turned out to be too arduous for Hattie, whose legs swelled up very badly, and transport had to be summoned to rescue her.

Hattie, who had hired a car immediately on arrival, was

invited to lots of events by expats, and Nigel happily acted as chauffeur driving his leading lady around. The RAF invited her to do a tour of the island by helicopter and they also travelled by junk to nearby Macau. During their stay at the Sheraton, the cast got to know a former 'All Black' rugby international, who owned a wildlife park where Hattie visited to feed the dolphins.

Hilary Gagan also went to Hong Kong as part of the backstage team and recalled that there was a running gag in the play that when Eric Sykes became irritated, he would stir the goldfish bowl, which contained an old bit of carrot. Every night, the talented Sheraton chef used to carve pieces of carrot in the shape of a perfect goldfish, which often resulted in complaints from some of the expats about animal cruelty when Sykes sent the 'goldfish' spinning!

Deryck Guyler and his wife Paddy were quite the opposite of Hattie when it came to spending money. They were tight-fisted and, being quite untheatrical and somewhat eccentric, were the perfect targets for practical jokes. On the last night of the engagement, Hattie and Hilary called room service and ordered absolutely everything on the breakfast menu – fourteen times – and listened outside the Guylers' door while 'Daddy and Paddy' anxiously discussed ways of getting out of paying for the lot!

On her return from Hong Kong, Hattie and Eric Sykes were invited to appear in the Royal Silver Jubilee gala performance which took place at the King's Theatre, Glasgow on 17 May 1977 and featured, among others, The Jackson Five, Frankie Howerd, David Soul and Dolly Parton. The producer David Bell, himself Scottish, was criticised for having so few Scots stars apart from Ronnie Corbett, who the *Glasgow Evening Times*, determined to be the star of the show.

A month later Hattie was back on television in a Thames Television hour-long special, *The Eric Sykes Show*. The *Daily Mail* reviewed it as 'a joy from start to finish'. Hattie played Native American Minnehaha and Sykes her Canadian Mountie lover. Peter Cooke played an infuriating stage electrician, Irene Handl was a Harrods customer in search of an elephant, Jimmy Edwards a stage psychiatrist, and Sykes played a doddering old stage-door keeper, recalling his younger days.

A Hatful of Sykes moved to Blackpool for the 1977 summer season and opened on 29 June at The Winter Gardens. Hattie wasn't very keen on spending the whole summer working in the show. She wanted a rest, and her ulcerated legs were giving her a lot of pain. Sykes, however, needed her and by playing on her loyalty persuaded her to be in the show.

Nigel Hamilton found accommodation for himself and Hattie in Sir Stanley Matthews' house. Sir Stanley and his wife, Lady Matthews, were divorced and every summer she would rent out the house and live in a caravan. Nigel also found a place for Sykes but this wasn't nearly as luxurious as Hattie's, and Sykes was somewhat miffed about this. Nigel and Hattie shared the house and there were lots of visitors. On occasion Hattie would receive 'gentlemen callers' and Nigel had to make himself scarce!

Hattie gave her first interview within two weeks of her arrival in the North West, 'It's the first time I've been in Blackpool but I'm already impressed by the warmth of the Lancashire people – everyone is so friendly, they can't do enough for you. I thought the show might be too gentle for Blackpool and that they might have wanted something a little more crude, but the audiences have been smashing and a pleasure to play to I'm quite happy about it, touch wood!'

She gave another interview to the *Daily Mail* on 22 July:

In Blackpool the audiences are wonderful and care so much about you. Humour is the most unsure realm of entertainment. In a theatre, one or two people can lead an audience. If they've had a bad day they can inhibit the rest. When you hear a giggly laugh at the start you think thank God for that woman in the second row. Last week we had an audience and you thought, well, golly, nothing is going to make this one laugh. You try harder and harder and the more you try the more wooden they are. You feel dreadful.

At the end of the first half when the curtain came down Eric said, 'Anyone want to buy an Equity card?'

Unlike the summer before in Torquay, the weather was terrible; it rained constantly, and the number of holidaymakers to Blackpool was much less than average. Consequently, business was poor in all the theatres. Matinee audiences were very small, and Eric Sykes was often less than enthusiastic about having to appear. It was left to Hattie to motivate the cast. She always gave of her best and remarked to Nigel, 'Don't forget, people in the audience may have saved up especially to come to the show – we must give it our all.'

There certainly wasn't the camaraderie at Blackpool that the cast had enjoyed at Torquay. No doubt, the lack of 'bums on seats' must have had an effect on morale, but generally the feeling in Blackpool was that it was all a bit of a struggle. Hattie even tried to repeat the fishing trips that they had all enjoyed in Torquay as a way of recapturing some of the spirit of the previous summer but surprisingly couldn't find anyone to take them out.

Most worryingly, the relationship between Hattie and Eric Sykes which had existed for nearly thirty years was beginning to suffer. Although they had never been great friends, they had always got on well and certainly enjoyed a mutual professional respect. Hattie's arthritis was giving her much discomfort and her ulcerated legs were extremely painful and she required daily visits from district nurses to dress the weeping sores. The dressing rooms at the Winter Gardens were situated up a flight of steep stairs and Hattie just couldn't manage them, sometimes having to crawl up the staircase on her hands and knees. In the end, she had to have a dressing room built on the ground floor to help her. According to Nigel Hamilton, Eric Sykes, far from being supportive of his co-star, was unhappy about this arrangement and felt that Hattie was receiving preferential treatment.

Eric Sykes began to act more reclusively and wouldn't join the rest of the cast for meals after the show. Nigel felt that, despite Hattie's poor health, Sykes drove her too hard. Sykes began to resent the fact that she was often given a bigger round of applause when she first appeared on stage and became increasingly grumpy with Hattie. He insisted she appear in curlers and wanted to her to look dowdier so that the audience were slightly bemused and wouldn't recognise her straightaway when she made her entrance. There was no real reason for this adjustment and Nigel felt it was done to belittle Hattie.

All the cast and production team were aware of Sykes' increasingly insecure behaviour. Hattie was naturally very upset and couldn't understand why her old friend would treat her in this manner. Nigel attempted to support Hattie and he was subsequently dropped from the production for the ensuing tour of Rhodesia.

Hattie was also subject to pangs of jealousy, although these were based on personal rather than professional feelings. Prior to the Blackpool show, Nigel had just met a new boyfriend, Roger, and excitedly told Hattie about him. Hattie never mentioned the subject again until several months later when they were both in Blackpool and she asked Nigel , 'Have you still got your young man? I'm worried that you're going to end up being hurt – he's so much younger than you.' In fact Roger was only three years younger than Nigel and while she may have been genuinely concerned about his welfare, Nigel felt that she was a little begrudging that he had found someone who might replace a little bit of her in Nigel's affections. In time, however, Roger was fully accepted and also became part of 'Hattie's set'.

There were other shows that rain-soaked summer in the seaside resort. Les Dawson, who lived at Lytham St Anne's, was appearing at the ABC Theatre. Danny La Rue was at The Opera House, and comedians Little and Large were also in town. Danny La Rue always insisted that his show was sold out but Les Dawson was slightly more realistic, admitting that he often had to open the show by asking the audience, 'Have you all come in one bus?'

Dawson was a great favourite of Hattie's – both personally and professionally.

There was some camaraderie between artistes in the town, once described as 'like Manchester but with sequins', and there was even a version of the popular television show, *It's a Knockout* in which cast members of the various theatres competed. During the Winter Gardens run, the cast participated in the *Midnight Matinee* at Lytham St Anne's, in which artistes from the other shows also appeared. The *Blackpool Evening Gazette* of 28 July 1977 reported:

> Dawn broke over the St Anne's skyline as an intrepid band of
> theatre goers crept out of the Ashton Theatre at 4.10 am today.
> The grand gala evening for the Queen's Silver Jubilee Appeal Fund,
> lived up to its name except that the evening started at 11.45 pm for
> a midnight matinee. The famous Sykes / Jacques / Corky trio
> delighted the audience – they set the pace for a show designed to
> conquer even the strongest impulse to yawn. Hattie Jacques,
> looking a little larger than life in an ample flowing evening gown
> was superbly entertaining in her petulant sister role. She even
> attempted a rough approximation of a Spanish gypsy dance with
> the ever henpecked Eric on guitar. Her act was predictably superb
> – easily the high spot of an all round good show.

All the stars gave their services free so the maximum amount of money could be raised for the Jubilee Fund. Audience figures were only a few short of the expected a numbers of 300, although by the time dawn began to break, almost half of the audience had departed. Not all of the performers were stars, 'Hard working Billy Fontayne's crisply delivered jokes kept up the tempo until his last appearance when he had visibly wilted. Also starring 'The Ashton Lovelies' and 'credit should also go to Junior Johnson singer dancer who brought a touch of the South Sea islands to St Anne's, with his hula-hula dancing – complete with grass skirt. At 4am, Les Dawson topped the bill.'

The Blackpool summer season was all a bit of a disaster, and Hattie was only too pleased when it came to an end and she could return to the safe haven of Eardley Crescent. Despite her differences with Eric Sykes, Hattie, who was always intensely loyal, ended the year by appearing with him in a Christmas television special.

During December, Hattie also filmed an advert for British Rail in Sevenoaks, publicising the 'Awayday' scheme. The idea was to convince viewers that travelling to London by train was quicker and more convenient than by car so that at the beginning, we see Hattie mounting a bicycle at the start of the 'Sevenoaks Grand Prix'. Jackie Stewart was supposed to be driving a racing car but, at the last minute, was unable to attend and so 'a stand in' took his place. The car speeds off, followed slowly by Hattie, who subsequently takes her bicycle to the station where she boards a train. Naturally she wins the race and beats 'Jackie Stewart' to the chequered flag. The advertising copywriter was quoted as saying, 'It was meant to be a bit like the tortoise and the hare – we chose Jackie Stewart because we like to think no-one can drive better than him and Hattie because she has such a warm personality and appeals to the public.' At the end of the shoot, a rather windswept Hattie was interviewed by the local newspaper and declared, 'I haven't ridden a bike for many years and I don't really think I'm going to take it on after this.' Earlier in the year, Hattie, Bruce Copp and Nigel Hamilton took a driving holiday in France. They started in Paris, staying near the Sorbonne and then travelled to the Loire Valley. Nigel, who did all the driving, described it as a fantastic holiday. Hattie was in a relaxed mood despite health concerns. He recalled that all three travellers smoked heavily so that the car was constantly fogged up with cigarette fumes. They used to book the evening's hotel accommodation every morning after a substantial breakfast. Apart from three sizeable meals a day, Bruce and Hattie also arranged snacks for the car and always visited the local boulangerie or patisserie before continuation of their journey. They referred to these titbits as 'tasty maisies' – a rather camp version of 'Mezes'.

Hattie always travelled with sundry items of food. Once, on a visit to her brother, Robin, who was living on the French Riviera and remarked that the only thing he missed from England was the traditional English sponge pudding 'Spotted Dick'. Hattie immediately went to her car, rummaged through the boot and returned to present Robin with one such pudding which she just happened to have in the car.

Actress Sheila Bernette started work at The Players' Theatre just as Hattie was ending her time there in 1960. Sheila recalled a day trip to France with Bruce Copp, Roger and Annie Hancock and Hattie, 'We stayed the night in Brighton and the following day, got the ferry across to Dieppe. Armed with copious amounts of food and drink, we were taken by taxi to the middle of a field where we had a fabulous picnic – a different wine with every course – only to be collected by the cab and returned to the French port.'

Sheila also remembers a fabulous dinner party at Eardley Crescent. Hattie had been preparing the meal since the morning and was in the middle of frying some croutons when the telephone rang and she had a chat, forgetting about the pan. Hattie returned to find the wallpaper and curtains aflame and she had to call out the fire brigade. Hattie didn't mention this at the dinner and the guests only found out about the drama days later. Even after all these years, Sheila can remember precise details of the evening, 'The table was beautifully set in lavender and pink. I had never seen such a beautiful table in my life. Everyone had their own menu and a choice of dishes. The dessert was ginger nut biscuits, dipped in cream coffee dotted with angelica and cherries. Delicious.'

Hattie never wrote a cook book but she did contribute to 'Entertaining with the Stars', a free booklet published by the icecream company Walls. Other contributions came from Gerald Harper, 'dinner parties need lots of good wine'; Rolf Harris, 'be organised and start with a game as an ice breaker'; and Katie Boyle, 'have informal dinner parties so you can let your hair down!' It was no surprise that the booklet also contained over seventy recipes for icecream.

The following year started with an inevitable series of *Sykes,* and Hattie also appeared on the *Multi-coloured Swap Shop* on 21 January with Noel Edmonds. *The Glasgow Evening Times* reported that although Hattie was very lovely, she was ill advised to wear false eyelashes at her age!

In spring 1978 Hattie was yet again rehearsing *A Hatful of Sykes.* Nigel Hamilton, who had displeased Eric Sykes, was replaced by Michael Sharvell-Martin, and the actress April Walker was added to the cast. April had studied drama at RADA, which she described as 'a baptism of fire' because among her contemporaries were John Hurt, Martin Jarvis, Ian McShane and Gemma Jones. Following graduation, April went into repertory and then joined the Royal Shakespeare Company, understudying Diana Rigg in Peter Hall's acclaimed production of A *Midsummer Night's Dream.*

April was then offered work in television, mainly comedy parts and appeared in *Fawlty Towers, The Two Ronnies* and *Yes Minister.* She was then cast in *A Hatful of Sykes* which was to tour Rhodesia, after a short run at the Theatre Royal, Lincoln. Just before she was due to open in Lincoln, April's boyfriend had to travel to Dubai and so the two of them had endured a tearful goodbye. Unknown to April, Hattie contacted the boyfriend before his departure, smuggled him into the Theatre Royal and provided champagne for them both in her dressing room after the show. April said it was a gesture that only Hattie could have thought of and carried out so expertly.

The cast flew to Salisbury (now Harare), Rhodesia, on 30 March 1978, and April remembers it as 'a terrifying flight, in which we had to endure a lengthy and rather dramatic electrical storm'. The company's first venue was the Seven Arts Theatre, Salisbury, and the cast were booked into the Monometapa Hotel. Eric Sykes describes the scene in his autobiography, 'It was so good to see Hattie sitting by the pool beneath an umbrella, smiling as she watched two white bathing caps keeping the sun off the heads of Derek Guyler and his wife Paddy as they swam in synchronised breaststroke back and forward . . . I sat under the umbrella next to Hattie. Peace, tranquillity and warmth.'

This calm and happy scene in the comfort of a luxury hotel, however, masked the fact that Rhodesia was very much in turmoil. Apart from the pressures caused by Ian Smith's declaration of UDI in 1965, which led to United Nations sanctions, thirteen years later the country was engaged in the 'Rhodesian Bush War', also known as the 'Liberation Struggle'. This armed conflict between the Rhodesian Army and members of the Zimbabwe African National Union (ZANU) and Zimbabwe African People's Union (ZAPU), trained in guerrilla warfare in Zambia and Mozambique, had been waged for over a decade.

April Walker recalled the tense atmosphere, 'Everyone was on full alert and nearly everyone seemed to be carrying guns.' The audience for *A Hatful* were mainly expats, and when the show moved to Gwelo (now Gweru) it consisted mainly of farmers, who had travelled long distances to attend the production. Because of this, they were offered a special deal in which they saw the show, spent a night at a hotel, and the following morning were able to take breakfast with the cast. The farmers were always asked to check their guns in at the hotel reception when they arrived.

As ever, Hattie acted as social secretary and ensured that the cast made use of their spare time: they visited Que Que Mosque, enjoyed a day at the races, went on a raft fishing trip and visited a crocodile farm. They went on a 'booze cruise' down the Zambezi, although the river banks were mined and there were guns trained on each side! Once, when having drinks in Selukwe Hills, April spotted a cobra. Hattie was all set to take a photograph, but before she had time, their guide took out his gun and shot the snake; then there was a frantic search for its partner, as cobras are apparently usually found in pairs.

Hattie and April also visited an African village, and in one of the huts a witchdoctor was seated on a tiny stool, offering 'a fortune telling' service for tourists. He beckoned to Hattie to enter and sit next to him on an equally inadequate perch but Hattie was worried about the precarious seating arrangement, whether she would ever be able to get up again and so asked April to take her place. The tribal leader prophesised that April would live until her eighties. Later on, when appearing in Bulawayo, Hattie, April and Eric went to see the Victoria Falls in a Piper Aztec aeroplane. Hattie was terrified at being in such a small aircraft and at one point said, 'April I'm so glad you're with me and that you're going to live until your eighties!'

Hattie, April and Michael Sharvell-Martin were totally dumbfounded by the extraordinary sight of the Falls which creates the largest mass of falling water in the world. The roar was deafening, and close to the edge of the cliff the spray shoots vertically like inverted rain. The whole effect was breathtaking and they stood silently 'in awe at the power of one of the world's great wonders.' After about ten minutes, Eric turned to the three of them and with his customary brilliant comedy timing asked, 'Is that all it does?'

The outing to the Victoria Falls had been arranged by the local Lions Club on the understanding that, in return, the actors would entertain the troops, which of course they did. Eric did a stand-up routine, Deryck Guyler played his washboard, Hattie sang and performed monologues, and April Walker danced with the soldiers, although, intriguingly, they all sought Hattie's permission first!

Hattie, April and Michael Sharvell-Martin decided to visit the Matobo Hills, the site of Cecil Rhodes' grave. Before they left, they had to check in at a local police station and were advised to arm themselves for protection. They followed this advice but fortunately did not have to use the firearm as none of them had ever fired a gun before! The intrepid explorers reached their destination after quite a difficult climb. The exertion of the ascent particularly exhausted Hattie, who needed a rest and promptly sat down on a conveniently placed mound. Still catching her breath, she and the others were surprised by the sudden appearance of a resplendent African Ranger who seemed to materialise from thin air. He viewed the group somewhat suspiciously and addressed Hattie in a polite but firm tone, 'Please do not sit on Cecil Rhodes's grave.'

Unfortunately Eric Sykes began to behave rather strangely towards the end of the trip to Zimbabwe, issuing a questionnaire to the cast about his performance and direction in the show and he even accused Hattie, to the amazement of the cast, of not being able to deliver a proper feed line! The tour ended on 6 May 1978, and Hattie returned home via Los Angeles to visit Robin, who was now working regularly with Rod Stewart and going out with Kim, a Bunny Girl who somewhat confusingly had a sister called Robin.

The Rhodesian tour caused some controversy at the time and was reported in the *Evening Standard*, 'TV comics Eric Sykes and Hattie Jacques leave London today to tour in the review "A Hatful of Sykes" in Rhodesia. Equity, [the actors union] of course, are furious. "We deplore our members visiting Rhodesia or South Africa," a spokesman said, "We offer them no legal representation there . . . so if a management defaults on payment, they're on their own." A leading theatrical agent explained actors breaking sanctions, "The money is fantastic – artists like Jimmy Edwards and Eric Sykes, who appeared there recently in *Big Bad Mouse* can get about £1000 a week."'

Equity, incidentally, never had a policy instructing members not to work in Rhodesia but the country had been starved of British entertainment since UDI was declared in 1965 and there is no doubt that theatrical tours of this sort did give some succour to the beleaguered minority rule of Prime Minister Ian Smith. Eric Sykes was a staunch supporter of Smith, who came to see the show with his wife in Bulawayo, and because of the war there were huge security implications. Michael Sharvell-Martin recalls that when the cast looked out at the audience from the stage, they could see Mr and Mrs Smith in the front of the stalls, surrounded by a number of armed guards. More disconcerting was a machine gun trained on the stage from the front of the circle – but even more frightening for the actors was their knowledge that during the show a couple of pistol blanks were fired offstage. Michael remembers praying that someone had informed Ian Smiths's security guards of these effects – otherwise the finale of *A Hatful of Sykes* might have ended up more like *The Wild Bunch*. Apparently Ian Smith later told the cast, 'I haven't laughed so much in years.' I'm not sure the actors found it quite so amusing at the time.

The next destination for *A Hatful of Sykes* was Canada. Michael Sharvell-Martin, who had already been booked to do pantomime, was replaced by Nigel Hamilton, who thanks to 'a bit of crawling' by Hattie and his own attempts to curry favour with Eric Sykes had succeeded in returning to the cast.

Hattie wasn't very keen on the trip as it meant flying out on Christmas Day 1978. 'I have never been away from home on that special occasion. Usually, I have 24 or so people at my house for a four-day binge of food and good, old-fashioned games,' she said. Although they had enjoyed drinks in the 'Maple Leaf Lounge' at Heathrow prior to the flight, there was no attempt at celebrating Christmas on the somewhat unoccupied Air Canada plane to Ottawa – an obvious anathema to Hattie and a bad start to the tour. The troupe was greeted on arrival in the capital by blizzards and temperatures of twenty degrees below freezing. Their accommodation, The Elgin Hotel, was described as 'unwelcoming and dour', and it being Christmas night, the kitchen was closed. One of the production team placed some Christmas crackers and nuts in Hattie's room to make it a little more festive but it was hardly what she was used to.

The cast spent two weeks in Ottawa. The National Arts Centre Opera was a vast arena containing a huge stage in the middle of which sat the play's small set. However, despite the lack of intimacy and the continuing bitterly cold weather, the show went very well – mainly thanks to large number of Brits in the audience, and the cast received a standing ovation every night.

The following is a review in Ottawa's newspaper *The Citizen* of a performance on 27 December 1978:

> The cast are adept at giving a ridiculously funny show and still leave the audience wanting more. To anyone who has watched the Sykes show on television, the format is familiar, but while the situation was vintage Sykes, the presentation was as fresh and breezy as a brand new production. There was Eric, the eternal dreamer who'd got himself engaged to a young woman he'd just met after an army reunion and his long suffering twin sister Hattie was trying to extricate himself from the planned marriage. . . each performer is given a chance to shine. Sykes is the main event, but Jacques and Guyler are given plenty of opportunities to pull off some good comic lines. April Walker and Nigel Hamilton were very competent in the supporting roles. *A Hatful of Sykes* is a very good evening of light entertainment with plenty of laughs, especially if you don't mind a few old chestnuts thrown in for good measure.

Hattie, as usual, suggested to Nigel Hamilton that they obtain some wheels, 'Darling, shall we have a car?' Nigel was more than wary, as the weather was extremely hazardous and he was unused to such driving conditions. However, Hattie was not to be dissuaded – she needed her sightseeing trips and Nigel soon found himself yet again acting as chauffeur. The only car available from the automobile rental company was a green car which Hattie was unhappy about. She remained deeply superstitious throughout her career: she would never wear green clothes and would shun anything in that colour. Hattie took theatrical folklore very seriously and maintained, 'No-one one must ever whistle in my dressing room, there must be no real flowers on the stage, nor must there be any knitting in the wings.' (Apparently that also included balaclavas created by Beryl Reid for Harry Secombe.)

Anyhow, Nigel and Hattie embarked on some tricky motoring adventures in the company of April Walker. Nigel was obviously keen to utilise the heater in the freezing weather, not only for reasons of comfort but also to assist visibility. Unfortunately, Hattie couldn't cope with such intense heat and was insistent that it was turned off regularly which made driving the car 'something of a nightmare'. On an outing to a ski resort outside Ottawa, Nigel had to brake suddenly, and in the icy conditions the car skidded one hundred and eighty degrees and mounted a bank. When the car came to a halt, Hattie, by now at a very unseemly angle and still puffing at a cigarette, calmly turned to Nigel and said, 'Oh dear . . . never mind . . . I'm afraid that's what happens when you drive a green car!'

A passing oil tanker stopped and Nigel explained to the driver that it was the celebrated English actress Hattie Jacques who was stuck in the front seat. Nigel and the star-struck tanker driver lifted up the car with Hattie still sitting inside, totally immobile. Nigel is still not sure whether Hattie couldn't or didn't want to leave her seat but whatever the case, she remained totally composed throughout the ordeal.

After Ottawa the production transferred to Newfoundland where the company toured for a couple of weeks by minibus and by air. Hattie didn't like small planes – she usually travelled first class because of her size. There were no seat belts and she used to slide across, ending up by occupying half of Nigel's seat.

There were a number of one-night engagements around the Province and although the show was never actually put on in a barn, they did perform for two nights in an aeroplane hangar. Both evenings were sold out! They also played in St Johns and Halifax, Nova Scotia. The tour ended in Hamilton, Ontario, on 27 January, and Eric Sykes, who was very generous to his fellow cast members, threw a party in his hotel suite. The hotel fire alarm went off during the night and everyone was evacuated, apart from Hattie who insisted on staying in her room. Deryck Guyler and his wife brought their Bible with them as a form of divine protection.

At the conclusion of the tour Hattie went to see an old friend in New York and as Nigel had never been to the city, Hattie paid for his air fare to accompany her. Eric Sykes described Hattie as, 'The life and soul of the party. Taking over the stewardship of our happy band of rogues and vagabonds, she was our counsellor, nurse, and barbeque cook, a make-believe sister to be proud of.'

Two weeks after returning from Canada, the show moved to South Africa. First stop, Cape Town, where they performed at The Opera House. Eric, Deryck and Hattie had travelled ahead to attend some publicity events and it transpired that Hattie was much better known than Eric Sykes due to her involvement in the *Carry On* films – although she wouldn't have been seen in *Carry On Dick*, which was banned by the South African authorities as being 'anti-Christian'. Although the Cape Town audience was not segregated, the cost of the tickets was completely prohibitive to the black population and so the theatre-goers were drawn mostly from the British expat community. Sykes was again unhappy at the fact that Hattie was receiving more of a response from the audience, and April Walker noticed that he began to tread on her lines when she was getting better laughs than him.

The production moved to the Civic Theatre in Johannesburg and Hattie initially occupied a swish hotel suite, while April Walker and Nigel Hamilton stayed nearby in self-catering apart-ments. Hattie soon decided to move so that she could spend more time with her friends and could also entertain more! During their stay, April and Hattie were browsing in the hotel's shop and April admired a rather expensive gold necklace, engraved with flowers and leaves but priced well beyond her budget. On April's birth-day, some weeks later, Hattie gave her a box with a card which read, 'Darling April, because we love you, Hattie and Nigel.' Inside was the very same necklace.

In Johannesburg, Hattie, April and Nigel did some sight-seeing, and it was during this time that Hattie began to comprehend the harsh realities of the apartheid regime. She was invited for dinner to a white family living in the suburbs. Hattie was horrified at their racist opinions and the fact that they openly admitted to the exploitation of the country and the indigenous population. Although she kept her cool and remained polite, she questioned the couple firmly about the treatment of their black servants and was courteously dismissive of their attempts to justify the situation. They, in turn, couldn't understand Hattie's attitude and her concern for the welfare of their black staff. According to Nigel Hamilton, Hattie just wouldn't let the subject rest and left the house quite appalled.

Hattie also met up with Cliff Richard, who was performing a concert in the city and agreed to attend a township church service the next day. Although she said that it was an important experience, she felt very uncomfortable being one of the few white people there and found it hard to come to terms with how the population was so divided. Another experience when she and Nigel mistakenly queued up in a 'Blacks Only' post office, further brought home to her the iniquities of a racially based society. Although Hattie must have been fully aware of what was happening in South Africa before her visit, it was only when she personally saw the effects of apartheid on individuals that she realised the true nature of the system and what it actually meant to the indigenous population.

In 1954 Equity had formally adopted a policy of anti-racism and offered to help members negotiate contracts for South Africa which would give them the freedom to perform in front of integrated and non-white audiences. This was strengthened in 1956 to become an instruction not to work in any theatre which operated a colour bar. In 1965 the South African government threatened to refuse work permits to any overseas performers who insisted on working in front of non-segregated audiences and integrated performances all but stopped. Equity decided to stop negotiating contracts for work in South Africa and to withdraw support for members who worked there. Legal advice was that support could not be withdrawn in that way, but a declaration against working in front of segregated audiences was signed by 3,000 members.

In October 1976, Equity members voted against changing its policy to one where members were instructed not to work in South Africa or Rhodesia but continued with the policy of asking members to sign the declaration that they would not work in front of segregated audiences. By performing in South Africa and before that Rhodesia, there is no doubt that Hattie was passively supporting racist governments. However, in her personal politics, Hattie could never be described as prejudiced. Quite the opposite in fact. She was politically naive and her experience in South Africa demonstrates this. She made it quite clear that she was opposed to the apartheid system but still agreed to tour there when it was very much frowned upon. Some of this could be explained by the fact that despite his behaviour towards her, Hattie's devotion to Eric Sykes was unshakable and he couldn't have done the show without her. It also wouldn't be too unfair to state that Hattie needed to make a living.

Bruce Copp felt that Hattie was unsophisticated in political matters – she disapproved of socialism and didn't understand it, but she acted much more like a socialist when it came to sharing her capital with fellow workers. Hattie was a traditional Tory voter, although not an actual member of the party or an activist. She never made the link between the personal and the political. She didn't approve of strikes but she was the first to give money to striking miners and their families when they needed help.

Hattie loved the English traditions and was always extremely patriotic as expressed in a piece in *The Northern Echo* in 1975:

'Carry On Britain' . . . that's the message from laughter-maker
Hattie Jacques yesterday. The big-hearted patriot was off to Canada
and unlike comedian Terry Scott she couldn't wait to get back.
The doleful Terry said at Heathrow on Monday that Britain was
'in a right mess'. It was being run by left wing 'nobodies and
communists' and 'for two pins he'd get on the next plane to South
Africa'. Before flying off from Heathrow yesterday, Hattie said he
had perhaps been influenced by what he had read whilst overseas:

'He might have got the impression that the dear old country is a lot worse off than it really is, but as far as I'm concerned, there is no other place for me. Of course times are hard but that was a good reason for everyone to rally around the old flag. My roots are here – there is something very special about the place . . . I enjoy being overseas but I would never leave the place for good.'

The following quote from *The Sunday Times Magazine* on 24 October 1976 in response to being asked, 'Is hunting cruel?' is pure Hattie: 'I don't suppose any animal likes being chased, but I can't help liking the traditional aspect of fox hunting. Those that do it seem such nice people. The other day I met an Irish priest who hunts. He is an enchanting man.'

Following their return from South Africa, the company embarked on a tour of the English regions: Lincoln for two weeks; Guildford; the Rex Theatre, Cardiff; Wilmslow; the Theatre Royal Norwich; and finally Brighton in July 1979. Nigel Hamilton had a flat in Hove and his parents lived in nearby Worthing; 'Hattie was lovely with my mother and father and we all enjoyed very pleasant times together.' Hattie worked very hard during the tour and struggled to maintain her usual extraordinary energy levels, quite often complaining of being tired. She slept a lot during the afternoon and the leg ulcers continued to cause her pain – one leg was particularly bad and the local district nurses sometimes visited more than once a day.

Whilst playing Brighton's Theatre Royal, Hattie invited Bruce Copp to have dinner. He arrived early and so waited in Hattie's dressing room while Hattie was still on stage. When the curtain had come down, Hattie entered her dressing room in floods of tears, 'Eric was so rude to me in front of the audience'. According to Bruce, Sykes reportedly said to her, 'You're supposed to be a working girl and you're behaving like a fucking duchess.' Bruce was incensed – he was ready to punch Sykes and had to be restrained by Nigel Hamilton and Hattie who didn't want a scene.

Bruce Copp had become increasingly angry about Sykes' behaviour towards Hattie during the last few years – particularly when they were touring. Sykes had gradually been reducing Hattie's part, he started to cut her laughs and even reconstructed the show so that he would get 'a bigger round' on entrance. However, it was clear that of the two stars, Hattie was much more popular with the public – the audience adored her and she also elicited a bigger response. 'Hattie was the one the public came to see and Sykes only realised this during the live shows,' according to Copp.

The relationship between Hattie and Sykes was rapidly deteriorating. They had been close professionally in the early days and it was clear that this was a symbiotic partnership: Eric found it difficult to work with other actresses and could always depend on Hattie. In turn, Hattie became increasingly reliant on Sykes for work. Publicly, Hattie was always fiercely loyal to him. In the Wogan television interview she said, 'I'd rather perform his scripts than anyone else's . . . the characters in the show are very much like our own characters, very protective of each other. We're great friends and just care for each other . . . he's a lovely man.' Privately, she confided to her closest friends how his behaviour and attitude towards her, particularly on tour, hurt and shocked her. In public, Sykes was always full of praise for Hattie.

Hattie started a two-month summer season in Bournemouth on 16 July 1979. Despite her burgeoning weight and mobility difficulties caused by her arthritis, she used to like outings to the country for pub lunches and also enjoyed going fishing every week in Studland Bay, getting to know a number of the Poole fishermen. Hattie inevitably cooked 'the catch' later in the day. Angling prowess seemed to be a family trait, because Robin Le Mesurier, visiting from California, went mackerel fishing and managed to land enough to feed the whole cast on one occasion.

Although they maintained a professional relationship, personal relations between Hattie and Eric Sykes, who was staying in Dickie Henderson's flat, were very poor and there was very little social contact between them. Fortunately, Hattie continued to attract lots of visitors from London and so most weekends were busy. Towards the end of the run of *A Hatful of Sykes*, Hattie was asked to judge the Miss Bournemouth beauty contest – a responsibility that she seemed to undertake every summer, whichever resort she was playing.

Despite their differences, Hattie returned to the television screen in October for yet another series of *Sykes*.

It was to be her last.

CHAPTER TWELVE

A Last Breath of Kindness

Death . . . like the rumble of distant thunder at a picnic

W H Auden

A FAMILIAR STORY WAS playing out at the start of the new decade: Hattie rescuing an old friend in need. Joan Sims had decided to move from her Fulham home because of a spate of muggings and burglaries. Her car was vandalised and she also witnessed a vicious attack by three men on a passer-by directly outside her house. Joan became very anxious and decided to rent a flat in Kensington Square, behind the High Street. This practical task was just too much for the fragile Miss Sims and she needed help in sorting out the clutter that she had accumulated over sixteen years:

As usual, the person who came and took charge was Hattie. For four days running she'd be driven over by her son Robin, laden with armfuls of cigarettes and food for lunch, and we'd get down to business. Hattie would take each item individually: 'Now, darling, when did you last wear this? Are you ever going to wear it again? At twelve thirty prompt Hattie would call a halt and waft down the stairs like an elegant battleship, flurry into the kitchen and produce a superb lunch. On moving day, Hattie supervised the whole operation. What would I have done without her? I've lost count of the number of times she scooped me up when I was down in the dumps, and her friendship, concern and advice had helped me through innumerable crises.

One morning in February Hattie telephoned her mother at 54 Waterford Road (she spoke to her mother every day no matter where she was). Mary told Hattie that she wasn't feeling very well and Hattie immediately went over to see her. Soon after Hattie arrived, Mary collapsed and died in her daughter's arms, having suffered a pulmonary embolism. According to her friends, although Mary was eighty, she was generally in good health. An affectionate and caring woman, Mary was much loved by all who knew her. She was intelligent, stylish and always radiated a presence which her theatrical background had bestowed on her.

Mary had been a significant influence on Hattie's career and had encouraged her daughter from an early age to follow the profession. Hattie had always been absolutely devoted to her mother and never came to terms with her death. Jake later moved into the Waterford Road house, which was subsequently willed to him and his brother, Robin.

Hattie, much affected by her mother's death, struggled on. Her breathing difficulties were exacerbated by her burgeoning weight but she continued to devote time to her charity work: she opened a rehabilitation unit in Poole and in July, she broke a giant bottle of whisky at The Carpenters Arms in Chiswick where over £200 had been raised for a talking newspaper for the blind. At the beginning of September Hattie opened the Chelmsford co-op's fete and sports day, proceeds of which were donated to a local charity and the same weekend she opened the Wrestlingworth Goodwill show and sale in Bedfordshire, threatening 'to turn upside down and shake anyone leaving with money unspent'. She judged the children's fancy dress show and decided that all the entrants were joint winners. Hattie visited every sideshow and stall, handing over money at every turn before signing autographs.

Despite their differences, it is a measure of Hattie's ambivalent feelings towards Eric Sykes that she appeared on his *This Is Your Life* and then began work on a film by him, *Rhubarb Rhubarb*, at Foxhill Country Club, Chertsey, Surrey on 21 April 1980. The television production, a thirty-minute comedy, in which the only word spoken is 'rhubarb' starred Beryl Reid, Jimmy Edwards and Roy Kinnear. The film features a very glamorous April Walker being taught to play golf by a lecherous Charlie Drake. Hattie plays a short-sighted nanny with coke-bottle glasses who is in charge of a baby in a pram. She is sitting on a bench reading a newspaper on the golf course, while Eric Sykes and Bob Todd are playing golf. Todd walks off with the pushchair instead of the golf trolley. Hattie gets up and wheels the trolley which she thinks is the pram. It is a very fleeting appearance and Hattie looks a little uncertain on her feet.

A month after *Rhubarb Rhubarb*, Hattie, Bruce Copp, Nigel Hamilton and his partner Roger organised a holiday in Greece – the plan being to hire a motor home and drive to Athens before embarking on a tour of the Greek islands. Unfortunately, just prior to departure, Hattie's doctors advised her that she was too ill to do all that travelling and so the quartet decided on Ireland instead. Hattie was indeed very breathless at times and had difficulty getting in and out of the car.

The foursome took the car ferry from Fishguard to Rosslare before driving to Waterford and visiting the Ring of Kerry and the Dingle peninsula. They used to alternate one night in farm accommodation and then the next in a hotel. Hattie was recognised everywhere she went and was treated with great kindness and care by the locals. She always sent flowers as a way of thanks – especially when she felt people had gone out of their way to make her trip so special. The holiday was a great success, there was lots of raucous laughter and the quartet had to be told to be quiet in a number of restaurants. In Dingle, they stayed at a hotel where there was a wake being held and according to Nigel Hamilton, 'We all got as merry as ticks.' It was, by all accounts, a most enjoyable trip, but although Hattie had a great time, she didn't look well and was struggling with her health.

On the return journey on the ferry, Hattie stood on the bridge for a while and was constantly being asked by fans for autographs to which she always agreed with great patience. At one stage, she put her hand on Bruce Copp's and said, 'You know I'm not going to live long.'

There was not much work awaiting Hattie in London other than a couple of game shows. She could not get health insurance for film work and she was becoming more dependent on repeat fees. Nigel Hamilton, who had been an accountant in a previous existence, was doing her books and was concerned at her lack of income. Hattie, of course, was undaunted and maintained her generous ways.

Jake was still living at Eardley Crescent and had taken over the huge basement flat which was a haven for his companions and hangers-on. Hattie occupied the first floor and kept the ground floor as somewhere where visiting pals could stay. There was some concern from Hattie's friends that Jake took his mother for granted – there was nothing that she wouldn't do for him. This was not particularly surprising as nearly everyone who met Jake found him lovable – never mind his adoring mother. He was described by Joan Le Mesurier as 'funny, bright, and mischievous'. Joan felt, however, that Hattie had lost some of her sparkle, 'It was as if one of the lights that made her so iridescent had gone out, like one or two lights in a chandelier. Things looked the same but slightly dimmer.'

Josephine Gordon went to see Hattie in the summer of 1980 and recollected that her friend looked very unwell and seemed quite unhappy. Hattie talked about how much she missed her mother and confided that she felt depressed. She also told Josephine that she was resigned to the fact that she wasn't going to be around for very much longer. In early September 1980, Robin Le Mesurier rang Hattie and told her that he was planning to get married at Christmas. Hattie was delighted but also insisted that he shouldn't wait until then and urged him to make plans earlier. Although she didn't tell her son, Hattie felt that her health was failing fast and clearly felt that she wasn't going to see another Christmas.

Nigel Hamilton recalled a typically enjoyably boisterous luncheon party in the company of Bruce Copp and Joan Sims at Eardley Crescent during the last weekend in September, 'It was a magical occasion. Hattie was on top form. It was almost as if she realised that she was very ill and was determined to enjoy herself even more than ever.' Her weight had ballooned even more and she was very breathless. Naturally Hattie was still smoking heavily but was mainly drinking water – in vast quantities.

Hattie's shortness of breath resulted in a hospital appointment and a brief admission to Charing Cross hospital at the beginning of October. She persuaded the medical staff to let her come home for the weekend without telling them that she was due to attend a charity event on the Sunday evening. However, during the day she admitted to Martin Christopherson that she was suffering from chest pains and he persuaded her to stay at home. Despite his protestations, Hattie refused to call a doctor, saying that all she needed was 'a good rest'. She and Jake also fell out over a domestic arrangement and had a heated argument. Unusually for her, Hattie retired early for the evening with a hot water bottle that Martin Christopherson had prepared for her.

By mid-morning the following day, Hattie had not appeared, and Jake, perhaps trying to make amends for the row the previous day, took her in a cup of tea in bed. He found her dead in her bed. Hattie had passed away sometime during the night. A distraught Jake rang Martin Christopherson, who had gone home to Waterford Road. Christopherson tracked down Bruce Copp, who was staying with his sister, Joan, in Saffron Walden. Bruce remembers he jumped in his car and drove immediately to Earls Court. When he left Essex, it was a beautiful golden autumnal day. As he pulled up outside 67 Eardley Crescent, the weather had deteriorated drastically and 'the heavens opened'.

Nigel Hamilton was informed by Martin Christopherson an hour after Hattie's death. He rang Joan Sims, who was inconsolable with grief. When the *Carry On* star recovered, she asked Nigel, 'What am I going to do now?' Kenneth Williams took the news of Hattie's death in his typical egotistical manner and as recorded in his diary, '*Monday 6th October 1980 'Hattie Jacques has died . . . curiously, I'd always thought of Hat as living a long time . . . the blow will hit me later on.'* Williams was asked to give an interview about Hattie on Radio London but refused.

John Le Mesurier received a dramatic telephone call from Jake, 'He was distressed and I caught the words, "Hattie's dead!"' Jake drove to Le Mesurier's Shepherds Bush flat and arrived, still in a state of shock. John telephoned Los Angeles but couldn't get hold of Robin and so left a message with Rod Stewart's manager, Billy Gaff, who later broke the news to Robin. John Le Mesurier also rang Hattie's brother, Robin, and then some of their closest friends before they heard the news on the television or radio.

Despite his own grief, Jake was concerned about how Joan Sims would cope, so he went over to her flat and brought her back to Shepherd's Bush so that she could be with her dearest friends. The group all spent the day together and Jake and Joanie Sims also stayed the night with the Le Mesuriers.

The following day, Jake returned to Eardley Crescent, feeling that if he didn't go home there and then, he never would. Eardley Crescent was as busy as ever, with many of Hattie's friends making an appearance, offering help but just really wanting to be together. Martin Christopherson started to sort out some of the practicalities and Bruce Copp prepared some food. Joan Le Mesurier recalled:

> The fridge was bulging as usual. There were cold meats and vegetables from the last meal Hattie had prepared. Bruce said that she would never forgive us if we didn't use up what was there and made an enormous pan of soup for everybody and a plate of cold cuts and cheeses. It seemed important to keep busy, to use the

house to comfort anyone who needed to come over, just as she would have done.

A couple of days later Robin arrived from Los Angeles, accompanied by wife Kim. Robin had realised that his mother's health had been deteriorating dramatically for some time and she was quite open with him that her body, which she had always resented for aesthetic reasons, was now failing her physically. She had told him that she'd had enough. 'I think she died because she couldn't take any more, she was tired and fed up with her health and wanted to move on.' Robin remembers that it rained solidly for two weeks following his return, apart from the actual day of the funeral, which was gloriously sunny.

Obituaries appeared in most of the national newspapers the day after Hattie's death and universally hailed the actress for her comedic talent. The *Daily Telegraph* stated that, 'Hattie Jacques was a leading popular entertainer for more than 30 years and a versatile actress of great accomplishment' and *The Times'* columnist wrote, 'Hattie Jacques will be remembered with affection by all who saw her in a clutch of *Carry On* films; heard her on the radio; and never missed her appearance with Eric Sykes . . . she was a very accomplished comedian, a 'feed' valued by many of the leading comedians of the day.' *The Sun* couldn't resist describing her as, 'The roly-poly, fifteen-stone comedy star'.

Tributes from friends and colleagues appeared in the press immediately; a very sad John Le Mesurier said, 'We have lost a very remarkable lady. I feel very shocked and full of grief. She had a wealth of talent which was often underestimated. Some people are dim-witted at times. They see a large lady and can't see further. She always showed tremendous generosity and kindness to other people and was a great giver of thought and help.' Hattie's agent, Felix de Wolfe, who had represented her since the 1940s, recalled, 'I was always trying to get her to take life a bit easier. She was gracious, considerate and her kindness was renowned. She became a big star, yet remained a very modest woman and totally unchanged from the day I met her.'

Eric Sykes was genuinely devastated, 'Hattie was really like a sister to me. I am deeply shocked by her death. She was an ideal partner to write and appear with. When you think about it about one third of my life has been spent with Hat. I miss her because she was so full of life and joy . . . her smile lit up my life for a long time.' The *Sykes* television situation comedy had run, in its various guises, for 127 episodes until Hattie's death. The BBC, desperate to continue the successful format, wanted Eric to write another woman into the show. But, to his credit, he was absolutely adamant that he wouldn't. Hattie was irreplaceable.

Kenneth Williams described Hattie as, 'The sort of woman one warmed to immediately. She was blessed with a marvellous personality, tremendous charm, and a consideration for all those on the film set. We had unforgettable times together.' He quoted an extract from a novel *A Life for a Life* by Dinah Maria Mulock, 'Oh the comfort, the inexpressible comfort of feeling safe with a person; having neither to weigh thoughts, nor measure words, but pour them all out, just as they are, chaff and grain together, knowing that faithful hand will take and sift them, keep what is worth keeping, and then with a breath of kindness, blow the rest away.'

Joan Sims was reported as saying, 'Team spirit among the *Carry On* gang was fabled, but naturally I became closer to some of the actors than others. Hattie Jacques was like a combination of sister and mother to me. Hattie has been my greatest friend and one of the great props of my life.' Kenneth Connor remarked that, 'However much she suffered she didn't talk about it or publicise it. She must have had the patience of a saint.'

An edition of *The Times*, on 8 October 1980, under the headline, 'No Inquest on Actress' reported that, 'Hattie Jacques, the actress, who was found dead at her home in Earls Court, London, Monday, died from a heart attack, a post mortem examination confirmed yesterday.' Hattie had also been suffering from kidney failure.

Hattie's funeral took place at Putney Vale Crematorium and was attended by family and close friends. The service was quite austere, without even a eulogy from the attending minister. Hattie had never participated in any organised religion and didn't attend church, but she did believe in God and was offended by people who ridiculed faith, which she felt was a great comfort to people. Peter Greenwell, Hattie's friend of many years from The Players', played a selection of some her favourite songs, including *Someone To Watch Over Me* on the chapel's piano. Hattie had issued specific instructions in advance, requesting no flowers, instead asking for donations to be made to her favourite charities. She also wanted everyone to enjoy a party afterwards but asked that there be no tears. Joan Le Mesurier later wrote, 'She might as well have asked the Thames to stop flowing.'

In spite of Hattie's request it was impossible for family and friends not to cry, and Robin and Jake sobbed throughout. The extremely proprietorial Martin Christopherson elevated himself to chief mourner and insisted on being the first to walk behind the coffin. He didn't, however, have his head bowed in customary manner, for fear of losing his precariously balanced wig.

Before the funeral, John Le Mesurier had encountered a group of Hattie's fans who had come to the crematorium to pay their respects. The actor invited them to attend, 'I can get a few of you in the back if you like.' But they declined saying they didn't want to intrude into the family's personal grief. However, at the end of the service, when John thanked them from coming, one of the women piped up, 'It's a shame, dear. We'll all miss her, but these things happen, don't they? By the way, I don't suppose, if you're going back via Fulham, you could give us a lift, could you?'

Unfortunately, the request was impossible owing to a lack of cars although Le Mesurier remarked that, if Hattie had still been around, she would somehow have managed to find a way of organising it.

Two people were missing from the funeral, who one would have expected to be present. Robin and Jake, upset at the way Eric

Sykes had treated their mother towards the end of her life, didn't want him to attend the ceremony or the subsequent memorial service. Sykes was naturally very hurt and couldn't understand why he had been excluded in this way.

The other notable absentee was a distraught Joan Sims, who stayed in her home and spent the day drinking, reading old letters from Hattie and wallowing in self pity. (Sadly, Joan Sims, who was much loved by Hattie's friends and family, drifted into an increasingly reclusive life, became totally dependent on alcohol and following the death of her mother, suffered a breakdown which required admission to a psychiatric hospital. She died in June 2001.)

After the funeral, there was a large wake at Eardley Crescent. Joan Sims was rescued from her gin-soaked grief by David Kernan and brought to Earls Court. And, as per Hattie's instructions, everyone got 'very pissed', shared their memories of Hattie and shed laughter and tears in equal amounts.

The Christmas following Hattie's death, Joan Le Mesurier hosted the festivities, determined to make the celebrations as 'lavish and sumptuous as Hattie had always done'. In the months before her death, Hattie had already bought and labelled presents for everyone in readiness for Christmas, another pointer to the fact that she really didn't believe she was going to live very long. Joan Le Mesurier wanted the event to last for a few days in true Hattie tradition but explained:

> We had a big party on Boxing Night where Jake was 'pulled' by two raunchy local girls and was missing for most of the following day. We kept him with us as long as we could but he was eager to return to his lair at Eardley Crescent, theoretically empty now except for him. The old friend who had lived on the top floor, John Bailey who had been there for the past fifteen years, had also gone. He found it too sad without Hattie's presence.

The deaths of Hattie and her mother in the same year created a number of practical and financial difficulties. When she made her will, Mary had decided to bequeath Hattie the Eardley Crescent house, which she still owned, and any savings would go to Hattie's brother, Robin. This was mainly based on the fact that although he cared very much for his mother, Robin had not been nearly as family orientated as Hattie, who had been totally devoted to her mother. Robin quite understood about this decision and there were no recriminations. When Hattie died some months later, everything was left to Robin and Jake, but there were now two lots of death duties to be paid.

When Hattie's will was made public, it was discovered, to everyone's amazement, that Martin Christopherson had been made executor. If Christopherson had been unpopular before with Hattie's friends, he became even more ostracised when he discharged his duties in a highly obtrusive manner. He insisted that the Eardley Crescent family home be put up for sale to cover the death duties, despite the fact that Hattie's friends implored Robin and Jake to find a way somehow of keeping the house. In the end, the property was sold very quickly at what was considered to be a bargain price of £80,000. Hattie's estate was later valued at £138,070.

The house at 54 Waterford Road remained in the family and was later occupied by Jake before being sold to television presenter, Gloria Hunniford. In 1995, a Comic Heritage blue plaque in Hattie's honour was added to the exterior of the house – the first for a comedy actress. Joan Le Mesurier was invited to attend the ceremony and was able to visit the house for the first time in fifteen years, 'Eardley Crescent passed into the hands of somebody who sliced all the grand and airy rooms into little plywood units and crammed it full. The lovely living-room where so many wonderful Christmas parties had taken place was now half its size, the beautiful marble fireplace was gone and the soul of the house had fled. Even the hall was now narrowed to two grim tunnels, one leading upstairs and one down to the basement flat.' The house has now been divided into over fifteen flats and bed-sitting rooms.

One of Hattie's last, and most candid, interviews was with *Annabelle* magazine in August 1980 just a couple of months before she died. She was asked about her busy lifestyle: 'I would love to live in a cottage in the country, but as I can't drive, life would be awkward. In any case, I don't suppose I would like the country permanently because I couldn't stand being on my own. I'm so used to having a large house with lots of people about.'

Hattie was also questioned about the difficulties of maintaining a private life in the presence of such public admiration and she replied, 'Having spent most of my life trying to get some recognition, it would be churlish to get upset about it when people recognise you and come up and talk.' When asked if she had ever thought of marrying again, her reaction was unequivocal, 'Oh no! Definitely not! I've got so used to living independently I'd be impossible to live with. I sometimes think the one reason I might want to marry again is so that I wouldn't get lonely – but then that's not a good enough reason, is it? I'm a very moody person and can become quite depressed. Music can make me weep and a sad play, unfairness and the rotten things people do to each other brings me to tears. And you think I'd be used to people saying supposedly funny things about me being fat, but that can make me cry. I don't like being fat, I hate it.'

Finally she was asked, 'If you weren't Hattie, who would you like to be?' Hattie said, 'Albert Schweitzer – he led a thoroughly useful and good life.' The philosopher, physician and humanitarian Albert Schweitzer based his personal ideology on a 'reverence for life' and a deep commitment to serve humanity through thought and action: a philosophy to which Hattie not only aspired but also succeeded in living for most of her fifty-eight years.

The Final Curtain

Clinging together, in all sorts of weather,
Dear old pals, jolly old pals,
Give me the friendship of dear old pals.

DEAR OLD PALS, THE PLAYERS' SIGNATURE TUNE

ACTRESS MARIE DRESSLER, star of the silent screen, has been quoted as saying, 'I enjoy reading biographies because I want to know about the people who messed up the world.' This couldn't be further from the truth when it comes to the subject of this biography. Hattie Jacques certainly didn't mess up the world. She made it a far better place in many different ways.

Describing Hattie as 'a larger than life character' is somewhat trite but goes some way to convey an accurate image of her charismatic personality, overwhelming kindness and zest for adventure. During her professional career, which spanned four decades, her most favourite role was that of Fairy Queen: a role which she also loved to play away from the footlights. Bestowing wishes on friends and family without the use of fairy dust is just what Hattie did in real life.

Hattie loved to please and would go to any lengths to help in any way that she could, be it practically, emotionally or financially. She remained ridiculously over-generous to the day she died, treating her friends to gifts and surprises, no matter what her financial circumstances. Even when she dined out, she made sure that the waiter or waitress received a bountiful tip. Once, when agent Richard Stone paid the bill and left what she considered to be a less than adequate tip, she replaced the half crown he'd left with a ten bob note when he went to the toilet.

Hattie was always great company, although in later years there was a perceived underlying sadness, which stemmed from a dislike of her own body. She was affected throughout her life by a lack of confidence in her appearance. Her low self-esteem and occasional melancholia didn't manifest itself in self-pity – instead, she threw herself into unselfish acts and grand gestures of kindness both on a personal level and in her endless charity work. She was certainly never sad in public and seldom exhibited that side of her – even to her closest friends.

It would be wrong, however, to paint her as a paragon of virtue: she could be caustic when fellow artistes failed to match her professional expectations, she had a tendency to be snobbish and she was certainly was no innocent when it came matters of the heart. She didn't suffer any qualms about having affairs with a number of married men. A 'sister' she wasn't. Her life was shaped by the death of her father when she was very young (a tragedy shared by her grandmother Adelaide) and this lack of a paternal influence could explain her attitude to anyone showing her affection, no matter what their own marital situation. Hattie certainly had a need to be loved and flattered . . . but then don't we all?

Another great British institution was born in the same year as Hattie. In 1922, the British Broadcasting Company (later Corporation) was created and it was with the BBC, through her involvement with ITMA, *Educating Archie*, *Hancock* and *Sykes* that Hattie was always synonymous. In addition, almost thirty years after her death it is difficult to find anyone of a certain age who isn't aware of her work in the *Carry On* films.

Her considerable shape, which prevented her from doing other more serious work, paradoxically also provided her with the opportunity to work steadily for most of her career. Hattie, who once said, 'I never remember wanting to be anything else but in show business,' was a supporting actress when perhaps she should have been a leading lady.

The memory of Hattie Jacques remains deep in the psyche of the nation, and her influence stretches far beyond the entertainment world and into some unlikely places: last year Hattie's name appeared on a Tottenham Hotspur website in response to a spate of injuries suffered by the football club, 'Ledley King is out for a while and Aaron Lennon may need knee surgery . . . perhaps the latest injury run is something to do with having a half-decent-looking club doctor in the sublime Charlotte Cowie. If they'd have employed a Hattie Jacques type in the treatment room, perhaps we'd have everyone reporting for football duty.'

The local government union Unison launched a poll to find the most famous nurses as part of a recruitment campaign. In the first place the public voted for Florence Nightingale, second came Edith Cavell and third they chose . . . Hattie Jacques. Hattie also had her day in Parliament – government minister Alistair Darling responding to an attack from Anne Widdecombe, 'Up until now I had been spared the sight of the Right Honourable Member for Maidstone and the Weald in full flow. I did not see the video of her at the Tory Party conference, but I have had the opportunity this afternoon to see something of a rather tormented and demented miniature Hattie Jacques!'

In the year 2000, thirty-four years after the title disappeared, the British government decided that it was time for matrons to make a long-awaited comeback in hospitals. The overwhelming demand for the reassuring presence to oversee the everyday running of hospital care had led ministers to draw up plans for their reintroduction. Christine Hancock, then General Secretary of the Royal College of Nursing, welcomed the idea, 'Patients have been crying out for someone they know to be in charge on hospital wards . . . it recognises the fact that when things go wrong, there is someone with the authority to put them right. The trouble is, say the word "Matron" and we all tend to think of Hattie Jacques.' Although it might be somewhat fanciful to believe that government terminology was shaped by the image of Hattie as portrayed in the *Carry On* films, it is interesting to think that she had such a huge influence that the new NHS position subsequently became known as 'A Modern Matron'.

Hattie's death at such an early age was certainly a devastating blow in its own right but the circumstances also contributed to another untimely tragedy some years later. Her son Jake blamed himself for his mother's death because of their argument on the day before she died. He felt somehow responsible for Hattie's heart attack and subsequently found it difficult to cope with the burden. He was quoted as saying, 'When mum died I couldn't get through it without drugs.' Jake had dabbled with marijuana ever since he was a young teenager but then started to involve himself with more serious substances.

Following Hattie's death he moved into 54 Waterford Road and ended up selling some of the furniture to an antique shop on the Kings Road to sustain his habit. Hattie liked to buy *objets d'art* wherever she went and had built up a large collection of china birds which she kept displayed on a chest of drawers in her bedroom. After she died, Jake put them all in a black rubbish bag with the intention of selling them. Unfortunately, on the way to the shop he dropped the bag and most of the china birds were smashed. He apparently didn't get a penny for his trouble.

Like his brother Robin, Jake was a well-respected musician, mainly playing the drums, but also writing songs, working with Roxy Music and Sade. David Malin, Joan Le Mesurier's son, was the same age as Jake and they became very close friends, 'Jake was a very gentle guy with a lovely, dry sense of humour. He was strikingly handsome and women adored him.' Jake never went looking for girlfriends – women found him, something that has also been said about his father. Another trait that he inherited from his father was an impractical nature which Jake stretched to the point of irresponsibility, on occasions going missing for days at a time with no-one knowing where he was.

The typically chaotic lifestyle of a heroin user led Jake to regular disappearing acts and despite attempts by Robin – who returned to London from Los Angeles to sort him out – there was little that anyone could do to change his habit. On one such occasion, in 1986, Joan Le Mesurier traced Jake to a London hospital where he had been admitted, suffering from meningitis. She took him to live in Sitges, near Barcelona, where she had bought a guest house and employed him doing odd jobs on the understanding that he had to 'stay clean'. Bruce Copp also helped him financially and for a while the arrangement was successful. Jake came off heroin, recovered his health and began to work again as a musician. Sadly, this was not to last for very long. He became involved with a female junkie who lived in a flat near The Ramblas in Barcelona and he got hooked again. Not only did she get him back on smack but she also stole all his belongings from his studio.

On 6 October 1991, Jake was spotted by friends in a Barcelona bar in a depressed state, crying and clearly distressed. Some hours later he was discovered in a squalid Barcelona squat with a needle in his arm and a large amount of heroin in his body. The day he died was exactly the eleventh anniversary of Hattie's death. He was aged just thirty-five. David Malin called Robin Le Mesurier, whose tearful response was, 'At least I'll always know where he is.' Robin is convinced that his brother's death was an accident and that Jake was not suicidal. He often needed to get 'out of it' when the anniversary came round.

Jake's father, John Le Mesurier, fortunately was spared the heartbreak of knowing about his son's death. He famously 'conked out' in November 1983 and his last words were recorded as, 'It's all been rather lovely.' Of the other principal characters in this book, Joan Le Mesurier is living happily in Ramsgate; and Robin le Mesurier is a very successful musician and song-writer, living in Los Angeles with his second wife, Jules, and their two Jack Russells, Harold and Maude. Since 1994 he has been playing, recording and writing for legendary actor and singer Johnny Halliday. Bruce Copp is a fantastically fit and engaging eighty-seven-year-old living in Barcelona. He remains a terrible flirt.

There is just one last postscript: Hattie used to meet a man regularly for secret passionate assignations in the 1970s. She later admitted to son Robin that it was the man whom she had always found irresistible . . . John Schofield.

Hattie never could resist the temptation of having a little fun . . .

Acknowledgements

Many thanks to the large troupe who helped me – not only the principal players but also the supporting cast. I am much indebted to Robin Le Mesurier, Joan Le Mesurier, Bruce Copp, John and Sally Jacques and Anne Valery, whose encouragement and enthusiastic participation have provided me with a wealth of information.

Grateful appreciation, especially to Ray Galton, Alan Simpson and Tessa Le Bars for interviews and script extracts, Peter Rogers, Barbara Windsor, June Whitfield, Jim Dale, Clive Dunn, Graham Stark, Dilys Laye, Roger Hancock and Annie Leake, Violetta, Daphne Anderson, Josephine Gordon, Pat Lancaster, Sheila Bernette, Ian Carmichael, Brian Rix, Bill Pertwee, Ernest Maxin, Sydney Lotterby, David Malin, George Evans, Nick Lowe, Peter Yeldham, Felix De Wolfe, Rob Harris, Paul Kelly and Roger Sansom.

A 'Hatful of help' was gratefully received from Nigel Hamilton, April Walker, Hilary Gagan and Michael Sharvell-Martin.

Thanks also to Brian Owen (Lady Margaret School), Malcolm Chapman, Louise North, Jaki Faulkner (BBC Archives), Charles Grant (The Actors' Church), Martin Brown (Equity), Emily Oldfield (British Red Cross), Douglas Osborne (Leukaemia Research Fund), Janet Holben, Bob Hollingsbee, Alan Taylor and Victoria Fisher. I was also assisted in my research by Jess Campbell, Daniel Merriman, Tessa Kulik, Mark Jones and Debbie Mortonson.

A special mention of gratitude to Rick Glanvill and finally thanks to my editor, Piers Burnett, for his patience and support.

Bibliography

BOOKS

A History of the County of Middlesex, Volume 12: Chelsea, 2004

The ITMA Years, Woburn Press, 1974

Briggs, Susan, *Those Radio Times*, Weidenfeld and Nicolson, 1981

Bright, Morris, and Ross, Robert, *Mr Carry On, The Life and Work of Peter Rogers*, BBC Worldwide, 2000

Galton, Ray, and Simpson, Alan, *Hancock's Half Hour*, Woburn Press, 1974

Hancock, Freddie, and Nathan, David, *Hancock, A Personal Biography*, Coronet Books, 1975

Lewis, Roger, *The Life and Death of Peter Sellers,* Century 1994

Lewis, Roger, *The Man who was Private Widdle – A Biography of Charles Hawtrey,* Faber and Faber, 2001

Lewisohn, Mark, *The Radio Times Guide to Television Comedy*, BBC Worldwide, 1998

McCann, Graham, *Spike and Co.,* Hodder and Stoughton, 2006

Mesurier, Joan Le, *Lady Don't Fall Backwards,* Sidgwick and Jackson, 1988

Mesurier, Joan Le, *Dear John,* Sidgwick and Jackson, 2001

Mesurier, John Le, *A Jobbing Actor*, Hamish Hamilton, 1984

Owen, Brian H., *A History of Lady Margaret School (1917–1992)*, 1992

Phillips, Leslie, *Hello*, Orion Books, 2006

Ross, Robert, *The Carry On Story,* Reynolds and Hearn, 2005

Sheridan, Paul, *Late and Early Joys at the Players' Theatre,* T.V. Boardman and Co, 1952

Sims, Joan, *High Spirits,* Transworld, 2000

Stark, Graham, *Stark Naked,* Sanctuary Publishing, 2003

Sykes, Eric, *If I Don't Write it, Nobody Else Will*, Harper Collins, 2005

Williams, Kenneth, *Just Williams*, J.M. Dent and Sons, 1985

Williams, Kenneth, *The Kenneth Williams Diaries*, Ed. Russell Davies, Harper Collins, 1993

Wilmut, Roger, *Tony Hancock, 'Artiste'*, Eyre Methuen, 1978

Wilmut, Roger, *The Illustrated Hancock*, Macdonald Queen Anne Press, 1986

MEDIA

Heroes of Comedy – Hattie Jacques, Thames Television 2001

The Unforgettable Hattie Jacques, Carlton Television 2000

Credits

The following list of Hattie's career is by no means exhaustive. She worked prolifically from 1944 until her death in 1980 and apart from her more significant projects, she made numerous guest appearances on radio and television and contributed extensively to theatrical charitable events.

THEATRE

4 May 1939	Amateur stage debut for The Curtain Club in *Borgia* and *Fumed Oak*, The Kitson Hall, Barnes
July 1944	Professional debut in *Late Joys* revue, The Players' Theatre
December 1944	*The Sleeping Beauty in the Wood*, Players' Theatre Pantomime
December 1945	Players' Theatre pantomime
December 1946– January 1947	Young Vic production of *The King Stag*, The Lyric, Hammersmith, and then national tour
December 1947	*Players, Please*, Players' Theatre Revue
Spring 1948	*Bates Wharf*, Whitehall Theatre
December 1948	*The Sleeping Beauty in the Wood*, Players' Theatre
December 1949	*The Beauty and the Beast*, Players' Theatre
May 1950	*Please Teacher*, The People's Palace
December 1950	*Ali Baba and the 39 Thieves*, Players' Theatre
1951	*Apartments, The Crystal Palace, Going Up*, Players' Theatre
December 1951	*Riquet with the Tuft*, Players' Theatre
December 1951–	*The Archie Andrews Christmas Show*,

222

January 1952	Prince of Wales Theatre
August–November 1952	*The Bells of St Martins*, St Martins Theatre
December 1952	*Babes in the Wood* (directed) Players' Theatre
December 1953	*Cinderella*, Players' Theatre
April 1954	*The Players' Theatre Minstrel Show* (directed)
July–October 1955	*Twenty Minutes South* (produced and directed 105 performances), St Martins Theatre
1956	*Chain of Guilt, The Two Mrs Carolls*, Players' Theatre
	Albertine By Moonlight, Westminster Theatre
May–December 1958	*Large As Life*, The London Palladium
December 1958	*The Royal Variety Performance*, London Coliseum
May 1960	*The Royal Variety Performance*, Victoria Palace, London
May 1977	*The Royal Silver Jubilee Gala Performance*, King's Theatre, Glasgow

A HATFUL OF SYKES

1976 Summer season	Torquay
February–March 1977	Hong Kong
1977 Summer season	Blackpool
Spring 1978	Lincoln, tour of Rhodesia
December 1978–January 1979	Tour of Canada
February-March 1979	Tour of South Africa
1979 Spring/summer	National tour
1979 Summer season	Bournemouth

RADIO

September 1947–January 1949	*ITMA* (three series, 54 episodes)
1949–1950	*April Revue, Clay's College, The Bowery Bar, Heloise*
1950–1958	*Educating Archie* (seven series, 184 episodes)
	Fine Goings On

1951	*Further Goings On* (one series)
April 1952	*Calling All Forces*
July 1952	*Arthur's Inn*
Christmas Day 1953	*The Santa Claus Show*
June 1954	*Archie in Goonland*
1954	*Paradise Street* (one series)
February–April 1955	*Mrs Dale's Diary* (eighteen episodes)
March 1955	*These Radio Times*
April–October 1955	*You're Only Young Once*
November 1956–January 1959	*Hancock's Half Hour* (two series, 40 episodes)
October 1961	*Desert Island Discs*
December 1963	*Hazy Days of Summer* (a talk from Hattie's house)
May–August 1964	*Housewife's Choice* (four programmes)
1965	*Souvenir* (13 shows)
	Twenty Questions
August 1968	*Sounds Familiar*
October 1969	*Pete's People* (interview with Pete Murray)
June 1971	*My Kind of Music, Today Programme* (Live Interview) *Morning Story*

TELEVISION

June 1946	*Late Joys Revue* (BBC Alexandra Palace Studios)
1948	*No No Nanette* (BBC Alexandra Palace Studios)
Summer 1954	*Happy Holidays* (BBC, six episodes)
1955	*The Granville Melodramas* (ITV, seven episodes)
	Plunder (BBC play)
	Pantomania (BBC variety show)
1956	*Tribute to Henry Hall* (BBC)
April 1956–June 1957	*Hancock's Half Hour* (five episodes, series 1)
March 1959	*Eric Sykes' Gala Opening*

1959	*Cup Of Kindness* (BBC)
October 1959	*Hancock's Half Hour* (one episode, series 5)
1960	*The Insect Play* (BBC play)
	Our House (ITV, three series, 39 episodes)
January 1960–	*Sykes And A . . .* (nine series, 60
November 1965	episodes)
1961	*Sally Ann Howes Variety Show*
	Juke Box Jury (BBC)
December 1961	*Billy Cotton Bandshow* (BBC)
February 1962	*Compact* (BBC)
December 1962	*That Was The Week That Was* (BBC)
25 December 1962	*A Christmas Night with the Stars*
February 1963	*This Is Your Life, Hattie Jacques*
August 1964	*Blithe Spirit,* (ITV Play of the Week)
1964	*Miss Adventure* (ITV, 13 episodes)
February 1965	*Cribbins* (BBC sketch show)
1966–1967	*Jackanory* (BBC, 10 episodes)
1967	*Sykes Versus ITV*
	The Memorandum (BBC 2 play)
	Titi-Pu (BBC version of *The Mikado*)
January–April 1968	*The World of Beachcomber* (one series, 12 episodes)
1968	*Knock Three Times, Inside George Webley* (ITV)
	Howerd's Hour (ITV sketch show)
1969	*Carry On Christmas, Pickwick, Join Jim Dale Rhubarb*
1970	*Catweazle, Charley's Grants* (ITV)
1971	*Sykes: With the Lid Off, Doctor At Large, Danger Point*
	Sykes and a Big Big Show (one series, six episodes)
	Frankie Howerd: The Laughing Stock of Television
	Ask Aspel (BBC interview)
1972	*Carry On Christmas* (ITV)
September 1972–	*Sykes* (seven series, 68 episodes)
November 1979	

1973	Appearances on *Pebble Mill at One* and *Call My Bluff*
1975	*Carry On Laughing*
1975	*Wogan's World* (interview)
1976	*Celebrity Squares*
1977	*Eric Sykes: A Few Of Our Favourite Things*
1978	*Multi-Coloured Swap Shop*
1980	*Rhubarb Rhubarb*

COMPILATION MATERIAL FOR TELEVISION

What's a Carry On? (1998)
Heroes Of Comedy (2001)
The Unforgettable Hattie Jacques (2000)
On Location: The Carry Ons (2001)
The Unforgettable Joan Sims (2002)

FILMS

Green for Danger (1946)	Uncredited
The Life and Adventures of Nicholas Nickleby (1947)	Mrs Kenwick
Oliver Twist (1948)	Singer at 'Three Cripples'
Trottie True (1948)	Daisy Delaware
The Spider and the Fly (1949)	Uncredited
The Chance of a Lifetime (1950)	Alice
Waterfront (1950)	Singer
Scrooge (1951)	Mrs Fezziwig
No Haunt for a Gentleman (1952)	Mrs Fitz-Cholmondley
Mother Riley Meets the Vampire (1952)	Mrs Jenks
The Pickwick Papers (1952)	Mrs Nupkins
All Hallowe'en (1952)	Miss Quibble
Our Girl Friday (1953)	Mrs Patch
The Pleasure Garden (1953)	Mrs Albion
The Love Lottery (1954)	Chambermaid
Up to His Neck (1954)	Rakiki
As Long as They're Happy (1955)	Party Girl

Now and Forever (1955)	Woman in sports car with dog
The Square Peg (1958)	Gretchen
Carry On Sergeant (1958)	Captain Clark
Left, Right and Centre (1959)	Woman in car
The Night We Dropped a Clanger (1959)	Ada
Follow a Star (1959)	Dymphna Dobson
The Navy Lark (1959)	Fortune-teller
Carry On Nurse (1959)	Matron
Carry On Teacher (1959)	Grace Short
Carry On Constable (1960)	Sergeant Laura Moon
School for Scoundrels (1960)	Miss Grimmet
Make Mine Mink (1960)	Nanette Parry
Watch Your Stern (1960)	Agatha Potter
Carry On Regardless (1961)	Ward Sister
In the Doghouse (1961)	Primrose Gudgeon
She'll Have to Go (1962)	Miss Richards
The Punch and Judy Man (1963)	Dolly Zarathusa
Carry On Cabby (1963)	Peggy Hawkins
The Plank (1967)	Woman with rose
The Bobo (1967)	Trinity Martinez
Carry On Doctor (1967)	Matron
Monte Carlo or Bust (1969)	Lady journalist
Carry On Camping (1969)	Miss Haggard
Carry On Again Doctor (1969)	Matron
The Magic Christian (1969)	Ginger Horton
Crooks and Coronets (1969)	Mabel
Carry On Loving (1970)	Sophie Plummet
Carry On at Your Convenience (1971)	Beatrice Plummer
Carry On Abroad (1972)	Floella Pepe
Carry On Matron (1972)	Matron
Carry On Dick (1974)	Martha Hoggett
Three for All (1975)	Security official

Index